Sense of Place and Sense of Planet

Sense of Place
and Sense of Planet

*The Environmental
Imagination of the Global*

Ursula K. Heise

OXFORD

UNIVERSITY PRESS

2008

OXFORD

UNIVERSITY PRESS

Oxford University Press, Inc., publishes works that further
Oxford University's objective of excellence
in research, scholarship, and education.

Oxford New York
Auckland Cape Town Dar es Salaam Hong Kong Karachi
Kuala Lumpur Madrid Melbourne Mexico City Nairobi
New Delhi Shanghai Taipei Toronto

With offices in
Argentina Austria Brazil Chile Czech Republic France Greece
Guatemala Hungary Italy Japan Poland Portugal Singapore
South Korea Switzerland Thailand Turkey Ukraine Vietnam

Copyright © 2008 by Oxford University Press

Published by Oxford University Press, Inc.
198 Madison Avenue, New York, New York, 10016
www.oup.com

Oxford is a registered trademark of Oxford University Press

Library of Congress Catologing-in-Publication Data
Heise, Ursula K.
Sense of Place and Sense of Planet : the environmental imagination
of the global / by Ursula K. Heise. — 1st ed.
p. cm.
Includes bibliographical references and index.
ISBN 978-0-19-533563-7; 978-0-19-533564-4 (pbk.)
1. Environmentalism—United States—History. 2. Globalization. I. Title.
GE197H.445 2008
333.720973—dc22   2007043073

Printed in the United States of America
on acid-free paper

For Rafael

ACKNOWLEDGMENTS

Book-length works of research tend to assemble themselves gradually, like jigsaw puzzles, pieced together out of a multitude of readings, conference papers heard and presented, formal and informal conversations, and the environments provided by universities and other scholarly institutions. While footnotes and bibliographies convey some sense of the intellectual matrix out of which an analysis has developed, they cannot convey an adequate sense of the many other debts accrued during such work. Needless to say, whatever these debts may be, remaining errors and shortfalls in this book are exclusively mine.

The Departments of English at Columbia and Stanford Universities have provided vibrant intellectual environments in which to pursue the project of *Sense of Place and Sense of Planet*, and my colleagues at both institutions have supported, encouraged and advised me in innumerable ways both large and small. At Stanford, the Woods Institute for the Environment has been an engagingly lively and interdisciplinary place to present and discuss parts of my work, and the comments and criticisms of colleagues from around the university caused me to rethink many of my arguments. Stacy Alaimo, Hannes Bergthaller, Michael Cohen, Catherine Diamond, Greg Garrard, Catrin Gersdorf, Christa Grewe-Volpp, Robert Kern, Sylvia Mayer, Patrick D. Murphy, Heather Sullivan, Robin Chen-Hsing Tsai, Alexa Weik, Louise Westling, and Chenkuei Yang, all at other universities and some on other continents, have become trusted conversation partners and welcome critics over the years. Rafael Pardo Avellaneda deserves particular thanks for introducing me to the intricacies of risk theory and patiently correcting many of my interdisciplinary errors and misunderstandings. Lothar Baumgarten generously granted me a conversation of several hours and a tour of his splendid New York City studio during my work on his complex nature documentary, *Der Ursprung der Nacht (Amazonas-Kosmos)*. Patrick Murphy, Dana Phillips, and an anonymous third referee at Oxford

University Press provided detailed feedback and criticism that caused to me to revisit and nuance many of my initial analyses. David Damrosch, Guillermina de Ferrari, Michael and Cherrymae Golston, Kristin Hanson, Winston James, Franco Moretti, Mario Ortiz-Robles, Martin Puchner, Ron Silver, and Miriam Wallace have shared not only their astonishing breadth of knowledge and acute insights in innumerable conversations on a wide range of issues but also the kind of personal warmth and friendship without which a project such as this one would soon run dry. Perhaps most of all, I owe a deep debt of gratitude to Cheryll Glotfelty, whose unfailing optimism and firm belief in the value of this book even at times when I myself despaired over its ever being completed inspired me to continue. Such enthusiasm and generosity from a colleague, even when our perspectives sometimes differed, are rare indeed; I feel extraordinarily fortunate to have had her support and advice over years of research and writing.

Combined research grants from the American Council of Learned Societies and the National Humanities Center (NHC) enabled me to take a year off from teaching and administrative tasks during 2001–2 and to complete the analyses that later turned into chapters 5 and 6. The NHC, in addition to its generous award of a fellowship for environmental studies supported by the John D. and Catherine T. MacArthur Foundation, provided a stimulating cohort of fellows across disciplines and plenty of opportunities for formal and informal intellectual exchange, as well as outstanding staff support for any and all research.

Chapter 2 was first written in a substantially different version for the journal *ISLE: Interdisciplinary Studies in Literature and the Environment* 8.1 (winter 2001) under the title "The Virtual Crowds: Overpopulation, Space and Speciesism." A part of chapter 3 appeared in *Comparative Literature Studies* 41.1 (2004) under the title "Local Rock and Global Plastic: World Ecology and the Experience of Place." Chapter 5 was first published as an article called "Toxins, Drugs and Global Systems: Risk and Narrative in the Contemporary Novel," *American Literature* 74 (December 2002), and chapter 6 as an essay in the collection *Nature in Literary and Cultural Studies: Transatlantic Conversations on Ecocriticism*, edited by Catrin Gersdorf and Sylvia Mayer (Rodopi, 2006). All of them are reprinted here with the permission of the original publishers. The John Cage Trust granted permission to quote from John Cage's poem "Overpopulation and Art." Special thanks are also due to John Klima for his extraordinary generosity in allowing me to reproduce an image from his multimedia work *Earth* in chapter 1 and to use another one for the book cover, and to UNKL for permission to include an image of their HazMaPo toy figures.

CONTENTS

Sense of Place and Sense of Planet

INTRODUCTION

Sense of Place and Sense of Planet

A rthur Dent is having a bad day. A bad Thursday, to be exact, on which local authorities roll bulldozers up on his front lawn to tear down his house in preparation for the construction of a new highway bypass. His clumsy protests against the demolition remain ineffectual, but that hardly matters, since the day quickly gets worse: a spaceship announces via a global public-address system that Planet Earth itself is about to be demolished to make way for a hyperspatial express route. The demolition crew aboard the spaceship, observing the worldwide panic this announcement causes, point out that "all the planning charts and demolition orders have been on display in your local planning department in Alpha Centauri for fifty of your Earth years, so you've had plenty of time to lodge any formal complaint." Apparently, they do receive an objection from someone on Earth, because a few minutes later they declare with irritation: "What do you mean, you've never been to Alpha Centauri? For heaven's sake, mankind, it's only four light-years away, you know. I'm sorry, but if you can't be bothered to take an interest in local affairs that's your own lookout. Energize the demolition beams." Earth is destroyed—to be replaced later by an identical copy of itself, manufactured in the same galactic factory that the original turns out to have come from.

This scene, of course, marks the beginning of Douglas Adams's science fiction comedy *The Hitchhiker's Guide to the Galaxy* (26), which propels the lone surviving earthling Arthur Dent into a universe of multiple galactic civilizations whose existence he had never so much as suspected. A rather obvious satire on the brutal tactics of urban development and the genocidal consequences of colonial invasion, the language of the alien technocrats derives much of its humor for the reader from the way it redefines the meaning of the word "local," which here encompasses not just all of Planet Earth but also distant solar systems where humankind has not even yet set foot. Whether Adams intended it that way or not, this sudden confrontation with a spatial, political, and economic context of previously unsuspected vastness also provides an apt metaphor for a cultural moment in which an entire planet becomes graspable as one's own local backyard. While such a globalist consciousness has forcefully been taking shape ever since space flight enabled the first views of Planet Earth from outer space in the 1960s, it has only more recently become a core concern of social and cultural theory.

Over the last decade and a half, the concept of "globalization" has emerged as the central term around which theories of current politics, society, and culture in the humanities and social sciences are organized. In literary and cultural studies, it is gradually replacing earlier key concepts in theories of the contemporary such as "postmodernism" and "postcolonialism." While studies of globalization tend to shift away from the aesthetic and cultural focus that dominated many analyses of postmodernism to a more economic and geopolitical emphasis, many of them nevertheless continue to be centrally concerned with the development of modernity in the late twentieth and early twenty-first centuries. Like other concepts that describe the most recent evolution of the modern—such as "late modernity" or "postmodernity"—globalization has elicited a spectrum of competing analyses and evaluations. While some sociologists (Anthony Giddens, for example) see it as a consequence of modernization processes as they have unfolded over approximately the last two centuries, others, for example Ulrich Beck, describe it as a departure into a different kind of modernity, and yet others (for instance, Martin Albrow) define it as a development that leaves the boundaries of the modern behind. Concurrently, some theorists (for example Immanuel Wallerstein, David Harvey, and Leslie Sklair) see globalization principally as an economic process and as the most recent form of capitalist expansion, whereas others emphasize its political and cultural dimensions, or characterize it as a heterogeneous and uneven process whose various components—economic, technological, political, cultural—do not unfold according to the same logic and at the same pace, an argument that has been proposed in different guises by Arjun Appadurai, James Clifford, and Néstor García Canclini.[1] All theorists of globalization would agree that even as the processes this concept describes affect a multitude of regions and nations the world over, they transform them in fundamentally different ways; opinions diverge, however, on whether this unevenness should be described as yet another dimension of the capitalist North's persistent attempts to dominate and exploit the South, or whether the power and interest structures it results from are more dispersed and complex.[2]

"Globalization," "globalism," and "globality," then, have evolved into complex theoretical notions that refer to a wide range of different phenomena and have been approached from a variety of analytical perspectives. In this multidisciplinary debate, the question of what cultural and political role attachments to different kinds of space might play, from the local and regional level all the way to the national and global, has assumed central importance. Literary and cultural critics as well as anthropologists, sociologists, historians, philosophers and political scientists have investigated the imaginative strategies and devices that allow individuals and communities to form attachments to these different types of spaces and to maintain them over time as an integral part of their identities, and have explored what overarching cultural and ideological purposes such commitments have been made to serve in different communities. These analyses began before globalization rose to prominence as an organizing intellectual term; from the early 1980s to the mid-1990s, they were centrally shaped by various poststructuralist philosophies and their shared resistance to what were perceived to be "essentialist" concepts of identity, that is, assumptions about the inherent characteristics of individuals and groups deriving from specific categories of nationality, ethnicity, race, gender, or sexual orientation. The thrust of the intellectual effort undertaken in those years was to show that such categories, which had earlier been assumed to be self-evident, natural, and sometimes biologically grounded, were in fact highly artificial and historically contingent, and were maintained and legitimated by specific practices, discourses, and institutions. Discourses about the nation and national identity, among others, were criticized as establishing "imagined communities," in Benedict Anderson's influential term, that often led to the denial and oppression of differences within the nation and aggression or imperialism between nations.

In search of countermodels to such nation-based concepts of identity, a wide range of theorists instead presented identities shaped by hybridity, creolization, *mestizaje*, migration, borderlands, diaspora, nomadism, exile, and deterritorialization not only as more politically progressive but also as potential grounds for resistance to national hegemonies. The abundance of studies focusing on such forms of identity often emphasized their marginal status in the mainstream culture and polity, a marginality that was viewed as both disabling and potentially empowering, insofar as it provided a view of the dominant culture from outside. Inevitably, a certain theoretical ambiguity accompanied the development of this line of argument, as hybridity, diaspora, and marginality sometimes turned into quasi-essentialist categories themselves, especially in some of the more emphatic validations of ethnicity, local identity, and "situated knowledge"; concurrently, other analyses emphasized the continued necessity of questioning essentialisms even in discourses that understood themselves as oppositional. The most important dimension of this phase of theoretical development for the purposes of the argument I will develop here is the fact that it produced an abundance of cultural studies that were skeptical vis-à-vis local rootedness and instead validated individual and collective forms of identity that define themselves in relation to a multiplicity of places and place experiences. Anthropologist James Clifford's influential work *Routes*—with its pun on the phonetic homonymy of "roots" and "routes"—proposed one of the most pointed formulations of this line of analysis by describing even the premodern and "locally rooted" communities that often form the anthropologist's object of study as "traveling cultures" associated with a wide range of places. Migration, in his work as well as that of other theorists, moved from the margins to the core of cultural identity—not only that of individuals but of entire societies.

In the later 1990s, as discussions of globalization spread from the social sciences to the humanities, studies of the relationship of identity to various kinds of space also shifted in emphasis to concepts such as "transnationalism" or "critical internationalism." Theorists from a variety of fields, at the same time, began to recuperate the term "cosmopolitanism" as a way of imagining forms of belonging beyond the local and the national. Philosophers Anthony Appiah and Martha Nussbaum, anthropologists James Clifford and Aihwa Ong, sociologists Ulrich Beck, Anthony Giddens, Ulf Hannerz, and John Tomlinson, political scientists Patrick Hayden, David Held, and Anthony McGrew, as well as literary critics such as Homi Bhabha, Pheng Cheah, Walter Mignolo, and Bruce Robbins, among others, have all engaged with this notion in the attempt to free it from the connotations of social privilege and leisure travel that accompanied it in earlier periods. While there are considerable differences in the way these theorists rethink cosmopolitanism, they share with earlier theorists of hybridity and diaspora the assumption that there is nothing natural or self-evident about attachments to the nation, which are on the contrary established, legitimized, and maintained by complex cultural practices and institutions. But rather than seeking the grounds of resistance to nationalisms and nation-based identities in local communities or groups whose mobility places them at the borders of national identity, these theorists strive to model forms of cultural imagination and understanding that reach beyond the nation and around the globe. In one way or another, all of them are concerned with the question of how we might be able to develop cultural forms of identity and belonging that are commensurate with the rapid growth in political, economic, and social interconnectedness that has characterized the last few decades.

Cogent as this reasoning is in its search for new forms of transnational cultural identity, it has not gone unchallenged. Historian Arif Dirlik, literary critic Timothy Brennan, and other theorists have recently reemphasized the value of local and national identities as forms of resistance to some dimensions of globalization. Critiques of the "essentialism" of local identities and of national belonging, Dirlik and Brennan argue, omit consideration of the ways localism and nationalism can serve progressive political objectives and legitimate emancipatory projects, especially in the developing world and in a context of rapid economic globalization (Dirlik, "Place-Based Imagination," 35–42; Brennan, *At Home in the World*, 44–65). Several recent anthologies—Prazniak and Dirlik's *Places and Politics in the*

Age of Globalization, Mirsepassi, Basu, and Weaver's *Localizing Knowledge in a Globalizing World*, or Jasanoff and Martello's *Earthly Politics*, for example—all seek to revalidate local and national foundations of identity as a means of resisting the imperialist dimensions of globalization.

With this wave of countercritiques, the theoretical debate has arrived at a conceptual impasse: while some theorists criticize nationally based forms of identity and hold out cosmopolitan identifications as a plausible and politically preferable alternative, other scholars emphasize the importance of holding on to national and local modes of belonging as a way of resisting the imperialism of some forms of globalization. Fredric Jameson sums up this quandary when he highlights how local and regional identities used to be pitched against the homogenizing force of the nation, only to point out that

> when one positions the threats of Identity at a higher level globally, then everything changes: at this upper range, it is not national state power that is the enemy of difference, but rather the transnational system itself, Americanization and the standardized products of a henceforth uniform and standardized ideology and practice of consumption. At this point, nation-states and their national cultures are suddenly called upon to play the positive role hitherto assigned—against them—to regions and local practices.... And as opposed to the multiplicity of local and regional markets, minority arts and languages, whose vitality can certainly be acknowledged all over the world uneasily coexisting with the vision...of their universal extinction, it is striking to witness the resurgence—in an atmosphere in which the nation-state as such, let alone "nationalism," is a much maligned entity and value—of defenses of national culture on the part of those who affirm the powers of resistance of a national literature and a national art. ("Globalization," 74–75)

This conflict between a conceptualization of national identity as either an oppressive hegemonic discourse or a tool for resistance to global imperialism, and of local identity as either an essentialist myth or a promising site of struggle against both national and global domination, leads Arif Dirlik even more pointedly to declare a theoretical stalemate. He acknowledges the

> intractability of the problem...with existing discussions of place/space in which the defense and the repudiation of place both carry considerable theoretical plausibility and for that same reason seem in their opposition to be confined within a theoretical world of their own out of which there is no exit that is to be revealed by theory. ("Place-Based Imagination," 23–24)

If Dirlik falls prey to a rather comical non sequitur by following up this categorical rejection of a theoretical solution with a sustained theoretical defense of place—against his own suggestion that the entire discussion should be shifted to the level of specific case studies—he and Jameson nevertheless accurately pinpoint the conceptual contradictions in many current discourses about place. It might be more useful to think of such contradictions as a starting point for reflecting on the kinds of categories and abstractions that are commonly used in cultural theory than to reject them wholesale, since such rejection would presumably lead back to the theory resistance and hyperspecific analyses of detail that were already rehearsed (and later abandoned) in cultural studies in the early 1990s. But Dirlik is surely right that no obvious theoretical solution presents itself to the conceptual dilemmas in current theories regarding the relationship of identity and place.

The argument proposed in this book evolved against the background of these waves of cultural critique and countercritique. While the advocacy of local, national, or global forms of identity, given the impasse these discussions have reached, may no longer make much sense at a very general and abstract level, it nevertheless remains an important issue in particular cultural and historical contexts. This book focuses on such a specific context, namely the discourses of the environmentalist movement since the 1960s (the American environmentalist movement in particular), as well as of the emergent research field of ecocriticism, which has evolved in literary and cultural studies since the early 1990s. Modern environmentalist thought, which has been intensely engaged with questions of the local and the global since its inception in the 1960s and 1970s, sits at an oblique angle to the theoretical debates I have outlined. Avant-garde and rearguard at the same time, environmentalism concerned itself with issues of global citizenship and activism long before such questions became fashionable in academia. But—in the United States at least—it also invested much of its utopian capital into a return to the local and a celebration of a "sense of place" that remained impervious for a long time to the kinds of antiessentialist perspectives that had become common currency in most other areas of American culture. While this tension may seem conceptually unsatisfactory, it has nevertheless been practically productive for a new social movement that in many ways has been surprisingly successful, given the relatively short span of its existence; certainly, this ambivalence has given American environmentalism part of its distinctive profile. Yet the contradictions remain problematic, especially since the rhetoric of place has now been absorbed into some strains of ecocritical research.

When I began to formulate the argument of this book, I did not envision it as a particularly Americanist project. Rather, it was my intention to explore strands of environmentalist and ecocritical thought that I perceived at the time to be shaped by impulses mostly unrelated to national or regional differences. As the research proceeded, however, I saw myself increasingly forced to address what turned out to be peculiarly U.S.-American inflections of environmentalism and ecocriticism. The marked emphasis in American environmentalist thought on the local as the ground for individual and communal identity and as the site of connections to nature that modern society is perceived to have undone certainly fits broadly into a pattern of critique of modernity that has been repeatedly articulated in western Europe and North America for at least two centuries. But many of the specifics of this critique draw their strength from cultural and rhetorical traditions particular to the United States, where rootedness in place has long been valued as an ideal counterweight to the mobility, restlessness, rootlessness, and nomadism that Americans themselves as well as observers from outside have often construed as paradigmatic of American national character. This cultural, political, and often even spiritual investment in the "sense of place" emerged for me in particularly stark profile in comparison with the highly successful environmental movement of my country of origin, Germany. The German environmental movement, unlike its American counterpart, could not look back on an unbroken tradition of thought and writing about place at the moment of its emergence in the 1970s. Since National Socialism had appropriated many of the Romantic symbols of connection to soil, place, and region in the 1930s and 1940s, localism has not played the same central role in German environmental rhetoric as in the United States. It was this difference that first led me to reflect on whether localism is indeed a necessary component of environmental ethics, as much U.S.-American ecodiscourse leads one to believe, or if it is rather the outcome of particular national traditions of thought and rhetoric.

If this observation has led me to include several German texts and films in my discussion, however, my intention has not been to outline a contrast between German and American environmentalisms: a thorough analysis of the various different traditions of environmentalist thought within what is usually perceived to be a relatively homogeneous cultural "West" or "North" would be the subject matter of another book. Since my textual analyses focus on works that offer conceptual and formal countermodels to ecolocalism, both the American and German texts, films, and artworks that I have selected are principally meant to point to ways of imagining the global that frame localism from a globalist environmental perspective. I hope, nevertheless, that the inclusion of texts in other languages, as well as the examination of how texts written in the United States draw on non-American sources and traditions, might serve as a comparatist reminder that neither environmentalism nor ecocriticism should be thought of as nouns in the singular, and that the assumptions that frame environmentalist and ecocritical thought in the United States cannot simply be presumed to shape ecological orientations elsewhere.

Chapter 1 presents a detailed analysis of the way the relationship between the local and the global has been imagined by American environmentalist thinkers and writers between the 1960s and the 1990s, but also presents a critique of what is in my view an excessive investment in the local. Some of this criticism will appear obvious, perhaps even banal, at this stage to those well acquainted with the debates over cultural identity and place of the last twenty-five years. But the fact is that such a critique has not been articulated with as much force or in as much detail in environmentalist discourse as it has, for example, for American conceptions of nation or race. To that extent, it remains a necessary critique.

Against the primary investment in the local, chapter 1 emphasizes the urgency of developing an ideal of "eco-cosmopolitanism," or environmental world citizenship, building on recuperations of the cosmopolitan project in other areas of cultural theory. While cosmopolitanism has generally been understood as an alternative to nationally based forms of identity, it confronts more local attachments in the case of environmentalism in the United States, which have been articulated by means of such concepts as "dwelling," "reinhabitation," "bioregionalism," an "erotics of place," or a "land ethic." Without denying that under certain circumstances such affirmations of local ties can play an important role in environmentalist struggles, I argue that ecologically oriented thinking has yet to come to terms with one of the central insights of current theories of globalization: namely, that the increasing connectedness of societies around the globe entails the emergence of new forms of culture that are no longer anchored in place, in a process that many theorists have referred to as "deterritorialization." Undoubtedly, deterritorialization, especially when it is imposed from outside, is sometimes accompanied by experiences of loss, deprivation, or disenfranchisement that environmentalists have rightfully resisted and should continue to oppose. Yet deterritorialization also implies possibilities for new cultural encounters and a broadening of horizons that environmentalists as well as other politically progressive movements have welcomed, sometimes without fully acknowledging the entanglements of such cultural unfolding with globalization processes that they otherwise reject. The challenge that deterritorialization poses for the environmental imagination, therefore, is to envision how ecologically based advocacy on behalf of the nonhuman world as well as on behalf of greater socioenvironmental justice might be formulated in terms that are premised no longer primarily on ties to local places but on ties to territories and systems that are understood to encompass the planet as a whole.

This book explores the implications of such a deterritorialized environmental vision in the realms of literature and art. The concluding section of chapter 1 addresses the question of what aesthetic forms might be most appropriate for articulating such a vision by proposing that allegories of the global have given way, in the most innovative works of literature and art, to forms that deploy allegory in larger formal frameworks of dynamic and interactive collage or montage: the iconic representation of the "Blue

Planet" seen from outer space has been superseded by the infinite possibilities of zooming into and out of local, regional, and global views enabled by, for example, the online tool Google Earth and the multiple databases, geographical positioning systems, and imaging techniques on which it draws. Chapters 2 and 3 investigate this question further by examining particular works. Chapter 2 focuses on the way fears about rapid global population growth were expressed in novels and films of the 1960s and 1970s through well-established narrative templates dealing with local urban overcrowding and the erosion of individuality. One of the novels that departs from this model, however, John Brunner's *Stand on Zanzibar*, moves toward a form that attempts to integrate a panorama of the whole planet with views from different localities through narrative strategies borrowed from the high-modernist novels of the early twentieth century. Brunner's collage technique is taken up in later treatments of population and ecology from David Brin's novel *Earth* to John Cage's poem "Overpopulation and Art," which use the virtual realms of electronic connectedness as a new site for imagining global multitudes without the earlier forms of urban paranoia, and give rise to new experiments with narrative and lyrical form. Chapter 3 moves from the city to the wilderness and juxtaposes two artworks, German installation artist Lothar Baumgarten's faux documentary *Der Ursprung der Nacht (Amazonas-Kosmos)* (The Origin of the Night: Amazon Cosmos) and Japanese American writer Karen Tei Yamashita's novel *Through the Arc of the Rainforest*. Both take the Amazon jungle, long a symbol of environmental crisis and concern, as a point of departure to explore via innovative visual and narrative forms how local ecological and cultural systems are imbricated in global ones. While some of the works discussed in chapters 2 and 3 offer more persuasive aesthetic solutions than others, all of them attempt to convey through their formal strategies, as well as their substance, facets of the kind of eco-cosmopolitanism I outline theoretically in chapter 1.

Part II links the analysis of the local and global imaginations to theories of risk, both because risk scenarios crucially affect forms of inhabitation, and because the idea of a coming "world risk society" has recently emerged as one of the most important ways of imagining global connectedness. Chapter 4 offers a brief survey of risk theory, an interdisciplinary field of research that has established itself in the social sciences in the second half of the twentieth century. The most empirically oriented part of this field studies how different individuals and social groups assess a range of risk scenarios, and what variables shape such assessments. The mostly statistical and cognitive assumptions that informed this research in the 1970s have increasingly been complemented—indeed, in some cases, contradicted—by social, cultural, and institutional perspectives that have led to a far more complex picture of how particular cultures select risks for awareness, interpret their meaning, and attempt to manage them. This research has also led to controversies about the nature of risk perceptions, their objective reality and social constructedness, about their cultural mediation through a variety of basic assumptions, forms of social organization and institutions, and about the ways specific risks should be prevented or mitigated. As I will argue, not only does this area of inquiry stand to benefit from the detailed analyses of risk-related narrative genres and images produced in cultural studies, but environmentally oriented studies of culture also have a vital intellectual stake in a field that has invested a great deal of research into the investigation of how social and cultural groups define their relation to the natural environment through perceptions of technological and ecological risk.

Chapter 4 will also present the more broadly formulated theories that address the relationship of risk to processes of modernization and globalization. Such theories, to the extent that they examine how certain types of risk are generated by and imbricated in complex and large-scale social and technological systems, contribute to the analysis of deterritorialization I outline in chapter 1, in that they foreground how practices of inhabitation are shaped by such systems. Theories of an emergent "risk culture" or "world risk society" such as those formulated by Anthony Giddens and Ulrich Beck assume particular importance in this context, as they postulate far-reaching changes in social structure as a consequence of global risk scenarios. I will show how such theories diverge from environmentalist thinking and where they dovetail with arguments of the environmental justice movement. Beck's "Cosmopolitan Manifesto," which postulates the emergence of new, transnational forms of solidarity and community on the basis of shared risk exposure, establishes such links at least implicitly, and adds a crucial dimension to the eco-cosmopolitanism discussed in chapter 1. At the same time, Beck's relatively simplistic assumptions about the connection of risk and culture need to be complemented by the analysis of difficulties in establishing transnational alliances that environmental justice advocates have highlighted, as well by the more sophisticated articulations of crosscultural literacy in recent theories of cosmopolitanism.

Environmentalists have sometimes objected to some of the basic terms of risk assessment, as well as to particular theoretical articulations. I address such objections throughout chapter 4 to show that many of them responded to an earlier stage of development in the field, and some of them to a conflation of risk assessment as a practical professional task with its anthropological or sociological study. Chapters 5 and 6 take these arguments onto the terrain of literary analysis by focusing on two sets of novels that illustrate some of the complex ways risk perceptions are translated into images and stories, and the way such tropes and narratives in turn shape the understanding of risk. Chapter 5 examines two American novels, Don DeLillo's postmodern classic *White Noise* and Richard Powers's *Gain*, which revolve around scenarios of chemical exposure that individuals undergo in their local environments. The analysis foregrounds how the perception of risk shapes the narrative forms these two novels deploy, and the way Powers's novel in particular constructs the relationship between local communities and the global reach of transnational corporations. Chapter 6 shifts the focus to two German novels that were written in the immediate aftermath of the nuclear accident at Chernobyl in 1986. Published in what were at the time the separate states of the German Democratic Republic and the Federal Republic of Germany, Christa Wolf's *Störfall: Nachrichten eines Tages* (Accident: A day's news) and Gabriele Wohmann's *Der Flötenton* (Sound of the flute) are principally concerned with how a risk scenario that unfolds hundreds of miles away from the protagonists changes their ways of inhabiting their local communities and of leading their everyday lives. The interplay between local, regional, and global processes, as well as the alternation between the irruption of an apocalyptic disaster and the normalcy of everyday routines, shapes both novels' psychological and political explorations, but ultimately takes each of them to a different narrative form and a different mode of accommodation to global risk. The conclusion, finally, takes a brief look at recent literary approaches to global warming as a way of understanding prevailing trends in the current environmental imagination of the global.

I intend this book, then, as a contribution to environmentally oriented literary and cultural studies in two ways. It puts environmentalist reflections on the importance of a "sense of place" in communication with recent theories of globalization and cosmopolitanism, in an attempt to explore what new possibilities for ecological awareness inhere in cultural forms that are increasingly detached from their anchorings in particular geographies. As the intensifying confrontation with ecological and technological risk scenarios forms part of globalization processes, the book also suggests that the study of risk perceptions and their sociocultural framing must form an integral part of an ecocritical understanding of culture. At the same time, this cultural analysis can make a significant contribution to risk theory by foregrounding how new risk perceptions are shaped by already existing cultural tropes and narrative templates. It is my hope that this examination of how environmental literary and cultural studies might fruitfully interact with other areas of theoretical investigation will contribute to an understanding of how environmentalist thought more generally might engage with the rapidly changing realities with which globalization confronts it.

PART I

World Wide Webs

Imagining the Planet

1

FROM THE BLUE PLANET
TO GOOGLE EARTH

Environmentalism, Ecocriticism, and
the Imagination of the Global

1. Vaster Than Empires

In her short story "Vaster Than Empires and More Slow," science fiction novelist Ursula K. Le Guin describes the encounter of a group of humans with an ecosystem that cannot be understood as encompassing anything less than an entire planet. When a team of scientific explorers arrives on the planet called only World 4470, after a journey that has taken just a few hours in their personal time but 250 years in Earth time, they find all its continents inhabited exclusively by plants, from grass-like to tree-like species. Their scientific study of this world is from the beginning impaired by the peculiarities of their life as a group: since only psychologically or socially alienated individuals volunteer for a mission that will take them 500 years into the future (returning to Earth will take another 250), conflicts continuously erupt between the team members. One of the scientists, Osden, proves particularly problematic, as his "wide-range bioempathic receptivity," a psychological condition that enables him to "share lust with a white rat, pain with a squashed cockroach, phototropy with a moth" (97), also leads him blindly to reflect back any human emotions he senses in his surroundings. Since most of his colleagues approach him with suspicion or latent hostility, he cannot help but respond with scorn and hatred, which ends up estranging even the most patient and compassionate among them. To minimize the disruptive effects of this condition, he moves away from the team to take on the biological exploration of a nearby forest.

But the tension that Osden's presence had caused is soon replaced by a vague feeling of unease that most members of the group experience in and around this forest. Lingering apprehension erupts into crisis when Osden misses his radio transmissions, and is found bleeding and unconscious on the forest soil by two scientists who go out to search for him. As they pick him up, they are seized by an overwhelming and irrational fear that they hardly know how to control. When they discuss their experiences as Osden regains consciousness, it becomes clear that the plant life in the forest has some kind of sentience that he was able to identify mostly by its fear: "'I suppose I could feel the roots. Below me in the ground, down under the ground.... I felt the fear. It kept growing. As if they'd finally *known* I was there, lying on them there, under them, among them, the thing they feared, and yet part of their fear itself. I couldn't stop sending the fear back, and it kept growing, and I couldn't move, I couldn't get away'" (113). Several of the scientists contradict him by pointing out that the tree-like plants have no nervous system that would enable them to react to their surroundings in such a way. But others observe that all the plants are linked by an intricate root system and a network of epiphytes so as to create what might be a far-reaching web of connections. One of them argues, "'sentience or intelligence isn't a thing, you can't find it in, or analyze it out from, the cells of a brain. It's a function of the connected cells. It is, in a sense, the connection: the connectedness'" (118). Osden sums up his experience of this utterly alien form of intelligence by characterizing it as "'sentience without senses. Blind, deaf, nerveless, moveless. Some irritability, response to touch. Response to sun, to light, to water, and chemicals in the earth around the roots. Nothing comprehensible to an animal mind. Presence without mind. Awareness of being, without object or subject. Nirvana'" (118).

In such an ecosystem, the only agent that could have attacked Osden is another human, and one of the scientists finally admits that he mistook the psychological effect of the forest for Osden's influence and wanted to rid the mission of his interference. To break the impact of the alien forest, the crew decide to relocate their camp to another continent. But the same unease as before revisits them on a vast prairie covered with grass-like plants, forcing them to realize, as the team's biologist points out, that the entire planet's vegetation constitutes one large "'network of processes.... There are no individual plants, then, properly speaking. Even the pollen is part of the linkage, no doubt, a sort of windborne sentience, connecting overseas. But it is not conceivable. That all the biosphere of a planet should be one network of communications, sensitive, irrational, immortal, isolated'" (122). Le Guin's title allusion to Andrew Marvell's well-known poem "To His Coy Mistress" with its reference to "vegetable love" is translated into "vegetable fear" as Osden infers that the planet's apprehension must have been triggered by its dawning awareness of other beings where there had never been anything but itself. As Osden and the other humans perceive and retransmit this fear to the alien intelligence, they are locked into a self-reinforcing feedback loop with their environment.

The only way to break this loop, Osden realizes, is either to leave the planet and thereby abort the mission or self-sacrifice. He chooses the latter, venturing into the forest on his own with a conscious effort to absorb rather than reflect back its fear, and to transmit the humans' absence of hostility. Doing so implies that he has to disrupt the psychic mechanisms that have allowed him to survive in human company, and he therefore remains in the forest when the rest of the expedition returns to Earth, merging with an intelligence that, in his perception, "'know[s] the whole daylight... and the whole night. All the winds and lulls together. The winter stars and the summer stars at the same time. To have roots, and no enemies. To be entire.... No invasion. No others. To be whole'" (123). The team members, for the rest of their stay, live immersed in this sentient environment whose planet-encompassing existence is unimaginably alien to their own:

> The people of the Survey team walked under the trees, through the vast colonies of life, surrounded by a dreaming silence, a brooding calm that was half aware of them and wholly indifferent to them. There were no hours. Distance was no matter. Had we but world enough and time.... The planet turned between the sunlight and the great dark; winds of winter and summer blew fine, pale pollen across the quiet seas. (127)[1]

Humans' interaction with a global environment is here articulated through a series of conceptual tensions: the forest's contemplative immobility versus the humans' movements; its indifference to them as against their investigation of it; its unconcern over space and time, which contrasts both with the humans' separation from their own world and history, and their longing to overcome the limitations of their biological form; its silence as against their language; its total unity (signaled here by the pollen, which connects the plants even across oceans) versus their plurality and individuality. At the same time, the lyrical quality of the passage, which culminates in the quotation from Marvell's poem and echoes the story's title, also conveys the sense that the forest possesses a kind of being that humans have always aspired to: a collective experience of "world enough and time," where temporality and space are no longer issues of existential concern. Even as the scientists, like Marvell's lovers, cannot share this experience, they seem to participate in it temporarily by "walk[ing] under the trees" (127): rootedness in its original, botanical sense and indifference to space coexist in the same experience.

Published in 1971, this short story articulates a vision of global ecology that had gained great popularity at the time. The idea that all the planet's life forms are linked in such a way that they come to form one world-encompassing, sentient superorganism echoes James Lovelock's well-known Gaia hypothesis, according to which Planet Earth constitutes a single overarching feedback system that sustains itself.[2] At the same time, the scientists' taxonomic approach to World 4470's biology—surveying the land, counting and identifying species, analyzing chemical processes—is complemented and in the end superseded by what the narrator calls Osden's "love," his willingness to merge physically and psychologically with the environment so as to communicate with it, in a transparent allusion to the holistic, synthetic modes of thought that were being advocated as superior to conventional, analytic science in the 1960s and 1970s. "Vaster than empires," this biosphere cannot be grasped in any of its parts unless their underlying planetary connectedness is understood first.

In asking how humans might be able to relate to such a planet-wide organic "network of communications," Le Guin responds to powerful allegorizations of the global in the 1960s, from the "global village" to "Spaceship Earth," and to some extent participates in their romanticizations of global connectedness as mergers with a technological or ecological sublime. Yet it is impossible to overlook that her short story also complicates such romanticizations, in that the global organism presents itself to the human observers as thoroughly alien, a world far from their own in both space and time. Osden's merger with it—enabled, it is worth noting, by psychopathology—comes at the price of his individual identity, while the other explorers remain just visitors who return to their own planets after a few months. Far from idyllic or utopian, the biosphere's total connectedness is what makes it even more strange than its remoteness or its unfamiliar species. Humans have no "natural" way of relating to such sentient connectivity, in whose context they themselves appear as alien Others. All the terms—cognitive, affective, and linguistic—by means of which they approach the planet have to be questioned as to whether they do not unduly project the terms of a quite different biological frame of reference, as one of the scientists implies when he refers to the tree-like plants of this "'totally alien environment, for which the archetypical connotations of the word 'forest' provide an inevitable metaphor'" (115). Rather than describing awareness of the global biosphere as a reassuring (re)turn to Mother Earth, Le Guin's story portrays it as a difficult and thoroughly mediated step for the human imagination.

This story fictionalizes some of the tensions that accompanied the emergence of the modern environmental movement in North America and western Europe in the late 1960s and early 1970s, a moment when new imaging technologies enabled humans to perceive their own planet as a whole from outer space for the first time and generated images some of which were soon to become icons of environmentalism. But the formation of this new social movement also occurred at a moment of looming global disaster from the dual threat of nuclear annihilation and environmental collapse. As environmentalism gradually established itself in this configuration of geopolitics, new science, and advanced technologies, it was initially fueled by powerful visions of the global, from the Gaia hypothesis to Spaceship Earth and popular slogans such as "Think globally, act locally." But the utopian political and cultural aspirations that seemed naturally connected to this holistic view of the planet found themselves from the beginning in a complex conjunction with darker visions of global collapse or conspiracy on the one hand and with the call to return to local environments and communities as a way of overcoming the modern alienation from nature on the other. Environmentalist discourses about the global between the late 1960s and the beginning of the third millennium, as the second part of this chapter will show, therefore evolved in a field of tension between the embrace of and the resistance to global connectedness, and between the commitment to a planetary vision and the utopian reinvestment in the local. The third section explores the specific features that this "sense of place" has acquired in various types of American environmentalist rhetoric, powerful critiques that have been formulated against it, and the reasons that this kind of discourse has nevertheless proven so culturally resilient. In spite of its persistence, however, I will argue in this chapter as well as throughout the book that the environmentalist emphasis on restoring individuals' sense of place, while it might function as one useful tool among others for environmentally oriented arguments, becomes a visionary dead end if it is understood as a founding ideological principle or a principal didactic means of guiding individuals and communities back to nature. Rather than focusing on the recuperation of a sense of place, environmentalism needs to foster an understanding of how a wide variety of both natural and cultural places and processes are connected and shape each other around the world, and how human impact affects and changes this connectedness.

Such a "sense of planet," as the fourth section of this chapter will show, might benefit from theoretical grounding in some of the insights of recent theories of globalization. Analyses of "deterritorialization," understood as the weakening of the ties between culture and place, point to the conceptual impasses of environmentalist considerations of the local, as well as to a different understanding of inhabitation. Recent recuperations of the concept of "cosmopolitanism" in the context of debates over nationalism and globalization, in addition, provide a useful basis for thinking about environmental allegiances that reach beyond the local and the national. What such a reconsideration might achieve, as I argue in the last section, is not only a more accurate understanding of how individuals and communities actually inhabit particular sites at the beginning of the third millennium but also a more nuanced understanding of how aesthetic forms such as allegory and collage have shaped the environmental imagination of the global. As I will show here and in later chapters, one of the crucial challenges for artists and writers, and beyond them, for all those engaged with environmentalist thought, is the creation of a vision of the global that integrates allegory—still a mode that is hard to avoid in representations of the whole planet—into a more complex formal framework able to accommodate social and cultural multiplicity. In this context, the transition from the image of the "Blue Planet" to the infinite zooming capabilities of the internet tool Google Earth marks a formal as well as conceptual shift with important implications for representations of the global across various forms of environmental art and thought.

2. Allegories of Connectedness: From Gaia to the Risk Society

From its beginnings in the 1960s, one of the founding impulses of the modern environmentalist movement was its attempt to drive home to scientists, politicians, and the population at large the urgency of developing a holistic understanding of ecological connectedness, as well as of the risks that have emerged from human manipulations of such connected systems. This concern to engage with the "Whole Earth" took several different forms that sometimes intertwined and sometimes conflicted with each other. Scientific assessments of the state of the planet and its future prospects have been one of the most important foundations for the environmentalist movement from the 1960s to the present day. Environmental science has proposed comprehensive ecological portraits of Planet Earth that have formed the backbone of many environmentalist organizations, initiatives, and policy suggestions: Paul Ehrlich's 1968 *Population Bomb*, Donella Meadows's well-known 1972 report to the Club of Rome, *The Limits to Growth*, and its two updates in 1992 and 2004, the 1980 *Global 2000 Report to the President*, the 1987 Brundtland Commission Report *Our Common Future*, the 1992 Rio de Janeiro Earth Summit, the Intergovernmental Panel on Climate Change reports of the 1990s and early 2000s, and the United Nations' Millennium Ecosystem Assessment, now to be followed by Ehrlich's Millennium Assessment of Human Behavior. While all of these reports on the state of the world have resonated beyond the domain of science and politics, their technical details have often remained inaccessible to the general population. To the extent that such scientific accounts reached a wide audience, it was through their recourse to a set of popular images and narrative patterns that were either generated by or became associated with the environmentalist movement in the 1960s and early 1970s.

No doubt the most influential of these was the image of the "Blue Planet" seen from outer space; this view first became available with the orbital flights of Yuri Gagarin and John Glenn in the early 1960s, and was popularized by the photographs of Earth rising above the Moon taken by the *Apollo 8* crew in 1968 and the famous "blue marble" picture obtained by the *Apollo 17* mission in 1972 (fig. 1.1). In spite of their technological—indeed, to some extent, military—origin, images of Earth in space were quickly appropriated by the environmentalist movement and prominently displayed at the first Earth Day in 1970. Set against a black background like a precious jewel in a case of velvet, the planet here appears as single entity, united, limited, and delicately beautiful. Thinkers as diverse as media theorist Marshall McLuhan and atmospheric scientist James Lovelock were deeply influenced by images such as this one; neither McLuhan's notion that the world had turned into a global village nor Lovelock's Gaia

Figure 1.1. Blue Planet. Photo taken by the Apollo 17 mission on December 7, 1972. Image courtesy of the Image Science and Analysis Laboratory, NASA Johnson Space Center, photo no. AS17-148-22727.TIF.

hypothesis of the Earth as a single superorganism can be dissociated from its impact.[3] The influence proved to be lasting: two decades later, the Brundtland Report, *Our Common Future*, began with an invocation of the same image accompanied by the claim that

> this vision had a greater impact on thought than did the Copernican Revolution.... From space, we see a small and fragile ball dominated not by human activity and edifice but by a pattern of clouds, oceans, greenery, and soils. Humanity's inability to fit its doings into that pattern is changing planetary systems, fundamentally. (World Commission on Environment and Development 1)

With historical hindsight, it is easy to indict this symbol and the globalist discourse that accompanied it for its inherent tensions: an antitechnological rhetoric relying on an image produced by advanced technology, an at least partially antiscientific discourse recurring to scientific insight to convey its message about the state of the world, and an emphasis on inter-connectedness that was variously used to demonstrate the planet's fragility or its resilience to human interference. Given the current intellectual investment in the inherent value of cultural, racial, ethnic, and gender difference, the Blue Planet concept is also an obvious target of criticism for its erasure of political and cultural differences (Jasanoff 40–41; Sachs, *Planet Dialectics* 110–28; Spivak, *Death of a Discipline* 72).[4] Yet in the context of a planet riven by the Cold War and struggles for colonial independence, in a world that many adherents of the new social movements of the time saw as dominated by the logic of capitalist exploitation, gender and race oppression, and increasingly lethal technologies, the enormous appeal of the image lay precisely in its suggestion of a unified and balanced world.

Lovelock's Gaia hypothesis attained vast popularity for similar reasons. In his search for the reasons life has been able to sustain itself on Earth for approximately three and a half billion years, he came to portray the planet in the vocabulary of cybernetics as "a complex entity involving the Earth's biosphere, atmosphere, oceans, and soil; the totality constituting a feedback or cybernetic system which seeks an optimal physical and chemical environment for life on this planet" (*Gaia* 10). But due to Lovelock's choice of an anthropomorphic name (suggested to him by his one-time neighbor, the novelist William Golding), it was easy in the popular reception of his theory to background its scientific and systems-theoretical vocabulary and to emphasize instead its mythological and spiritual resonances. For the burgeoning environmental movement of the 1970s, as well as for ecofeminist and New Age philosophies in the 1980s, Gaia became readily associated with age-old images of Mother Earth, as well as with John Muir's famous dictum that "when we try to pick out any thing by itself, we find it hitched to everything else in the universe" (245). Understood as an echo of such older views of global connectivity, the popular conception of the Gaia hypothesis became a shorthand for holistic approaches to the natural environment that emphasized balances, interdependencies, and the need for preservation rather than scientific analysis and technological exploitation.[5]

In 1963, Buckminster Fuller similarly described Planet Earth in terms of systems theory and cybernetics through his allegory of Spaceship Earth. Fuller envisioned Earth as "an integrally-designed machine which to be persistently successful must be comprehended and serviced in total" and argued that "up to now we have been mis-using, abusing and polluting this extraordinary chemical energy-interchanging system for successfully regenerating all life aboard our planetary spaceship" (52). The economist Kenneth Boulding took up this metaphor of an intricate organic machine in his well-known essay "The Economics of the Coming Spaceship Earth" (1966), in which he contrasted the seemingly inexhaustible resources of the open "cowboy economy" of the past with what he called the "spaceman economy" of the future, "in which the earth has become a single spaceship, without unlimited reservoirs of anything, either for extraction or for pollution, and in which, therefore, man must find his place in a cyclical ecological system" (11). The influence of the image of the Blue Planet floating in space is palpable in these conceptualizations of Earth as a spaceship with finite resources for survival, an allegory that highlights the sophistication and fragility of this extremely complex system as much as its self-enclosure.

Garrett Hardin's central metaphor from 1968 is inspired by more ordinary and earthly models. His suggestion that many of the Earth's resources are subject to the same exploitation and lack of long-term foresight that in earlier centuries afflicted village commons open to use by all inhabitants led him to postulate the imminent tragedy of the "global commons." Instead of the inherent intricacy of global ecological systems that Lovelock's and Fuller's allegories foreground, this metaphor emphasizes the human usage of limited resources. While quite different analyses of such usage as well as its historical precedent were proposed in the decades following Hardin's essay, the concept of the global commons continues to be used to the present day in discussions of resources that are not or only partly subject to the control of individual nations, such as the management of oceans or the atmosphere.

In spite of their conceptual differences, what all of these ecological allegories share in common is a sense that the Earth's inhabitants, regardless of their national and cultural differences, are bound together by a global ecosystem whose functioning transcends humanmade borders. It is easy to see how such a conception of ecology, derived from an attempt to practice science in a more synthetic and holistic fashion, lent itself to extrapolation into the political and social sphere. Countercultural aspirations toward global peace and the "brotherhood of man" could effortlessly be associated with the image of the Blue Planet and indeed be understood to derive directly from the planet's ecological functioning. Ecological systems, in this understanding, are naturally balanced, harmonious, and self-regenerating, and much of the utopian energy of the 1960s derived implicitly or explicitly from the inference that sociocultural systems might also return to such a state if they were freed from artificial constraints and distortions. Whatever the critiques one might want to formulate vis-à-vis this understanding of ecology and its sociocultural ramifications from the perspective of current cultural theory—justifiably much more suspicious of such notions of the natural—one cannot underestimate the galvanizing influence such thinking exerted on the burgeoning environmentalist movement, as well as on other new social movements in the 1960s.

But as Hardin's warning about the possible "tragedy" of the global commons already indicates, visions of global connectedness did not always entail utopian sociocultural projects. Ehrlich's *Population Bomb*, the Meadows's *Limits to Growth*, and Lester Brown's *Twenty-Ninth Day*, on the contrary, emphasized the possibility of catastrophic collapse on a planetary scale if contemporary trends in demographic growth, resource use, and pollution continued. The widespread use of apocalyptic narrative in environmentalist rhetoric of the 1960s and 1970s is well documented,[6] as is the transfer of Cold War language to environmentalist scenarios in Ehrlich's metaphorization of population growth as a "bomb" or Rachel Carson's description of chemical pollution as a "grim specter stalk[ing] the land" (3). Environmentally oriented science fiction stories, by both scientists like Paul Ehrlich himself and literary authors, similarly portrayed global agricultural landscapes gone so toxic they could only be worked by robots (as in Brian Aldiss's 1967 *Earthworks*), nightmarish urban crowding, food riots, and famine (in a multitude of texts and films that will be discussed in more detail in chapter 2), or the entire planet laid to waste in misery, pollution, and disease (as in John Brunner's 1972 novel *The Sheep Look Up*). As Killingsworth and Palmer have pointed out, the horror of such millennial scenarios was in many cases intended less as a probable assessment of things to come than as a means of driving home the urgency of the environmentalist call for social change (41); the presentation of collapse as global rather than local or national functioned as one important way of conveying the deadly seriousness of the crisis.

If nuclear fear and environmental concern shared such narrative patterns, derived in the last instance from biblical apocalypse, a more subtle but no less terrifying vision of global connectedness emerged from fears of corporate conspiracy that had circulated since the 1950s and made themselves explicit in the countercultural resistance to "the Man" or "the System." While social critics in earlier decades had emphasized the dangers of totalitarian states that might expand to worldwide rule, from the 1950s on, transnational corporations became the prime suspects of aspirations to global hegemony. Anticipated in novels such as Cyril Kornbluth and Frederik Pohl's *Space Merchants* (1953), this fear found its most influential cultural expression in the indictments of the corporate "moloch" and characters' persistently paranoid states of mind in the poetry and fiction of Allen Ginsberg, William Burroughs, and above all, Thomas Pynchon. As a form of resistance to capitalism and specifically to the mass consumerism that escalated in scale and scope after 1945, this paranoid vision of a global corporate conspiracy aiming to control the lives of individuals, communities, and nations, up to and including the triggering of world wars, was not in its original formulations specifically environmentalist. But it made its way into environmental rhetoric in the 1970s, when it surfaced in, for example, Edward Abbey's ecoclassic *The Monkey Wrench Gang* (1975), whose protagonists struggle against what they perceive as a "megalomaniacal megamachine" (167):

U.S. Steel intertwined in incestuous embrace with the Pentagon, TVA, Standard Oil, General Dynamics, Dutch Shell, I.G. Farben-industrie [*sic*]; the whole conglomerated cartel spread out upon half the planet

Earth like a global kraken, pan-tentacled, wall-eyed and parrot-beaked, its brain a bank of computer data centers, its blood the flow of money, its heart a radioactive dynamo. (172)[7]

Part of today's antiglobalization rhetoric, with its allegorization of villainous transnational corporations, descends directly from this corporate-conspiracy discourse of the 1960s and 1970s.

This intensely ambivalent legacy of global visions may help explain why the environmentalist movement today is uneasily extended from organizations that operate internationally and regularly make their voices heard in global political affairs using the diplomatic, economic, legal, and social languages of international institutions, all the way to a fervently antiglobalist wing of activists who demonstrate in the streets against the actions of precisely such institutions. The current political influence of international environmental nongovernmental organizations depends on their willingness to engage in and shape global processes in view of environmentalist goals, while the running battles of activists against the police at the Seattle World Summit in 1999 and the G8 Summit in Genoa in 2001 reflect a different assessment of globalization as dominated by corporate interests and therefore in need of being vigorously resisted. While the term "antiglobalization movement" has become popular in the media, many activists prefer the terms "anti–global capitalism movement" or "global justice movement," as they seek to foreground their opposition to the way politics has been dominated by transnational corporations.

But while this ambivalence of engagement in and resistance to the global, as I have shown, has a history that is several decades old, both the apocalyptic and the utopian dimensions of environmentalist visions of the planet have substantially weakened. Frederick Buell has persuasively demonstrated how the expectation of future collapse, prevalent in the 1960s, has transmuted into an awareness of ongoing crisis in the present (177–208). Instead of anticipating disaster, he argues, most populations have learned to live with, and sometimes to accommodate to, a multitude of daily ecological risk scenarios. Utopian hopes have diminished along with all-encompassing millennial visions. Attempts to project a future course for the planet under the label "sustainable development," widely discussed since the 1987 Brundtland Report, and more recent revisions of the development philosophy that undergirded this notion in the context of "environmental justice," are themselves contested and have not to date generated the kind of powerful images that dominated the debates of the 1960s and 1970s.[8] To the extent that most environmentalists see the world as unified today, it is either as a world dominated by corporate capitalism or as a world at risk.

Lawrence Buell has argued that in some ways the idea of the risk society holds out the idea of a permanently destabilized globe, in diametrical opposition to Lovelock's vision of an enduring and balanced planetary ecosystem (*Future* 90). I will examine this concept of a global "risk society," to use German sociologist Ulrich Beck's term, in more detail in chapter 4. But clearly, it is the ambivalence toward the notion of global connectedness dating back to the 1960s, in conjunction with the weakening of the utopian impulses that still formed part of the cultural imaginary surrounding the Blue Planet, which account for the persistent utopian reinvestment in the local in much environmental literature, philosophy, and cultural criticism.

3. Localism and Modernity: The Ethic of Proximity

In examining Western environmentalist discourses that arose around the photograph of the Blue Planet, science studies scholar Sheila Jasanoff has argued that they rely on a globalizing approach to ecological issues, which she contrasts with the more localizing perspectives of environmental movements in the developing world (46–50). But any study of American environmentalist literature of the last forty years reveals a very different and far more complex picture, some of whose dimensions emerge in the following description of an environmental studies course:

> On a balmy September afternoon, about a hundred students at one of the finest public universities in the nation are gathered under a sprawling Monterey pine. "What kind of tree is this?" a professor asks. Silence. "How many of you don't know any more than that it's a tree?" Most students raise their hands. They can converse knowledgeably about chlorofluorocarbons and the ozone hole, but most can't tell a pine from a fir, or even an oak. The professor is perturbed. "I don't think we have a chance of changing our relationship to the natural world if you don't know what's around you," he says. (Hamilton, http://www.asle.umn.edu/archive/intro/sierra.html)

This scene from a course taught by Berkeley professor and poet Robert Hass articulates a familiar idea in American environmentalist discourse: in order to reconnect with the natural world, individuals need to develop a "sense of place" by getting to know the details of the ecosystems that immediately surround them. The fact that the students who fall short in their identifications of local plants do seem to have a fairly detailed understanding of larger-scale ecological phenomena such as the depletion of stratospheric ozone is dismissed here as too abstract a kind of knowledge. The basis for genuine ecological understanding, Hass seems to claim, lies in the local.

The insistence on individuals' and communities' need to reconnect to local places as a way of overcoming the alienation from nature that modern societies generate, as well as long-standing ambivalences about the global are two of the most formative and characteristic dimensions of American environmentalism that Jasanoff misses in her description. In the United States—but less so in other regional varieties of environmentalism—place has figured since the 1960s as a countervailing tendency to what Allen Ginsberg called "Globe-Eye Consciousness" in one of his poems (528). Environmental philosopher Paul Shepard, for example, has claimed categorically that "knowing who you are is impossible without knowing where you are" and that the relationship to place serves to "both reflect and create an inner geography by which we locate the self" (32, 28). Neil Evernden has similarly insisted that "the establishment of self is impossible without the context of place" and, indeed, that "there is no such thing as an individual, only an individual-in-context, individual as a component of place, defined by place" (101, 103). On the basis of such perspectives, place continues to function as one of the most important categories through which American environmentalists articulate what it means to be ecologically aware and ethically responsible today.

Due in part to its long persistence, the rhetoric of place in U.S. environmentalism cannot be reduced to a single philosophy but encompasses a whole range of sociocultural projects, from Wendell Berry's Jeffersonian agrarianism and the bioregionalist movement founded by Peter Berg and Raymond Dasmann in the 1970s all the way to the emphasis on minority communities, traditions, and rights in the environmental justice movement. Place-oriented discourses associated with movements such as these variously deploy notions of "dwelling," "(re)inhabitation," "land ethic," "bioregionalism," or, more rarely, "land erotic" as their anchoring concepts. Unsurprisingly, the localisms articulated through such concepts are not all alike. White male environmentalist writers between the 1950s and the 1970s often put the emphasis on the (usually male) individual's encounter with and physical immersion in the landscape, typically envisioned as wild rather than rural or urban.[9] In its more literary versions, this vision leads to individuals' epiphanic fusions with their natural surroundings, not unlike Osden's merger with the forest in Le Guin's "Vaster Than Empires." Edward Abbey, for example, describes an extended stay alone in Havasu Canyon during which he gradually lost a sense of the identity of his human body and began to see a leaf when looking at his hand (*Desert Solitaire* 250–51). Aldo Leopold portrays a merger of his body with the surrounding marsh landscape in one of his sketches, as does Gary Snyder in his poem "second shaman song"(*No Nature* 56).[10] Berry's extensive writings about his homesteading on an Appalachian farm, by contrast, foreground an agricultural landscape and the careful use of and work with the land. Women writers and some Native American authors later criticized the individualist focus of these writings and instead shifted the emphasis to more communal forms of inhabitation. Writers and activists in the environmental justice movement drew attention to glaring social, racial, and gender differences in exposures to risk, possibilities of coping with them, and the divergent modes of encountering nature resulting from such gaps. Rather than superseding the older forms of place imagination, these more recent perspectives have added to what is by now a considerable range of environmentalist visions, some of whose advocates are antagonistic to each other.

Yet certain elements of the place imagination tend to reappear across different types of political and cultural orientation. Snyder and Abbey's earlier scenarios of bodies fused with their surroundings may seem dated, but the much more recent idea of a "land erotic," formulated in the creative writings of Terry Tempest Williams and more theoretically in the work of ecofeminists such as Louise Westling, returns to the idea of human bodies merged with their natural environments.[11] More broadly, a fundamental investment in a particular kind of "situated knowledge," the intimate acquaintance with local nature and history that develops with sustained interest in one's immediate surroundings, recurs across otherwise quite different discourses. This type of knowledge is often portrayed as arising out of sensory perception and physical immersion, the bodily experience and manipulation of nature, rather than out of more abstract or mediated kinds of knowledge acquisition. Walking through natural landscapes, observing their flora and fauna, hunting, fishing, gathering fruits or mushrooms, plowing a field, and tending animals are some of the ways the human body is perceived to reintegrate itself into the "biotic community."

Similarly, elements of pastoral tend to reassert themselves in unexpected ways. While the American environmentalist movement's early preference for wilderness and natural spaces untouched by humans has by now been thoroughly criticized for its involvement in a history of indigenous displacements and its disregard for native populations that use their environments sustainably (Cronon; Guha), it has retained a galvanizing force for radical groups, including Earth First! and Friends of the Earth, as well as for some conservation efforts. But the idea that either wild or rural places might function as an antidote to the corruptions of modern, industrial, and urban society—an idea Leo Marx analyzed in detail in his classic study *The Machine in the Garden*—informs innumerable environmentalist novels, poems, and essays that revolve around farming, gardening, hiking, rafting, mountain climbing, or "roughing it." Even in the more industrial and urban landscapes that form the backdrop for much environmental justice literature, pastoral tends to recur by way of the alternative communities and surroundings the movement endeavors to create.[12]

In this context, local autonomy and self-sufficiency often present themselves as desirable goals at the level of either individual families or of larger communities: building one's own house, homesteading on one's own farm, or becoming self-sufficient in terms of food and energy tend to be achievements that are held up as models for individuals, while the rejection of large cities, the nation-state, and economic globalization along with an emphasis on local production, consumption, and reinvestment, local currencies or trading systems, decentralized power, egalitarianism, and grassroots democracy shape corresponding visions of local communities (see Naess, *Ecology* 141–46 and Sale chaps. 6 and 7). Such autonomy and self-sufficiency, in the view of many advocates of place, can only be achieved through prolonged residence in one place and the rejection of high mobility. Wendell Berry has argued that

> at present our society is almost entirely nomadic . . . and it is moving about on the face of this continent with a mindless destructiveness . . . that makes Sherman's march to the sea look like a prank. Without a complex knowledge of one's place, and without the faithfulness to one's place on which such knowledge depends, it is inevitable that the place will be used carelessly, and eventually destroyed. Without such knowledge and faithfulness, moreover, the culture of a country will be superficial and decorative. ("Regional Motive" 68–69)

Scott Russell Sanders's tellingly entitled book *Staying Put: Making a Home in a Restless World* (1993) echoes this sentiment as it portrays his

> attempts to fashion a life that is firmly grounded—in household and community, in knowledge of place, in awareness of nature, and in contact with that source from which all things rise. I aspire to become an inhabitant, one who knows and honors the land. . . . My nation's history does not encourage me, or anyone, to belong somewhere with a full heart. A vagabond wind has been blowing here for a long while, and it grows stronger by the hour. I feel the force of it, and brace my legs to keep from staggering. . . . I wish to consider the virtue and discipline of staying put. (xiii–xv)

Associating geographical mobility with "nomadism" or "vagabondage" rather than with the more ecologically grounded concept of "migration," these and other environmentalist writers seek to "ground" or "root" their philosophy in long-term residence in one place.

Environmental justice activists have often taken issue with the underlying assumptions of race, class, and gender that tend to be taken for granted in the environmental ethics of white, male, middle-class writers, including Berry and Sanders. They have rightly emphasized not only that the privileges of encounters with nature as well as the risks associated with some branches of agribusiness and industry are unevenly distributed but that in fact this uneven distribution has in some instances helped to perpetuate environmentally unsound practices whose consequences have often not been suffered or even noticed by the middle class (Reed 151). Given the environmental justice movement's leftist, antihegemonic, and radical political rhetoric, it comes as somewhat of a surprise to find one environmental justice ecocritic deploring how "globalization . . . alters traditional values of place, life, and meaning" and "trigger[s]...chaos" (Sze 168), as if tradition and order were self-evidently worth perpetuating, and to see others relying on conceptions of place-based identity that do not differ from those of the white, male, middle-class environmentalists they criticize as much as one might expect. In his study of the Latino *acequía* communities of the southwestern United States, for example, Devon Peña delivers a precise and clearheaded account of how such communities combine ecological with cultural practices, and how the usufruct principles of collectively managed *acequía* irrigation systems legally conflict with the Anglo principle of "prior appropriation" of water. But Peña oscillates between affirming that such traditional forms of community are capable of change and adaptation to the social conditions created by modernization and describing modernization processes as irreversible injuries done not only to the material practices but the spiritual essence of individuals and the community. "At the root, hispano mexicano environmental ethics seem governed by an intense and even militant attachment to place (and to staying in place) and therefore by an unwavering principle of local autonomy. The environmental ethics of hispano mexicanos are thus an ethics of place and are derived from localized identities," he argues (65), in a vocabulary that echoes that of Sanders and Berry.

> The destruction of the Culebra forests is the extirpation of a man's soul, a rupturing of his spiritual connection to the land, mountains, and water. His sense of place is violently disturbed by the industrial exploitation that radically altered the landscape of his childhood. The actual biophysical anchors of memory are displaced, producing a sense of being violated and emptied of spirit. (66)

Whatever the merits of this elegiac portrayal of trauma may be, the concepts it relies on are clearly remote from the sociological and economic account Peña delivers of how modernization affects the ecological bases of the livelihood of a specific social group; they slide from a materialist analysis of place into the speculative psychology that the concept of "spirituality" often also introduces into meditations on the sense of place in white, male, and middle-class environmentalist writings. This uneasy mix of a materialist analysis ultimately, if for the most part indirectly, informed by Marxist assumptions, and a New Age–inflected rhetoric of spirituality underlies quite a few environmental justice texts, though usually in more covert form.[13]

The models for self-sufficient and rooted communities, in first-wave as well as environmental-justice ecocriticism, are frequently premodern societies. In U.S. environmentalism, it is often Native American cultures that are credited with having—or having had in the past—a closer connection to the land, a conception that surfaced perhaps most visibly in the

1970s poster of "Iron Eyes" Cody in Native American attire crying over the despoliation of the land.[14] More recently, Leslie Marmon Silko's essay "Landscape, History, and the Pueblo Imagination" has functioned as a touchstone for Native American traditions of thought about inhabitation. Silko describes an alternative type of community reliant on a mythological mode of perception that accepts neither a fundamental dividing line nor a fusion between nature and human culture. Instead, it infuses every feature of the contemporary landscape with mythological origins and significance. Silko refers specifically to southwestern Laguna Pueblo culture and should not be unproblematically taken to represent the several hundred different native cultures of North America, some of which were historically sedentary and others nomadic. Her essay, however, has often been understood to sum up in paradigmatic fashion the premodern awareness of peoples with a deeply rooted and intimate relationship to their places of inhabitation.[15] While environmental historians have pointed to a more mixed record of premodern cultures and their relationship to their natural habitats (see Bahn and Flenley; Diamond; Krech), such cultures nevertheless often continue to function as models for envisioning an alternative relationship to place in the contemporary imagination.

I would argue, then, that in spite of significant differences in social outlook, certain features recur across a wide variety of environmentalist perspectives that emphasize a sense of place as a basic prerequisite for environmental awareness and activism. Many of them, as I have attempted to show, associate spatial closeness, cognitive understanding, emotional attachment, and an ethic of responsibility and "care." Put somewhat more abstractly, they share what philosophers Hans Jonas and Zygmunt Bauman, as well as the sociologist John Tomlinson, have in a broader context called an "ethic of proximity." As Bauman puts it,

> the morality which we have inherited from pre-modern times—the only morality we have—is a morality of proximity, and as such is woefully inadequate in a society in which all important action is an action on distance.... Moral responsibility prompts us to care that our children are fed, clad and shod; it cannot offer us much practical advice, however, when faced with numbing images of a depleted, desiccated and overheated planet which our children, and the children of our children will inherit and have to inhabit in the direct or oblique result of our collective unconcern. (217–18)

Bauman sums up the dilemma that this approach to ethics raises in an increasingly global context by claiming that

> the cancelling of spatial distance as measured by the reach of human action—that sometimes applauded, but ever more often bewailed feat of modern technology—has not been matched by the cancellation of

moral distance, measured by the reach of moral responsibility; but it should be so matched. The question is, how this can be done, if at all. (219)

This skepticism as to whether an ethical code based on what is geographically or socially nearby will be able to cope with larger contexts such as the nation or the transnational realm is echoed by many environmentalist thinkers. The Norwegian philosopher Arne Naess, for example, a highly influential figure for American environmentalism, declares categorically that "the nearer has priority over the more remote—in space, time, culture, species" ("Identification" 268). His call for "a coherent, local, logical, and natural community" (*Ecology* 144) assumes, as do many other celebrations of the sense of place, that sociocultural, ethical, and affective allegiances arise spontaneously and "naturally" at the local level, whereas any attachments to larger entities such as the nation or beyond require complex processes of mediation.

Frequently, the assumption that there can be no compelling ethical interpellation other than that of proximity becomes the foundation for a more general critique of modern sociopolitical structures in environmentalist thought, a deep-seated skepticism vis-à-vis the long-distance, mediated, and abstract structures and institutions that shape modern societies. Naess himself is quite explicit about his rejection of social modernity: "Locality and togetherness in the sense of community are central key terms in the deep ecological movement. There is, so to say, an 'instinctive' reaction against being absorbed in something that is big but not great—something like our modern society" (*Ecology* 144). For this reason, the bioregionalist movement, which is heavily indebted to Naess, has consistently advocated a geographical, political, and economic reorganization of nations into bioregions whose boundaries would follow ecological dividing lines like climate zones, species distribution, watersheds, or mountain ranges. Such a reorganization, according to prominent bioregionalist Kirkpatrick Sale, would liberate people from the large-scale social structures that interpose themselves between people's actions and the visibility of their consequences:

> The only way people will apply "right behavior" and behave in responsible ways is if they have been persuaded to see the problem concretely and to understand their own connections to it directly—and this can be done only at a limited scale....[P]eople will do the environmentally "correct" thing not because it is thought to be the *moral*, but rather the *practical*, thing to do. That cannot be done on a global scale, nor a continental, nor even a national one, because the human animal, being small and limited, has only a small view of the world and a limited comprehension of how to act within it. (53)

Sale's central idea, that the ecologically right course of action will impose itself as the obvious one at the local but not at larger levels of scale, may seem something short of compelling to anyone who has ever engaged in local politics (a point I will return to later). What persuasive power it has surely derives from its widely shared mistrust of the large-scale, abstract, and often invisible networks of authority, expertise, and exchange that structure modern societies.[16]

This critique of modernity in American discourses of place derives not infrequently from the European phenomenological tradition, as is obvious in the case of Sale's reliance on Naess, who is himself heavily influenced by Martin Heidegger. Heidegger and Maurice Merleau-Ponty both attempt to think beyond what they perceive to be the limitations of modern thought and society in works whose influence on American environmentalism continues to be palpable. In his well-known essay "Bauen Wohnen Denken" (Building Dwelling Thinking, 1951), Heidegger holds against the "homelessness" of modern society the well-known image of the Black Forest farmhouse, which exemplifies a mode of inhabitation in which construction is not so much a mere process of turning a set of materials—stone, timber, slate—into particular objects as part of the very process of living itself. Such dwelling, for Heidegger, should ideally give expression to the essence of human existence, and should also aim to give other forms of being an occasion—or a "location"—to manifest their own presence. Merleau-Ponty, especially in his late work *Le visible et l'invisible* (The Visible and the Invisible, 1961), seeks to overcome the separation between subject and object by anchoring the perception of phenomena in the living body, and by foregrounding that the encounter with the world, the natural world included, is a physical, material encounter that can be described in terms of metaphors drawn from erotic rhetoric.[17] Both of these different phenomenological approaches to the relationship between humans and their habitats have exerted a shaping influence on American environmentalist and ecocritical thought, and have sedimented in various articulations of the ethic of proximity as articulated by Jonas and Bauman, who themselves refer to the same tradition.[18]

Aldo Leopold's concept of the "land ethic" is often mentioned, along with Heidegger and Naess's writings, as one of the basic sources for contemporary environmentalist approaches to place. Indeed, Leopold at times sounds bitterly critical of modern culture and the way it alienates people from the land:

> our educational and economic system is headed away from, rather than toward, an intense consciousness of land. Your true modern is separated from the land by many middlemen, and by innumerable physical gadgets. He has no vital relation to it; to him it is the space between cities on which crops grow. Turn him loose for a day on the land, and if

the spot does not happen to be a golf links or a "scenic" area, he is bored stiff. . . . In short, land is something he has "outgrown." (223–24)

Yet Leopold legitimates his notion of a land ethic by arguing that it would follow a tradition of political and legal thought that is—even though he does not say so—distinctively modernist. Leopold points out that over the course of time, basic rights have been extended to members of the human community that were formerly considered outside their bounds, such as women and slaves. In his view, the extension of these rights to nonhuman subjects is merely another step in the same direction:

> All ethics so far evolved rest upon a single premise: that the individual is a member of a community of interdependent parts. . . . The land ethic simply enlarges the boundaries of the community to include soils, waters, plants, and animals, or collectively: the land. . . . A land ethic of course cannot prevent the alteration, management, and use of these "resources," but it does affirm their right to continued existence, and, at least in spots, their continued existence in a natural state.
> In short, a land ethic changes the role of *Homo sapiens* from conqueror of the land-community to plain member and citizen of it. (203–4)

The explicit vocabulary of rights and citizenship Leopold deploys, along with his obvious underlying assumptions about gradual enlightenment, emancipation, and social equality are all distinctively modernist in ways that he himself does not acknowledge, and that put him to some extent at odds with the European phenomenological critique of modernity. Leopold also diverges from the ethic of proximity as formulated by Bauman in the way he envisions the meaning of "community." In his analysis, land-community is not defined in advance by the natural or social environment, but has to be culturally imagined and can, on the evidence of historical precedent, be "enlarged" to include members not previously thought to have formed part of it: the promise of Leopold's land ethic rests entirely on the hope that such a cultural reimagination beyond existing boundaries is possible. Clearly, the idea that existing communities can be ethically broadened beyond the parameters that previously defined them offers a different foundation for thinking about modern sociopolitical structures than the assumption that a compelling ethical code can only be grounded in the local.

If some of the most important intellectual sources for contemporary environmentalist discourses about place are not entirely commensurate with each other in their vision of modernity, it may come as no particular surprise that globalism, understood as the worldwide spread of modernization processes, is also envisioned in ambivalent and sometimes self-contradictory ways. One prominent example is the place philosophy of the geographer Yi-Fu Tuan, which is not itself articulated in explicitly environmentalist terms but is often alluded to by ecologically oriented thinkers and writers. In his exploration of "topophilia," the affective bonds that tie humans to particular places, Tuan rejects the nation as too large and abstract an entity to command human affection, but simultaneously affirms that attachments to the planet as a whole are possible and desirable. "Just as the pretense to 'love for humanity' arouses our suspicion, so topophilia rings false when it is claimed for a large territory. A compact size scaled down to man's biologic needs and sense-bound capacities seems necessary," he argues. "The modern state is too large, its boundaries too arbitrary, its area too heterogeneous to command the kind of affection that arises of experience and intimate knowledge.... [The state's] reality for the individual depends on the ingestion of certain kinds of knowledge" (101,100). If this claim seems to suggest, oddly, that knowledge is desirable if it is "intimate" but not if it appears in any other guise, his aspiration toward planetary topophilia is even more openly self-contradictory:

> If both empire and state are too large for the exercise of genuine topophilia, it is paradoxical to reflect that the earth itself may eventually command such attachment: this possibility exists because the earth is clearly a natural unit and it has a common history.... Possibly, in some ideal future, our loyalty will be given only to the home region of intimate memories and, at the other end of the scale, to the whole earth. (102)

Even as Tuan generally bases his theory of topophilia on the privileging of direct sensory experience in the way many phenomenologically influenced environmentalist writers do, he omits any reflection on what cultural mediations, abstract knowledge, and technological apparatus necessarily go into a perception of the Earth as a "natural unit" with a "common history." In fact, what Tuan articulates here is a version of the Blue Planet perspective, which is able to take in the entire planet at one glance and perceive it as a shared whole without conflicting histories or cultures—a perspective that, as I showed earlier, is inconceivable without the intervention of advanced technology, and whose meaning depends on a particular cultural moment.

Many environmentalist writers are a good deal more logically consistent in their approaches to the global than Tuan. Yet the spectrum of perspectives reaches from those who reject globalism outright to those who perceive it as a seamless extension of the local. Garrett Hardin, for example, mocks what he calls the Global Pothole Authority, that is, global institutions designed to deal with problems that would be much more efficiently solved at the local level: "Long experience has shown that local problems are best dealt with by local action.... Globalization favors evasion. The wise rule to follow should be plain: *Never globalize a problem if it can possibly be dealt with locally....* Globalism is usually counterproductive" (*Filters against Folly* 144).[19] Wendell Berry shares this feeling when he points out that "The adjective 'planetary' describes a problem in such a way that it cannot be solved.... The problems, if we describe them accurately, are all private and small" ("Word and Flesh" 198). John Haines, who has described his forty years of living self-sufficiently in Alaska in many of his poems and essays, takes a more ambivalent stance by anticipating the necessity of a global consciousness, but regrets the passing of a sense of place that it entails in his view:

> When our imaginations have grown enough, perhaps we will understand that the local must one day include the continent, and finally the planet itself. It seems likely that nothing else will allow us to thrive as a species. But it is also true that meanwhile we are painfully aware that an honored and durable way of life has disappeared, leaving an empty place in our lives. (9)[20]

In other cases, environmentalist writers and thinkers have expressed a desire to connect the local with the global. René Dubos's well-known 1970 slogan "Think globally, act locally," formulated at a time when globalism was still associated with utopian social ideals, articulates the hope that local politics can be positively reshaped through its persistent framing in terms of global issues. Other activists and writers have equally reached for a bottom-up connection from the local to the global by proposing that global connections present themselves as a kind of addition or multiplication of local scenarios. Snyder suggests in one of his essays that "a place on earth is a mosaic within larger mosaics—the land is all small places, all precise tiny realms replicating larger and smaller patterns" ("Place" 27). Sanders similarly claims that

> we can live wisely in our chosen place only if we recognize its connections to the rest of the planet. The challenge is to see one's region as a focus of processes that extend over the earth and out to the edges of the universe; to realize that *this* place is only one of an infinite number of places where the powers of nature show forth. (xvi)

In both cases, the local is presented as a miniature version of the globe and indeed the cosmos.

Both the rejection of the global and its seamless integration into the local pose considerable conceptual and political difficulties. Denying that a global perspective might yield useful insights and solutions implies either that one deprives oneself of a fair number of ecological insights, as well as an understanding of present political and economic realities, or that one is forced to make a large number of exceptions. Arguing that the local connects seamlessly with the global means ignoring that access to an understanding of global ecological as well as political and cultural configurations usually relies on different types of knowledge and experience than an understanding of the local, and that precisely these kinds of knowledge and experience are often rejected as inauthentic or adulterated by environmentalists. More recent attempts to articulate an environmentalist vision of the global have therefore adopted a somewhat different strategy: they aim primarily at an understanding of global structures, but retain the emphasis on the local as a matter of political or didactic practicality rather than as an issue of the existential or spiritual significance that was postulated in earlier writings. Paul and Anne Ehrlich, for example, discuss a sense of place mostly as a matter of expediency when they argue in *One with Nineveh* (2004) that

> one clear need...is more emphasis on maintaining people's sense of place...[L]ocalization can strengthen that sense of place, that attachment to an immediate environment, which is still a major part of the identity of most human beings. An understanding of local surroundings permits many people to gain awareness of the ecosystem services upon which their lives depend. (324–25)

A similar shift marks Mitchell Thomashow's attempt to consider the role of place in an increasingly global context in his book *Bringing the Biosphere Home: Learning to Perceive Global Environmental Change* (2002). Thomashow's primary objective is not a conventional advocacy of place but the question of how large-scale ecological developments such as climate change, soil erosion, or shrinking biodiversity might become part of the awareness of average citizens. Arguing that "there is no such thing as a local environmental problem" because all such problems form part of a network of global processes and issues, Thomashow indicates that his own thinking about global ecology was initially shaped by the image of the Blue Planet and Dubos's slogan "Think globally, act locally" (7). But Thomashow is acutely aware that thinking about the relationship between experiences of the local and global processes involves complex shifts of conceptual register, and involves knowledge of scientific principles and processes as well as recourse to metaphor. "It takes a chain of conceptual leaps and assumptions to perceive that an enormous globe filled with six billion people and several hundred countries has a shared destiny, a co-ordinated plot," he argues (26). In his attention to such conceptual leaps and the metaphors that often undergird them, Thomashow moves considerably beyond more conventional environmentalist discourses of place. Nevertheless, he continues to insist that the way to an understanding of the global can only proceed through a prior engagement with the details of the local environment, in what he calls a "place-based perceptual ecology," because "people are best equipped to observe what happens around them—what they can see, hear, smell, taste, and touch. These observations are poignant in their home places, where they are likely to spend lots of time, have many relationships, and be most in touch with the natural world" (5). If this sounds like a return to Naess's and Sale's affirmation that people are likely to get attached to what is "closest" to them in some sense, Thomashow pays a great deal more attention to what might complicate such a relatively simple assumption. Migration, he argues in some detail, is so common and widespread a phenomenon in both human history and ecology that rootedness in one place cannot plausibly be claimed as the most "natural" form of relating to place; instead, "place-based transience" might be a better concept for thinking about the kinds of mobility that characterize many species' relation to their habitats (180–82).[21]

At the same time, Thomashow recognizes that media such as television and the internet have made it possible for average people to experience a multitude of faraway places in unprecedented sensory detail and imaginative scope, and sees benefits for the environmentalist project in this connectedness. Early in his book, he imagines locally rooted observers building a network of information sharing around the globe through the use of such new media; thereby, he argues, "the patterns of global environmental change emerge seamlessly out of deep engagement with local natural history. Nodes of local observers form a global environmental change interpretive network—the biosphere observes and interprets itself" (*Bringing* 7). This systems-theoretical vision of observers linked by a global network of information exchange leads Thomashow to a detailed exploration of the highly mediated and culturally conditioned forms by means of which individuals and communities come to imagine the global. Within such a framework, the imperative to reconnect to the local transmutes into a matter of pragmatic convenience rather than a claim to ontological foundations:

> I am just passing through this landscape.... No matter how this landscape molds and shapes me, it can only modify my diasporic origins.... Yet I am not willing to let go of this place-based philosophy. Not only does it make good educational sense but it speaks to the possibility of ecological fidelity, and lends me a sense of rootedness (however transient) in a world of ceaseless motion. (176–77)

This sounds like an eminently sensible way of thinking about place attachments today—except that one might ask, as I will shortly, why the kinds of connections between people's daily lives and global connectedness Thomashow points to really require any special emphasis on place at all. But Thomashow is clearly uncomfortable with leaving matters there. In his last chapter, he reinserts what is otherwise a largely pragmatic approach to global ecological awareness into a vaguely defined spirituality:

> Through familiarity and intimacy, you learn how to pay closer attention to the full splendor of the biosphere as it is revealed to you in the local ecosystem. In those moments when you can wade through the distractions of business and task, when you catch a glimpse of the unfathom-

able world at your doorstep, you open yourself to biospheric perception. Through a deliberate place-based gaze, by learning how to move between worlds, you allow those glimpses to last a little bit longer each time. By developing appreciation for the biosphere, in liberating your sense of wonder, in summoning praise and reverence, in contemplating the mystery and circumstances of processes that you can never fully understand, you feel a sense of gratitude and appreciation. You learn to honor biogeochemical cycles as intrinsic to your breath and thirst. You find your origins in the history of life on earth. You forge alliances and affiliations with people and species from all corners of the globe as you watch them pass through your neighborhood. You summon praise for whatever lies behind this outstanding journey—Gaia, God, evolution? With the passing of praise comes cause for celebration. (*Bringing* 212)

This mixture of Thoreau, New Age, and Judeo-Buddhist mysticism is obviously light-years away from Thomashow's earlier systems-theoretical description of the biosphere coming to observe itself. Even as he stakes out new and useful territory in his exploration of how bridges might be built between the small-scale details of everyday life and global ecological functioning, Thomashow here tries to connect back to an older environmentalist tradition that puts the emphasis on a spiritual immersion in place. Indeed, "biospheric perception" in this passage seems simply a paraphrase for experiences of the sublime ("moments of great awareness and serendipity, when you feel that you are deeply touched by something unfathomable," 212–13) that can only be described by means of tautology: "by developing appreciation . . . you feel a sense of . . . appreciation."

The obvious incongruence between this tautological foray into the postmodern ecosublime and Thomashow's otherwise quite pragmatically and empirically oriented investigation of how mediation and migration modify the contemporary experience of local and global spaces indicates just how tenuous the sense-of-place rhetoric has become for environmentalism. Thomashow holds on to this rhetoric even though much of his own analysis shows how questionable it has become, forcing him to adopt such oxymoronic phrases as "place-based transience" and "diasporic residency." By the same token, his argument, like that of many other writers who have insisted on a sense of place as the basis of ecologically aware practices, remains tenuously suspended between the assertion that the local provides a familiar ground from which to expand one's awareness to larger scales and the uneasy realization that the local itself is thoroughly unfamiliar to many individuals, and may be epistemologically as unfathomable in its entirety as larger entities such as the nation or the globe.

The persistence of place and place-attachments as a basis of environmentalist thinking also made itself felt in the emergence of ecocriticism as a new area of research in literary and cultural studies in the mid-1990s. In her programmatic introduction to the first highly visible textbook of the new field, *The Ecocriticism Reader*, Cheryll Glotfelty asked: "In addition to race, class, and gender, should *place* become a new critical category?" and seemed to answer her own question by saying that "as a critical stance, [ecocriticism] has one foot in literature and the other on land" (xix). Somewhat more indirectly, Lawrence Buell defined an "environmentally oriented work" in his seminal study *The Environmental Imagination* as one in which the *"nonhuman environment is present not merely as a framing device but as a presence that begins to suggest that human history is implicated in natural history"* (7), with his examples indicating that "nonhuman environment" refers mainly to landscape or setting. Robert Kern expanded this approach by arguing that "all texts are at least potentially environmental (and therefore susceptible to ecocriticism or ecologically informed reading) in the sense that all texts are literally or imaginatively situated in a place, and in the sense that their authors, consciously or not, inscribe within them a certain relation to their place" (259).

Quoting such groundbreaking texts in the establishment of the field is not meant to imply that their association of the ecocritical venture with the study of (representations of) place was uncontested. Scholars such as Glen Love and Joseph Carroll suggested a very different point of departure by anchoring ecocritical investigation in the Darwinist idea of the "adapted mind," that is, the idea that culture is, generally speaking, a mechanism of evolutionary adaptation (Carroll, *Evolution* and *Literary Darwinism*; Love, esp. chap. 2). But theirs remained a minority position, and they did not choose to articulate it as a form of opposition to the dominant place paradigm, which manifested itself not only in theoretical statements of the kind I have focused on here but also in innumerable studies of place in the works of a wide variety of authors from Henry David Thoreau, John Muir, and Willa Cather to Mary Austin, Edward Abbey, Gary Snyder, Barry Lopez, Terry Tempest Williams, and many others.

The underlying problem that persists in the writings of those environmental and ecocritical thinkers who recognize the importance of the global is that they do not, by and large, question the assumption that identity, whether individual or communitarian, is constituted by the local. The crucial insights of the last twenty years of cultural theory into the ways local and national identities depend on excluded others, how they rely on but often deny their own hybrid mixtures with other places and cultures, and in what ways real and imagined travel to other places shapes self-definitions have not left any lasting marks on American environmentalist and ecocritical thought. Where the importance of transnational and global frameworks of reference is acknowledged, it is generally as an addition to a fundamentally localist conception of the subject, not as perspectives that might unsettle such a conception. The ethic of proximity I outlined earlier relies on the assumption that genuine ethical commitments can only grow out of the lived immediacies of the local that constitute the core of one's authentic identity. In this respect, I would argue, ecocriticism in particular, but also much environmentalist thought more generally, has not connected to the foundational idea in much recent cultural theory that identities are at their core made up of mixtures, fragments, and dispersed allegiances to diverse communities, cultures, and places—or that precisely these mixtures might be crucial for constituting "identities" politically as "subjects."

One brief example might help clarify this claim. Perhaps no other writer has been as influential for the American environmental movement, as well as for ecocriticism, as the poet and essayist Gary Snyder. More than many other environmentalist writers, Snyder seems to be in a privileged position to address issues of transnationalism. He studied Chinese and Japanese in the 1950s, lived in Kyoto from the late 1950s to the late 1960s, and has consistently incorporated classical Chinese and Japanese literature and philosophy, as well as Native American storytelling traditions, into his writings. Moreover, some of his titles and key concepts, such as that of an "earth house hold," highlight a planet-wide perspective, even as much of his work focuses on precisely the knowledge of local nature and history and the kind of localist ethics I outlined earlier. Snyder's work, therefore, entirely deserves the detailed attention environmentalists and ecocritics have bestowed on it, and I would not venture to claim that I can explore its full complexity here. Yet I would argue that the persistent presence of other cultural spaces and traditions in Snyder's writings does not in the end translate into a theory of why local inhabitation *needs* any encounter with cultures one does not inhabit, how such an encounter might reshape the identity and experience of the local in its basic terms, what problems might arise from transferring the nature philosophies of the rice-growing regions of East Asia to the slopes of the western Sierra Nevada, or what systematic role commodity exchange, consumption, or advanced technologies of transportation and information might play in structuring such transfers. In an essay first published in 2001, for example, Snyder suggests, by way of a utopian vision, that national borders might disappear from the North American continent:

> Why not try the bioregional approach and declare the boundaries between the United States and Mexico, the United States and Canada, null and void. Natural regions, and their capacities, would be the touchstone. A bunch of gringos could move south if they had the will to learn. Let the Chicanos who want to move north and give their work and loyalty to the Cascades or the Great Basin. (The Arctic Inuit already have a hemicircumpolar nation of their own.) All of us together will...learn our ecosystems—together...in Spanish, English, and Navajo, and Lakota. Multiracial patriots/matriots/ of Turtle Island. (*Back on the Fire* 19)

One is tempted to label this appealing utopia "multicultural": it is and is not. It is, in the sense that Snyder envisions cultural communities shaped by the divergent ecological frameworks of their bioregions. It is not, in the sense that it does not articulate any sense of how differences between one's region and culture of origin and one's region and culture of residence might transform one's mode of inhabitation, or any vision of how different cultural frameworks (for example, Hispanic vs. Anglo vs. indigenous) might condition quite divergent perceptions of what the local ecology consists of, what it requires from humans, or what an appropriate way of responding to it might be. Snyder's underlying assumption seems to be, in other words, that cultural identities will be shaped and reshaped by whatever place one chooses to live in, rather than that cultural migrations will in any fundamental way unsettle the terms of local inhabitation—perhaps all the way to the notion of the "bioregion" itself.

This assumption becomes even more explicit when Snyder turns to considering migrants from outside the continent: "Offshore immigrants— new ones from Asia, Africa, Europe . . . will be called on to learn not just U.S. history and the Constitution, but the landscapes, watersheds, plants, and animals of their new home. . . . Each person will come back out of the sweat-lodge purified, reborn, no longer an immigrant, but a person whose work and heart are here in North America" (*Back on the Fire* 19). Snyder here relies on the ecologically inflected version of a U.S.-American myth of complete cultural assimilation whose basic terms have been persistently questioned over the last twenty years. What if immigrants—just as other people—are not reborn but constantly reassembled out of the many changing experiences of their life histories, of which North American identity is only one piece? What if work and hearts are not confined to one continent but sustain ties to several? What if migration is not a life phase that is concluded once and for all with the visit to the sweat lodge but a basic mode of inhabitation, as Thomashow suggests? If Snyder does not consider questions such as these, it is because in the last instance he, like many other environmentally oriented writers, sees the transnational and global realms as supplements to locally based identities rather than as a possible positive alternative to them.[22]

The persistence of the sense-of-place rhetoric in writers such as the Ehrlichs, Thomashow, and Snyder, as well as in new research areas such as ecocriticism, raises the question why this discourse has proven so resilient even for thinkers whose own arguments seem to point beyond it. I would argue that this question cannot be answered for environmentalist discourse alone but requires a look at the role that the return to the local has played more generally in debates about American identity over the last few decades, as well as at the critiques that have been raised against this renewal of localism. A good deal of cultural critique during the 1980s and 1990s emphasized local places as sources of identity, of "situated knowledge," and as possible sites of resistance to hegemonic social structures. Much of the postmodernist resistance to universality, "totalization," and "grand narratives" during the 1980s crystallized around such concepts of situatedness and local knowledge, understood as both epistemological strategies (in the skepticism vis-à-vis abstractions and generalizations that might in some way be assumed to rely on a transhistorical human subject) and as ethical imperatives (in the avoidance of any intellectual gesture that would usurp the position and voice of the Other). In the 1990s, identity politics reinforced the investigation of the local with the personal roots and histories it was assumed to anchor, as a means of laying the groundwork for alternative and pluralist concepts of subjectivity. Critiques of the nation-state and nationality as organizing concepts in the understanding of individuals and communities that arose in part from identity politics have been pursued more recently under the rubric of "postnationalism": while nation-states are redefining themselves in a context of increasing political and economic globalization, they have in many cases also come under pressure from the subnational level, where their legitimacy is being questioned from the perspective of regional, ethnic, religious, or local agendas. In this context, the question of place and its claims on individual and community identities plays a crucial role.[23]

Two sets of criticisms have been raised against these as well as specifically environmentalist discourses of place, one revolving around definitions of the local and the other around its presumed epistemological, ethical, and political ramifications. One problem in defining the local, as Lawrence Buell has pointed out, is that its scale can vary enormously: "What counts as a place can be as small as a corner of your kitchen or as big as the planet" (*Future* 62). This variability becomes problematic insofar as ecologically oriented discussions of place, as I mentioned earlier, tend to rest on the assumption that only a relatively small and directly experienceable spatial and communal framework will yield affective attachments and ethical commitments. The claim that ecology itself gives rise to natural boundaries that define place can sometimes run directly counter to the stipulation of such small places. Donald Alexander points out in his critique of bioregionalism not only that different ecological criteria—watersheds, vegetation zones—can define a region in very different ways but also that a bioregion such as the Great Lakes in the United States encompasses a population of 30 million people, more than many nations. In other words, the commitment to naturally defined places and the commitment to small communities do not always go smoothly hand in hand.

The shifting scales at which the local is defined in different types of discourse already show that developing a "sense of place" cannot mean a return to the natural in and of itself, but at best an approach to the natural from within a different cultural framework. In the view of many cultural theorists, the assumption that places possess inherent physical as well as spiritual qualities to which human beings respond when they inhabit them must be replaced by an analysis of how such qualities are either "socially produced" or "culturally constructed." The idea of the social production of space has been pursued by geographers working in the Marxist tradition of Henri Lefebvre. In *The Production of Space* (1974), Lefebvre argued for envisioning space as a "social product" in large part created and experienced through social structures and processes, and imbricated in patterns of domination and inequality (26). Geographers such as Neil Smith, David Harvey, and Doreen Massey have elaborated the implications of Lefebvre's theory for more recent forms of localism by emphasizing that a consideration of the particularities of places cannot be separated from processes of uneven economic development, and that casting such particularities as inherent properties can easily serve to mask the power relations that make them visible and experienceable in the first place. Even and especially an experience of the local as "natural," "wild," or "authentic," in this view, is enabled by social processes that define what such an experience feels like and means.

The idea of the "cultural construction" of place similarly revolves around the assumption that places are not simply given in advance of human understanding, but its emphasis lies more on the cultural practices of particular communities in creating them than on the mechanisms of capitalist economies. Both the characters of particular places and the modes of belonging to them are defined by human intervention and cultural history more than by natural processes, cultural constructionists argue; local citizenship, far from coming naturally, is painstakingly established and safeguarded through a multiplicity of political, social, and cultural practices and procedures. As anthropologist Arjun Appadurai has argued, this is even and especially the case in premodern tribal communities: against a view of such communities as more spontaneously and directly bonded to place than modern societies, Appadurai insists that on the contrary, elaborate rituals of home building, gardening, or initiation can all be read as strategies to define an always uncertain and embattled local citizenship rather than as signs of its self-evidence and stability (183–86). More broadly, the basic goal of work in cultural studies for the last twenty years has been to analyze and, in most cases, to dismantle appeals to "the natural" or "the biological" by showing their groundedness in cultural practices rather than facts of nature. The thrust of this work, therefore, invariably leads to skepticism about the possibility of returning to nature as such, or of the possibility of places defined in terms of their natural characteristics that humans should relate to.

A somewhat different, but related, set of criticisms has emphasized not so much the difficulties of defining the local as the ambivalent ethical and political consequences that might follow from encouraging attachments to place. In the passage quoted earlier, for example, Kirkpatrick Sale assumes that at the local and regional level, environmentalist considerations will simply impose themselves as the most "practical" course of action because people will be directly aware of and affected by the consequences of their decisions. But it remains unclear why this would be the case. Surely in a local or regional context, decision-makers have to weigh different kinds of "practicalities" against each other just as those in national or transnational contexts do: the interests of different social groups, short-term versus long-term practicalities, the interests of present versus future generations, diverging predictions of what consequences a particular course of action might entail, competition between different interests the community holds in common (e.g. the need for access to transportation vs. the interest in preserving natural areas), and so on. Since many such decisions depend on value judgments about the kind of community and environment that are considered most desirable, and on courses of action whose outcome cannot be predicted with complete certainty, "practical" reason of the kind Sale postulates cannot function as an unambiguous guide for how communities should reconnect to nature. A change in scale from large to small entities, therefore, does not in and of itself guarantee anything in the way of more ecologically sustainable modes of living. The history of environmental politics includes many examples of local communities voting in favor of their own economic interest and against environmental preservation, decisions that have sometimes been overruled by a national community with fewer direct gains to hope for from development or exploitation of local resources. Similarly, supranational entities such as the European Union have in some cases passed environmental laws whose stringency exceeds national and local ones.

As quite a few critics of deep ecology have pointed out, in addition, one of the risks in attempting to derive political and ethical norms and imperatives directly from nature is that of underestimating the diversity of political projects at whose service such derivations can be put. The most extreme and frequently quoted example is no doubt the National Socialist rhetoric of Germans' natural connectedness to "blood and soil" (Blut und Boden), which helped legitimate fascist political structures, military expansion of the "life space" (Lebensraum), and unprecedented violence both within and outside what was claimed to be Germans' legitimate space of domination in the 1930s and 1940s (Biehl 131–33; Biehl and Staudenmaier; Bramwell). But there is no need to rely only on this in many ways extraordinary case to argue that a sense of place can lend equal support to both conservative and progressive politics. From tracing one's own roots in a particular locale and defending it against despoilation, it is sometimes but a small step to a class-based or even racially tinged politics of exclusion that seeks to preserve it for the benefit of a specific social group against the interests of others. Discussions over how the interests of affluent tourists and local residents should interact to shape policies of preservation in popular vacation destinies, for example, often involve questions of socioeconomic privilege as much as of ecology,[24] and David Harvey's analysis of the Guilford district of Baltimore provides an instructive urban example of how attempts to preserve the distinctive character of a locale can be intertwined with questions of social and racial exclusion (*Justice* 291–93). The political consequences of encouraging people to develop a sense of place, therefore, are far from straightforward and predictable, and environmentalists need to be aware that place awareness can be deployed in the service of political ideals they may not judge desirable. There is nothing in the idea of localism itself that guarantees its connection with the grassroots-democratic and egalitarian politics that many environmentalists envision when they advocate place-based communities.

Questions of social and financial privilege attach even to some of the most individually based projects that are held up as examples by writers advocating for a sense of place as the basis for reconnection to nature. Wendell Berry's Appalachian farm, Gary Snyder's Kitkitdizze, and Scott Russell Sanders' self-built home are all portrayed by their owners as attempts at autonomy, self-sufficiency, and a lifestyle that is envisioned as an alternative to the mindless consumerism of the mainstream. There is unquestionably much to admire and learn from these writers' passionate dedication to learning about and caring for the places they inhabit, and their careful reflection on how they might minimize their own negative impact on the land. Yet, considering their projects as paradigms of how to live in an environmentally conscious way, one must also ask what social groups typically have access to the financial means, education, occupational flexibility, and time to carry out such endeavors. Surely, for large parts of the lower and middle classes in the United States in the early twenty-first century, working one's own fields and building one's own home are not viable paths toward reconnecting with the land—and that does not even include a consideration of the ecological consequences of millions of urban residents lighting out for the territory to return to subsistence farming. While Berry's and Snyder's projects in living with the land are valuable thought experiments in the same way Thoreau's stay at Walden Pond was earlier, they become imaginative dead ends when they are held up as the principal models of what it means to think and live in an environmentally conscious way.

With these critiques in mind, let me return to the question why the rhetoric of place has proven so enduring for environmentalism. I would argue that its persistence has little to do with its immediate usefulness for the environmentalist project—as I will show, there are many other ways one can imagine individuals and communities developing an awareness of ecology. Rather, its resilience is due to a long discursive tradition in which Americans are deploringly or admiringly portrayed, by themselves as well as others, as a highly mobile people, nomads without roots forever on the road. Already in 1835, Alexis de Tocqueville marveled in *Democracy in America* at how

> in the United States, a man will carefully construct a home in which to spend his old age and sell it before the roof is on....He will settle in one place only to go off elsewhere shortly afterward with a new set of desires....And, if toward the end of a year of unremitting work he has some time to spare, he will trail his restless curiosity up and down the endless territories of the United States....At first, there is astonishment

at the sight of this peculiar restlessness in so many happy men in the midst of abundance. Yet this is a sight as old as the world; what is new is to see a whole nation involved. (623)

Historian William Leach has traced this tradition through Nathaniel Hawthorne's remark in 1855 that "no people on earth have such vagabond habits as ours," George Perkins Marsh's complaint in his 1864 *Man and Nature* about "the restless love of change which characterizes us, and makes us almost a nomad rather than a sedentary people," and Harvard philosopher Josiah Royce's 1902 observation that "in America today, nobody is at home" all the way to the later part of the twentieth century, when books such as *The Moving American* or *The Homeless Mind* by journalists and scholars such as Vance Packard, George W. Pierson, and Peter Berger all emphasized mobility as a distinguishing characteristic of American culture (9–30).[25] Recent scholarship has perpetuated this stereotype. Wayne Franklin and Michael Steiner, in the preface to their 1992 anthology *Mapping American Culture*, accumulate a long list of quotations on Americans' placelessness reaching from Domingo Faustino Sarmiento's 1847 travel writings to Thornton Wilder and Charles Tomlinson only to conclude: "A deep love of place eludes most urban, nomadic Americans. In our relation to place, we are profoundly absent-minded" (8). And one might add to this list the entire genre of road novels and road movies, starting with Jack Kerouac's famous assertion in his epoch-making novel *On the Road* that "we were leaving confusion and nonsense behind and performing our one and noble function of the time, *move*. And we moved!" (134). In this context, Berry's and Sanders's indictments of American nomadism come to lose some of their specifically environmentalist inflection and reveal themselves to be deeply rooted in a cultural rather than an ecological logic. For at least two centuries, Americans have seen themselves as modern nomads, and have always felt ambivalent about their mobility, perceiving it by turns as their greatest social asset and their deepest cultural deficiency; only in this context does authentic rootedness in place—which Americans often portray as something others possess, whether they be Native Americans, Europeans, or cultures of the past—come to seem as a particularly desirable goal to achieve, or as a means of resistance to mainstream culture. It is this cultural tradition that gives the insistence on a sense of place much of its persuasive power in environmentalist discourse today, and it is this power that accounts in large part for its recurrence in otherwise more globally minded arguments. Once one recognizes the influence of this tradition in American thought and writing, it becomes possible to redeploy some of the useful insights articulated by a theorist such as Mitchell Thomashow from a different perspective that approaches the environmentalist rhetoric of place with some of the insights of current theories of globalization in mind.

4. Deterritorialization and Eco-Cosmopolitanism

In his by now classic 1984 essay "Postmodernism, or, The Cultural Logic of Late Capitalism," cultural theorist Fredric Jameson incisively formulated the challenge that globalization poses for individuals' sense of situatedness. This formulation emerges in his architectural analysis of the Bonaventure Hotel in Los Angeles, whose emptiness, symmetry, and camouflaging of spatial boundaries creates what he calls a "postmodern hyperspace," a space that defies orientation, spatial recognition, and memory. "This latest mutation of space," Jameson suggests,

> has finally succeeded in transcending the capacities of the individual human body to locate itself, to organize its immediate surroundings perceptually, and cognitively to map its position in a mappable external world....[T]his alarming disjunction point between the body and its built environment...can itself stand as the symbol and analogon of that even sharper dilemma which is the incapacity of our minds, at least at present, to map the great global multinational and decentered communicational network in which we find ourselves caught as individual subjects. (*Postmodernism* 44)

This difficulty of mapping individual positions in a set of extremely complex global networks also confronts environmentalist discourses of place. As I have suggested, environmentalism has met this challenge in two ways between the 1960s and the turn of the millennium: first, by creating allegorical visions of the global that over the course of time have shifted from a utopian to a more dystopian emphasis; second, by developing a set of perspectives that share an emphasis on the importance of a "sense of place," the attachment to or "reinhabitation" of the local through prolonged residence, intimate familiarity, affective ties, and ethical commitment. While the two perspectives are often, implicitly or explicitly, assumed to complement each other, they are also quite frequently at odds—in part because of the rejection of abstract and mediated kinds of knowledge that characterizes some versions of environmentalism, and in part because of the resistance to certain forms of economic globalization over the last decade.

Such problems in rethinking the relation of local inhabitation to global citizenship are by no means limited to environmentalist rhetoric but have surfaced in a variety of fields from identity politics to globalization theories. As I pointed out in the introduction, several waves of debate about notions involving rootedness in the local or the nation on the one hand and concepts such as diaspora, nomadism, hybridity, *mestizaje,* borderlands, and exile on the other have led to an impasse, where advocacies of local and of global consciousness have achieved equal plausibility when they are formulated at an abstract theoretical level. It no longer makes sense to rely mechanically on a particular set of terms with the assumption that it always describes the ideologically preferable perspective: for example, the frequent assumption that hybridity is inherently preferable to claims to cultural authenticity, that an emphasis on migration and diaspora is superior to one on rootedness or, conversely, that nomadism is destructive while place attachments are not. But acknowledging this impasse does not imply that such arguments no longer make sense or that they have become superfluous in specific political and discursive contexts. Environmentalist and ecocritical discourse in the United States, for the reasons I outlined in sections 2 and 3, remains constrained in its conceptual scope by an at least partially essentialist rhetoric of place as well as by its lack of engagement with some of the insights of cultural theories of globalization. Such an engagement, I would suggest, might begin with two concepts that have played a central role in globalization theories: deterritorialization and cosmopolitanism.

Deterritorialization in literary and cultural criticism is most centrally associated with Deleuze and Guattari's attempt philosophically to reconceptualize social, spatial, and bodily structures outside the classifications, categorizations, and boundaries usually imposed on them.[26] But it has also been widely used in anthropologically and sociologically oriented studies of how experiences of place change under the influence of modernization and globalization processes, as a shorthand for the way "locality as a property or diacritic of social life comes under siege in modern societies" (*Appadurai* 179), and it is mainly in this sense that I will use the term here. More specifically, it refers to the detachment of social and cultural practices from their ties to place that have been described in detail in theories of modernization and postmodernization. Sociologist Anthony Giddens, for example, has examined the "disembedding" that occurs when modernization processes shift structures of governance and authority away from villages and counties to more distant locations and give rise to networks of exchange via symbolic tokens (such as money), of expertise (such as that which guarantees that buildings are constructed safely and food does not arrive contaminated at the store), and of social trust in the legitimation and enforcement procedures of large-scale social communities (*Consequences* 21–36). Expanding this type of analysis to the processes he considers typical of the postmodernization of the second half of the twentieth century, geographer David Harvey has similarly pointed to the "time-space compression" that forces distant locales closer together and triggers movements of homogenization as well as differentiation of places under the umbrella of global capitalism (*Condition of Postmodernity; Justice, Nature and the Geography of Difference*). Sociologist Roland Robertson, from a somewhat different theoretical perspective, has introduced the related notion of the "glocal" to capture "the extent to which what is called local is in large degree constructed on a trans-or super-local basis.... Much of what is often declared to be local is in fact the local expressed in terms of generalized recipes of locality" (26). Néstor García Canclini's analysis of different modes of modernization in the developing world also emphasizes deterritorialization as "the loss of the 'natural' relation of culture to geographical and social territories" (229). While some studies of modernization processes foreground above all increased mobility as the main cause of deterritorialization (see Lash and Urry 252–54), other analyses highlight the ways it transforms the experience of place even and above all for those individuals and communities that stay put.[27]

This aspect is addressed in detail by the sociologist John Tomlinson, who emphasizes that while mobility—whether the voluntary one of the leisured traveler or the involuntary one of the migrant worker—forms an important part of the forces that dissociate culture from place, "the paradigmatic experience of global modernity for most people... is that of staying in one place but experiencing the 'dis-placement' that global modernity *brings to them*" (9). This displacement is caused by the availability of internationally produced and distributed consumer products, cultural artifacts, and foods, the presence of media such as radio, television, and the internet, which bring faraway places and problems into average citizens' living-rooms, and the experience of what Tomlinson, following French anthropologist Marc Augé, calls "nonplaces," locales such as airport terminals, supermarkets, or gas stations that are configured quite similarly across a variety of regions and countries (108–28). Tomlinson is well aware that these elements describe the ordinary life of populations in Europe and North America better than in other parts of the world. Yet he argues that even and perhaps mainly those who live in less privileged regions of the world are also affected by deterritorialization, precisely because processes of exploitation involve them deeply in globalization. Workers in the developing world who are forced to follow the flows of capital experience deterritorialization in this way, as do farmers whose choices of products to cultivate are dictated by the needs of First World markets (Tomlinson 136) or whose agricultural success has become dependent on seeds, fertilizers, and pesticides sold by transnational corporations. In urban contexts, in addition, many of the same products (goods, foods, media) that are available in the First World are becoming available across the globe. Therefore, Tomlinson argues,

what is at stake in experiencing deterritorialized culture is not, crucially, level of affluence, but leading a life which, as a result of the various forces of global modernity, is "lifted off" its connection with locality....[I]t is possible to argue that some populations in the contemporary Third World may, precisely because of their positioning within the uneven process of globalization, actually have a sharper, more acute experience of deterritorialization than those in the First World. (137; see also 135)

Tomlinson does not discuss the important dimension of risk as an experience with similar power to transcend geographical, political, and social boundaries, as I will show in chapters 4–6. Some recent ecological and technological risk scenarios (regional ones such as the nuclear accident at Chernobyl in 1986 or truly global ones such as atmospheric warming and the depletion of the stratospheric ozone layer) affect populations that are geographically, politically, and socially distant from the places where these risks originate. In addition, risks that emanate from political or economic crisis have similar potential to work across national and social borders and affect populations with little control over their causes. They lend additional support to Tomlinson's conclusion that

> globalization promotes much more physical mobility than before, but the key to its cultural impact is in the transformation of localities the mselves....[C]omplex connectivity weakens the ties of culture to place. This is in many ways a troubling phenomenon, involving the simultaneous penetration of local worlds by distant forces, and the dislodging of everyday meanings from their "anchors" in the local environment. Embodiment and the forces of material circumstance keep most of us, most of the time, situated, but in places that are changing around us and gradually, subtly, losing their power to define the terms of our existence. This is undoubtedly an uneven and often contradictory business, felt more forcibly in some places than others, and sometimes met by countervailing tendencies to re-establish the power of locality. Nevertheless, deterritorialization is, I believe, the major cultural impact of global connectivity. (29–30)

Even though deterritorialization thus understood implies profound social and cultural upheaval, Tomlinson is at pains to emphasize the ordinariness of many of the daily experiences it involves. Most of the changes they bring are, in his view, quickly assimilated by those who undergo them and become part of what is considered normality (128). Indeed, much of the importance of the deterritorialization process derives from the fact that its effects so quickly come to be accepted as part of individuals' daily routines. Ulrich Beck has described the same process as the "cosmopolitization" or "banal cosmopolitanism" of lifeworlds, which quite often occurs without conscious awareness on the individual's part (*Der kosmopolitische Blick* 65–67).

Within this theoretical framework, the environmentalist call for a reconnection with the local can be understood as one form of "reterritorialization," an attempt to realign culture with place. But the framework also shows why this attempt is bound to remain both practically and theoretically problematic. In practical terms, it shows how global connectedness makes an in-depth experience of place more difficult to attain for more people. As I mentioned earlier, remaining in one place for many decades, taking care of a house or farm, intimately knowing the local environment, cultivating local relationships, being as self-sufficient as possible, resisting new technologies that do not improve human life spiritually as well as materially are options no longer available to many. Deterritorialization implies that the average daily life, in the context of globality, is shaped by structures, processes, and products that originate elsewhere. From the food, clothes, and fuel we buy to the music and films we enjoy, the employer we work for, and the health risks we are exposed to, everyday routines for most people today are inconceivable without global networks of information and exchange. And while it is possible to "reterritorialize" some of these dimensions by, for example, buying locally grown produce or supporting local artists, a more complete detachment from such networks is surely not within the average citizens' reach. To say this is not in and of itself to question the desirability of reestablishing a sense of place, but it does limit its viability as a model for thinking about the future of significant portions of the population.

Apart from such practical considerations, the concept of deterritorialization also points to a more theoretical problem in environmentalist calls for an ethic based on a sense of place. For it is not just that local places have changed through increased connectivity but also the structures of perception, cognition, and social expectations associated with them. Joshua Meyrowitz, in a seminal study of the impact of television, has shown how basic social parameters, such as the distinction between public and private places and the structures of authority associated with them, are altered by a technological medium that not only broadcasts public events into private living rooms but also gives social groups unprecedented insight into how other groups live and behave. As women see how men act in the absence of women, or the poor observe the lifestyles of the middle and upper classes in abundant visual detail, Meyrowitz shows, social relations themselves change. Structures of authority and of group inclusion and exclusion, as well as social inequalities, come to be perceived and have to be legitimated differently (69–126, 185–267). Along somewhat different lines, Beck has pointed to changes in the structure of affect and empathy through the embedding of daily life in transnational media networks (*Der kosmopolitische Blick* 67). Such changes in social relations cannot simply be undone, even in the unlikely event that a majority of the population decided to turn off their television sets permanently. Related arguments surely have to be made for other media and other dimensions of increased global connectedness: once we have to perceive and live in our own places with the expanded awareness of other regions that media such as radio, television, telephony and the internet provide, our relationship to local places changes irreversibly.

The problem with environmentalist advocacies of place, from this perspective, lies in that most of them assume that individuals' existential encounters with nature and engagements with intimately known local places can be recuperated intact from the distortions of modernization.

Analyses of media and studies of globalization, by contrast, suggest that the essence of such encounters and engagements itself has changed. Some of these changes may be subtle and for the most part unconscious—the fact that most citizens of Western countries can now compare their own locale with a much greater number of other places they have visited than previous generations, that our perception of the local natural world is inflected by media images of other ecosystems that we may never have seen in person, or that the materials and technologies by means of which we are able to inhabit particular places (from building materials to hiking gear or optical equipment) are fundamentally different. But some dimensions of this change are quite obvious—perhaps most saliently the fact that whatever knowledge inhabitants acquire about a particular place is for the most part inessential for their survival. Unlike tribal peoples, peasants, or hunters in past centuries, whose subsistence depended on their familiarity with the surrounding ecosystems, most citizens of modern societies are free to acquire such knowledge or not, or to learn some parts of it and ignore others. Some distinctly modern forms of intimate acquaintance with nature—highly specialized hobbies such as bird-watching or orchid collecting—depend precisely on their being leisure activities rather than existential necessities; and they are often quite far removed from any genuine ecological understanding, focusing as they do on one particular aspect of ecology rather than its systemic functioning. A sense of place and the knowledge that comes with it, in other words, is something that most people quite rightly perceive as a kind of hobby, something that may be useful and entertaining to acquire but on which basic existence does not depend, however desirable it might be from the viewpoint of the social collective.

This deterritorialization of local knowledge does not necessarily have to be detrimental for an environmentalist perspective, but on the contrary opens up new avenues into ecological consciousness. In a context of rapidly increasing connections around the globe, what is crucial for ecological awareness and environmental ethics is arguably not so much a sense of place as a sense of planet—a sense of how political, economic, technological, social, cultural, and ecological networks shape daily routines. If the concept of deterritorialization foregrounds how cultural practices become detached from place, it also points to how these practices are now imbricated in such larger networks. As a consequence, a wide range of different experiences and practices can serve as the point of departure for understanding these networks—some that are associated with a conventional "sense of place," others that are unrelated to it. Thomashow rightly points to such a variety of starting points when he argues that observations of local weather or reflections on the migration patterns of birds showing up at a local feeder can lead to an intensified awareness of processes that shape regions far beyond the local (*Bringing* 96–98). Yet he proves in the end unable to break with the conventional assumption that somehow all of them still have to be rooted in local perceptions and experiences. It is true that becoming familiar with local songbirds, for example, might lead one to inquire into their migratory patterns and the conditions of their remote seasonal habitats; or observing damage on local trees might give one the incentive to explore the origin of the acid rain that falls in one's region: familiarity with the local might lead one "naturally" to the global. But if one grants the usefulness of such an exploration, one would also have to encourage avenues of inquiry into ecological connectedness that do not take their starting point in a familiarity with the local environment. If studying local plants is valuable because it can lead one to questions of global connectivity, so is exploring where the bananas one buys come from and under what conditions they were grown; under what circumstances and with what waste products one's TV set was put together; or how the shipping out of waste from one's own city might affect the community where it will be deposited. All of these inquiries open the local out into a network of ecological links that span a region, a continent, or the world.

Once one pursues such questions, one might also want to value concerns and types of knowledge that are even further removed from the local environment: individuals who have no leisure to pursue local knowledge—immigrants from another country, for example—may know a great deal about the climatological and socioeconomic difficulties of farming in their place of origin; some of those who are more affluent and move often to new places of residence have an acute sense of the consequences of urban sprawl; persons who would not be caught dead in a pair of hiking boots have intensely felt concerns over the impact of air pollution and pesticide use on their health; others are stirred into curiosity and sometimes into action by seeing a documentary about orangutan extinction on television; yet others who spend most of their time in front of a computer screen rather than in protests outside the local nuclear plant turn out to know a great deal about statistical trends in global agricultural production, population growth, or economic development; and some, like the students in Robert Hass's course, may know a great deal about global atmospheric change even though they are unable to identify local plants. If a knowledge of one's local place has value because it is a gateway to understanding global connectedness at various levels, then nonlocal types of knowledge and concern that also facilitate such an understanding should be similarly valuable. The challenge for environmentalist thinking, then, is to shift the core of its cultural imagination from a sense of place to a less territorial and more systemic sense of planet.

Such a reimagination of the global has been in process in many areas of cultural theory, where it has usually been shaped by its opposition to national imaginaries. Throughout the 1980s and 1990s, theorists in anthropology, philosophy, sociology, political science, and literary and cultural studies critically examined concepts of the nation and national identity, highlighting the practices, discourses, and institutions that served to legitimate and make appear natural what most of these approaches cast as highly artificial and historically contingent entities—Anderson's "imagined communities." Identities defined by nation or nationalism tended to be viewed as oppressive, while those shaped by hybridity, migration, borderlands, diaspora, nomadism, and exile were valued not only as more politically progressive but also as potential grounds for resistance to national hegemonies, raising "hopes that transnational mobility and its associated processes have great liberatory potential (perhaps replacing international class struggle in orthodox Marxist thinking). In a sense, the diasporan subject is now vested with the agency formerly sought in the working class and more recently in the subaltern subject" (Ong 15). Anthropologist James Clifford's influential work *Routes,* among others, expanded this analysis by showing how entire cultures, even native villages conventionally thought to be most clearly place-bound, are diasporic in nature, in that they derive their identity from connections to a variety of places ("routes") rather than their anchoring in just one locale ("roots").

Different types of theoretical projects emerged from this founding critique of nation-based identities. While a great deal of intellectual energy was invested in studies of particular borderlands identities or diasporic communities, other lines of research sought to define forms of belonging that would transcend exclusive commitments to a particular nation, culture, race, or ethnicity in favor of more global modes of awareness and attachment. In this context, scholars across a wide variety of disciplines sought to recuperate and redefine the concept of "cosmopolitanism" as a way of imagining what such deterritorialized identities might look like. From the mid-1990s on, a profusion of studies revolving around this concept appeared, including work by Appiah and Nussbaum in philosophy; Clifford and Ong in anthropology; Beck, Giddens, Hannerz, and Tomlinson in sociology; Hayden, Held, and McGrew in political science; and Bhabha, Cheah, Mignolo, and Robbins in literary and cultural studies, among many others.[28]

Theories of cosmopolitanism circumscribe a field of reflection rather than a firmly established and shared set of concepts and assumptions. All of them are concerned with the historical, political, and cultural circumstances under which modes of awareness that reach beyond the local and the national emerge and sustain themselves. With the long history of cosmopolitanism in mind—from the Stoics to sixteenth-century Spanish reflections on the nature of indigenous peoples in the new colonies and all the way to Kant—theorists seek to dissociate the term from connotations of European upper-class travel and to redefine it as a way of envisioning contemporary modes of consciousness that might be commensurate with intensified global connectedness. Many foreground a basic sense that nationally and regionally defined identities, far from emerging naturally, are established and maintained by means of complex sets of sociocultural practices, so as to explore how larger-scale affinities have emerged or might do so in the future. But within this general framework, theories of cosmopolitanism vary considerably. Many of them include both a descriptive component and a normative one. Descriptively, they seek to capture the ways people live connected to a wide variety of places and spaces that are geographically and often culturally far removed from each other, aiming at many of the processes and phenomena that other researchers have investigated under the label "deterritorialization." Normatively, these theories attempt to outline an ideal form of awareness or cultural disposition. This dual orientation has in some ways been detrimental, in that it has led to a neglect of solidly empirical studies aimed at determining under what circumstances, with what subjects, and by what means affective and ethical attachments to the global arise (Skrbis et al. 119–21, 131–32); yet it has in practice also been productive, making cosmopolitanism a concept around which analytical perspectives as well as forward-looking political projects have crystallized.

Theories of cosmopolitanism also differ in other ways. Some of them focus centrally on the experience of the middle classes, sometimes specifically on intellectuals—as in Bruce Robbins's work—while others approach the question of global consciousness from the perspective of formerly colonial, marginalized, or disenfranchised populations and the kind of cosmopolitan awareness that results from international trade, labor migration, political displacement, or exile (for example, in the "vernacular cosmopolitanisms" of Homi Bhabha or the "colonial difference" that Walter Mignolo emphasizes).[29] Cosmopolitan perspectives emerge in some approaches as a more or less mechanical consequence of global circumstances and in others as a self-conscious adoption of values (Skrbis et al. 117); historically as well, cosmopolitanism is sometimes claimed to consist either of practices that have always formed part of even the most locally rooted human cultures or of a project that still awaits realization and is by definition always incomplete.[30] Similarly, the questions whether cosmopolitan awareness ultimately rests on a core of shared humanity or an acknowledgement of human difference and whether national and subnational affinities are antagonistic or complementary to such an awareness have been matters of controversy, especially in the debate about Martha Nussbaum's well-known essay "Patriotism and Cosmopolitanism."[31] Scholars have also approached the basis for generating and sustaining a cosmopolitan disposition from different angles, with some theorists foregrounding increased knowledge, a kind of transnational cultural literacy, as the foundation and others foregrounding particular forms of affect, while yet others have tended to see it mostly in a framework of ethical questions of responsibility or have investigated what kinds of sociopolitical institutions might further it.

Given this range of approaches, it is unsurprising that critiques of cosmopolitanism have also varied widely, in debates that cannot be unfolded here in detail. As I noted in the introduction, scholars such as Timothy Brennan, Arif Dirlik, and Karen Caplan have pointed to the continued importance of local, regional, and national claims to identity in the context of political struggles that many of the theorists who advocate various forms of cosmopolitanism would most likely endorse. The significance, for an analysis of environmental discourses, of these debates about local, national, and global modes of belonging lies in the way they highlight how attachments to a particular category or scale of place can shift in value and function when considered in different political contexts. Advocacies of the local can play a useful political and cultural role in one context and become a philosophical as well as a pragmatic stumbling block in another. As I argued earlier, it seems to me imperative to reorient current U.S. environmentalist discourse, ecocriticism included, toward a more nuanced understanding of how both local cultural and ecological systems are imbricated in global ones. This argument for an increased emphasis on a sense of planet, a cognitive understanding and affective attachment to the global, should be understood not as a claim that environmentalism should welcome globalization in every form (there are good reasons to resist some of its dimensions) or as a refusal to acknowledge that appeals to indigenous traditions, local knowledge, or national law are in some cases appropriate and effective strategies. Rather, it is intended as a call to ground any such discourses in a thorough cultural and scientific understanding of the global—that is, an environmentally oriented cosmopolitanism or "world environmental citizenship," as Patrick Hayden calls it (see 121–51).

An indispensable first step in the direction of such an eco-cosmopolitan awareness is the acknowledgment of "varieties of environmentalism," as Ramachandra Guha and Juan Martínez-Alier have labeled the divergent motivations of efforts for the protection of nature in different regions of the world. Most importantly, Guha and Martínez-Alier distinguish between a First World environmentalism and the "environmentalism of the poor." First World environmentalism, they argue, tends to arise from a matrix of what Ronald Inglehart called "postmaterialist values," that is, a set of cultural values, including the preservation of the natural environment, that move to the forefront once societies have attained a certain level of affluence. In many developing countries, by contrast, poor and sometimes not-so-poor communities struggle for the pursuit of traditional ways of using nature, or simply for control of natural resources that are essential for their survival. Far from any "postmaterialist" motivation, such fights for the sustainable exploitation of local forests, against the construction of large dams, or against the contamination of groundwater involve the most basic necessities for the survival of the affected communities. Since such struggles tend not to be anchored in any deep-ecological valuation of nature for its own sake, Guha and Martínez-Alier argue, they have often not been recognized as "environmentalist" by ecologically oriented movements in the industrialized world. Yet they aim at the preservation of natural ecosystems and their sustainable human use in just the same way (16–21).

Guha and Martínez-Alier admit that the opposition may not be as simple as one between materialist and nonmaterialist struggles for the environment. The fight against pathogenic waste disposals or nuclear armament in developed countries is no less a struggle for survival than that of communities in the developing world for access to crucial resources for their livelihood. In addition, Guha and Martínez-Alier acknowledge that some theorists—Vandana Shiva, for example—have attributed an essentially nonmaterialist approach to nature to some Eastern forms of spirituality as well as to certain indigenous cultures or to women. They therefore end up with a fourfold division between developed and developing countries' and materialist and nonmaterialist environmentalisms (36). Such distinctions provide a first route of access to a broader understanding of what forms the interactions between nature and culture and, more specifically, between different socioeconomic systems, cultures, and natural environments at risk might take. Still, Guha and Martínez-Alier's schema remains strikingly general in its assumptions. It provides no easy way, for example, to account for substantial differences in the cultural perception of genetically modified foods between the United States and western Europe; the deep wariness of nuclear technology that distinguishes German and Japanese culture from the traditional French perception of nuclear plants as icons of progress; the importance of animal rights in British environmentalism, which sets it apart from its continental European counterparts; or representations of nature as rugged and wild in traditional Chinese culture, as opposed to representations of it as constrained, small-scale, and domesticated in Japanese culture, to name just a few examples.[32] What I mean to suggest here is not that varieties of environmentalism necessarily line up with the boundaries of national cultures (though the latter certainly do play an important role in shaping them, as do different indigenous traditions) but that the study of such varieties from an eco-cosmopolitan perspective will need to develop finer-grained distinctions than the very general ones proposed by Guha and Martínez-Alier between First and Third World or materialist and nonmaterialist motivations.

Yet even such an expanded understanding of how different cultures approach nature, which parts they consider most worth preserving, and what they perceive to be the most important dangers threatening it still leaves at least one crucial distinction intact between this kind of eco-cosmopolitan project and the political and cultural theories of cosmopolitanism I have mentioned. The strength of these theories lies in the way they use the cosmopolitan concept to provide a shorthand for a cultural and political understanding that allows individuals to think beyond the boundaries of their own cultures, ethnicities, or nations to a range of other sociocultural frameworks. But whether this understanding is framed as thinking in terms of a shared humanity or in terms of access to and valuation of cultural differences, cosmopolitanism in these discussions is circumscribed by human social experience. Eco-cosmopolitanism, by contrast, reaches toward what some environmental writers and philosophers have called the "more-than-human world"—the realm of nonhuman species, but also that of connectedness with both animate and inanimate networks of influence and exchange.[33] While some environmentalists have claimed that biological diversity is closely associated with cultural diversity (see Nabhan), which might tempt one to conclude that an understanding of other cultures might easily be linked to an interest in the state of other species, the interaction between the two projects is arguably more complex than that. Undoubtedly, environmentalists will encounter scenarios in which the interests of particular human populations cannot be easily lined up with the needs of the nonhuman environment. Eco-cosmopolitanism will not be able to provide an easy template for making such difficult choices in all cases, but at least it would allow those who are charged with making these choices to base their decisions on a thorough understanding of the cultural as well as the ecological frameworks within which they will play themselves out. In this context, clearly, the question of how the rights (or more generally, the affectedness) of nonhuman parts of the biosphere should be legally, politically, and culturally represented takes on central importance (Eckersley, 111–38; Murphy, "Grounding" 429–32; Stone); but this question itself needs to be considered from within the different frameworks of cultures that cast their own relationships to other species in quite divergent terms.

Eco-cosmopolitanism, then, is an attempt to envision individuals and groups as part of planetary "imagined communities" of both human and nonhuman kinds.[34] While the cultural mechanisms by means of which allegiance to national communities is generated, legitimated, and maintained have been studied in depth, ecocriticism has only begun to explore the cultural means by which ties to the natural world are produced and perpetuated, and how the perception of such ties fosters or impedes regional, national, and transnational forms of identification. Too often, as I have shown, the temptation on the part of environmentalist writers, philosophers, and cultural critics has been to assume that such ties emerge "naturally" and spontaneously in the process of inhabiting particular places, while allegiances to larger entities—modern society, the nation-state—have to be created by complex and artificial means. But as analyses of nation-based forms of identity have shown, individuals in certain cultural contexts readily identify themselves as belonging to very large-scale and abstract entities of which they have only partial personal experience, a kind of commitment that place-oriented environmentalists tend to consider highly artificial and arbitrary. As well they should—but not without acknowledging at the same time the possibility that a sense of the local is simply the analogous outcome of a different set of cultural commitments and habits rather than a "natural" foundation. To call entities such as the nation "abstract" in this context, at any rate, may well be to misunderstand the work culture accomplishes; arguably, it is precisely through culture that national belonging—just as local belonging—comes to appear concrete, obvious, and woven into the texture of one's own thoughts and feelings.[35] The point of an eco-cosmopolitan critical project, therefore, would be to go beyond the aforementioned "ethic of proximity" so as to investigate by what means individuals and groups in specific cultural contexts have succeeded in envisioning themselves in similarly concrete fashion as part of the global biosphere, or by what means they might be enabled to do so; at the same time, as the work of Vandana Shiva, among others, highlights, such a perspective needs to be attentive to the political frameworks in which communities begin to see themselves as part of a planetary community, and what power struggles such visions might be designed to hide or legitimate.

In this context, "the issue isn't so much that all places are connected (one of the great clichés of modern environmental studies), as it is understanding which connections are most important," as Thomashow argues (*Bringing* 194). Precisely—but Thomashow is mistaken in concluding that a sense of place will invariably be the privileged cultural means by which such a systemic understanding is achieved. While it can be a helpful tool in some cases and for some people, the focus on the local can also block an understanding of larger salient connections, as I argued earlier. Besides the valuation of physical experience and sensory perception, therefore, an eco-cosmopolitan approach should also value the abstract and highly mediated kinds of knowledge and experience that lend equal or greater support to a grasp of biospheric connectedness. McKenzie Wark has made this point forcefully and humorously in an essay that reflects on the enormous role that computer modeling and simulations have played in the scientific description of global ecological processes, as well as on the way these modeling techniques have trickled down to the popular entertainment sphere in the shape of computer games such as SimEarth. The capabilities of such software tools, Wark argues, make it possible for users to understand the consequences of even minor changes in one variable for the system as a whole, and thereby enable an understanding of global ecology that is very difficult to attain through direct observation and lived experience: "It is only by becoming more abstract, more estranged from nature that I can make the cultural leap to thinking its fragile totality," he concludes (127).

Computer images of various types have played an increasingly important role in the cultural imagination of global ecology, a point to which I will return in the last section. But they are only a small subset of a much larger array of cultural strategies and devices by means of which Planet Earth has become perceivable and experienceable as a complex set of ecosystems over the last forty years. The task of ecocriticism with a cosmopolitan perspective is to develop an understanding and critique of these mechanisms as they play themselves out in different cultural contexts so as to create a variety of ecological imaginations of the global.

5. Forms of the Global

The main objective of this book as part of such an eco-cosmopolitan investigation is to trace some of the narrative and metaphorical templates in the rhetorical as well as visual realms that have shaped perceptions of global ecology in Western societies over the last forty years—particularly in the United States, but also in western Europe—and to investigate how they negotiate the connection to the imagination of the nation and the local. Such templates and the cultural traditions they derive from, I would argue, exert an influence as important as—or more important than—factual information on environmental issues, and environmentalists and ecocritics need to be extremely cautious about turning such particular cultural devices into foundations or prerequisites for ecological awareness and ethics. As I showed in section 3, the insistence on the necessity of a sense of place owes much of its persuasiveness to its grounding in a long discursive tradition about the rootlessness of American culture rather than its specific ecological insights. Images and stories about the global need to be approached with similar attention to the cultural sources and traditions—often nationally specific ones—from which they derive. The interpretive chapters of this book, therefore, focus on works that deploy some conventional articulations of the relationship between local and global environments only to twist them into more experimental forms that reach toward an innovative understanding of global ecology or that highlight the ways the more conventional images might be problematic.

The rhetorical figure that predominated in the textual as well as visual representations of Planet Earth that surfaced in the 1960s and 1970s was undoubtedly allegory, broadly understood as the figuration of abstract concepts and connections by means of a concrete image. As discussed earlier, from McLuhan's "global village," Fuller's "Spaceship Earth," and Lovelock's "Gaia" to visual portrayals of Planet Earth as a precious, marble-like jewel exposed in its fragility and limits against the undefined blackness of outer space, these representations relied on summarizing the abstract complexity of global systems in relatively simple and concrete images that foregrounded synthesis, holism and connectedness. The efficacy of these tropes depended not only on their neglect of political and cultural heterogeneity, as I noted, but also on a conception of global ecology as harmonious, balanced, and self-regenerating. This view has been discredited by biologists' more recent emphasis on the dynamic and often nonequilibrated development of ecological systems even in the absence of human interference. As biologist Daniel Botkin has pointed out,

> until the past few years, the predominant theories in ecology either presumed or had as a necessary consequence a very strict concept of a highly structured, ordered, and regulated, steady-state ecological sys-

tem. Scientists know now that this view is wrong at local and regional levels.... Change now appears to be intrinsic and natural at many scales of time and space in the biosphere. (9)

This altered scientific perspective has momentous consequences for environmental literature and ecocriticism, which, as Dana Phillips and Greg Garrard have shown, have often continued to rely on a Romantic and pastoral notion of nature that they claimed to be grounded in ecological science long after ecologists discarded such views.[36] Allegorical representations are generally ill suited to reflect dynamic changes in global ecosystems, even as it is difficult to imagine tropes for the planet as a whole that do not in some way invoke allegorical mechanisms. Recent authors, therefore, often use allegory in combination with other genres in a wary kind of experimentalism, attempting to capture both a sense of the planet's many types of connectedness and of cultural heterogeneity as well as ecological dynamism. Epic, one of the oldest allegorical forms of narrative in which the fate of the entire known world is usually at stake, has made a comeback as a way of establishing a planetary scope in storytelling, though only in combination with sometimes radically modernist narrative strategies. Novelists including David Brin (*Earth;* see chap. 2 here) and Karen Tei Yamashita (*Through the Arc of the Rainforest;* see chap. 3 here), in their search for modes of representation that might accommodate ecological dynamisms, disequilibria, and disjunctions along with ecosystems' imbrications in heterogeneous human cultures and politics, combine allegory with modernist and postmodernist experimental modes that resist any direct summing up of parts into wholes or any simple foregrounding of connectedness at the expense of disjunction and heterogeneity.

Redefining the parts of an aesthetic work in their relation to the whole as something other than simple subordination was, of course, one of the central goals of the high modernist techniques of collage and montage. The texts and artifacts I will examine attempt to develop aesthetic forms that do justice both to the sense that places are inexorably connected to the planet as a whole and to the perception that this wholeness encompasses vast heterogeneities by imagining the global environment as a kind of collage in which all the parts are connected but also lead lives of their own. Some of the new forms that result from such combinations of conventional literary strategies with the innovative techniques of the twentieth century are more aesthetically persuasive in their results than others; but in all of them, imagining a global ecological and cultural environment is as much a question of linguistic and visual form as a matter of particular thematic issues. Narrative, lyrical, or cinematographic form, in other words, conveys its own figuration of the local-global dialectic that may or may not line up with the representations of the global that the work proposes by way of its substance.

In this search for new forms, many theorists as well as creative writers have gravitated toward the trope of the "network," usually envisioned as a decentralized system of nodes connected by multiple links. In itself an abstract concept that can be used in the context of ecology, economics, politics, or culture, the network is often most immediately associated with information and communications technologies—most obviously the internet (more accurately called the World Wide Web) and the telephone, now spreading rapidly in their highly mobile wireless forms, but also older media such as television, radio, and newspapers. Obviously, information and communications technologies assume this crucial role because they are the primary means by which even individuals and communities who remain sedentary most of the time relate to global processes and spaces. Yet in a curious twist, technological connectedness also quite frequently becomes a metaphor by means of which ecological connectedness can be represented, inverting more conventional tropes that figured human communities and systems of exchange as organic. Informational networks, which in industrialized regions may well appear more immediately palpable and imaginable than ecological systems, become themselves allegorical—concrete instantiations of an organic connectedness that eludes the grasp of the senses. In some instances, indeed, as Le Guin's "Vaster Than Empires" already indicates, ecological connectedness is envisioned as a particular kind of informational exchange. The textual analyses in the following chapters will show that such metaphorical uses of communications networks serve as convenient shorthands for just the combination of decentralized heterogeneity and encompassing holism that linguistic and visual experimentations also aim to convey.

What the analysis of genres such as allegory and collage, and of tropes such as that of the network, suggests is the importance of formal choices in the imagination and representation of the global. Through such choices, existing ideas and ideologies of collectivity and totality, some with very long cultural traditions, are deployed in the attempt to envision global ecological belonging. An awareness of such forms and their cultural background and implications is part and parcel of an environmentally oriented cosmopolitanism that not only seeks to explore how global systems shape local forms of inhabitation but also is aware of how this exploration itself is framed by culturally specific assumptions. The following chapters will explore such techniques in literary and film texts, but I would like to conclude here with a brief foray into the rapidly expanding realm of new-media art.

John Klima's installation *Earth*, a version of which was exhibited at the 2002 Biennial at the Whitney Museum, takes up the 1960s image of the Blue Planet but inserts it into both new informational systems and networks of different viewers. The installation exists in several different forms—as a stand-alone combination of a computer, monitor, and trackball input device, as a java browser module, and as a more complex object with two input stations at the Whitney—a plurality that itself suggests something of the transformability of data into different images that forms the core of Klima's portrayal of the global. The work consists of software that gathers internet data about topography and weather for the Earth and projects them onto a three-dimensional model of the planet, in such a way that the user can zoom in and out of different regions and see them displayed in terms of six different layers of data about the Earth as a whole as well as the specific places the viewer zooms in on. In the stand-alone installation, which is hooked up to the internet, other online viewers are represented by icons of positioning satellites; in an interesting twist, since online users cannot be readily identified in terms of their geographical position, the system has to attempt a good guess at their location in order to represent them in this way. At the Whitney installation, two viewers could use the system simultaneously and see each other's views, which were also being projected on a transparent weather balloon positioned above the computer stations. Through the possibilities of zooming in and out as well as the accessibility of other viewers' perspectives, *Earth* gestures formally toward the kind of ecological cosmopolitanism I have outlined here. Klima's installation generates images that combine different spatial scales into striking visual collages like the one of Patagonia shown here (fig. 1.2). The view of the "Blue Planet" is here overlaid with detailed, three-

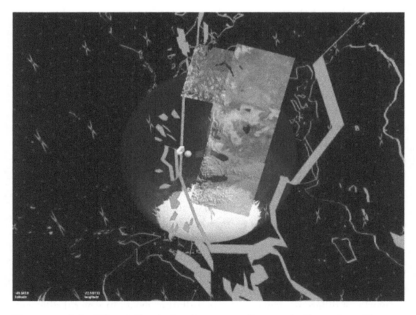

Figure 1.2. John Klima's Earth: Landsat-7 over Patagonia. Reproduced by permission of the artist (http://www.cityarts.com/earth/).

dimensional profiles of the local terrain, as well as the regional coast outline and an indicator of the viewer's position. The geometrical, square-
by-square representation of the topography contrasts with the jagged
coastline as well as with the familiar blue sphere against black space,
which here appears at an unusual tilted angle. In its combination of different imaging techniques and scales, the dynamic manipulation of the
data by the viewer, and connectedness to both informational and social
networks that span the world, *Earth* suggests some of the complexities an
eco-cosmopolitan imagination of the global must take into account at the
beginning of the third millennium.

Klima's installation uncannily prefigured one of the most recent internet tools to have come into common usage. Google Earth, an application
that was originally developed under the name Earth Viewer by Keyhole
Inc. and acquired by the search engine company Google in 2004, allows
users to travel virtually around the globe, to zoom in and out of different regions and locations, and to display different sets of data about these
sites. Like Klima's *Earth*, it builds on data inputs from a variety of sources
such as aerial photography, satellite images, and geographic information
systems that are projected on to a model of the planet, with some cities and
natural sites available for three-dimensional viewing. Because this application is able to display satellite images from around the globe in very high
resolution and in close-up, allowing the viewer even to discern structures
such as trees and cars in many cases, it has become not only a popular entertainment but also a threat to governments and institutions who would
prefer to keep certain parts of their territory shielded from public view.[37]
This latest metamorphosis of the Blue Planet image into a searchable and
zoomable database in the shape of a virtual globe signals and sums up
some of the crucial transformations that have taken place in the imagination of the global since the 1960s. No longer relying on allegorical images
of the planet, Google Earth instead instantiates what media theorist Lev
Manovich has called the "database aesthetic" of much new media art, in
his view a new aesthetic configuration that is neither narrative nor metaphorical in its basic structure but instead presents infinitely expandable
sets of data with the possibility of establishing different sorts of sets and
linkages between them (Manovich 212–43). In its ability to display the
whole planet as well as the minute details of particular places in such a
way that the user can zoom from one to the other and focus on different
types of information, Google Earth's database imaginary may well be the
latest and post-postmodernist avatar of modernist collage, which has now
turned global, digital, dynamic, and interactive. It also, more metaphori-
cally, points the way to some of the information, as well as formal structures, that eco-cosmopolitanism of the kind I have described here can rely
on, and through which it can express itself.

2

AMONG THE EVERYWHERES

Global Crowds and the Networked Planet

In the environmental vision of the planet as it emerged in the 1960s and 1970s, few issues galvanized political debates as well as the cultural imagination as much as what was then referred to as "overpopulation." Demographers and environmentalists pointed not only to the growth of Earth's human population—from approximately five hundred million in 1650 to one billion around 1850, two billion in 1930, and three billion in 1960—but also the rapidly accelerating pace of this increase, warning that it might lead to unprecedented environmental devastation and human misery. Annual percentage increases in populations, they pointed out, might appear deceptively low, but a yearly increase of 2 percent means a doubling in thirty-five years, while a 3 percent increase implies a doubling in twenty-four years. Few countries, they argued, are prepared to double their food and energy supplies, housing, and educational and medical facilities in so short a time, and as a consequence they forecast dire panoramas of mass starvation and immiseration. Governments and international institutions were encouraged to take resolute measures to limit further increase in the growth rates, though the reproductive momentum of the already existing population implied that growth itself would continue for decades to come. "POPULATION EXPLOSION: Unique in human experience, an event which happened yesterday but which everyone swears won't happen until tomorrow," novelist John Brunner summed up the problem sarcastically in his novel *Stand on Zanzibar.*

The political controversies that ensued from this concern are well known. Millions of people did starve in the developing world in the 1970s and 1980s, though not at the rate environmentalists had predicted. Leftist critics, especially, argued that these deaths were due to problems in food distribution and more generally to staggering social inequalities rather than any overall scarcity. Population control measures, including the one-child policy in China and widespread sterilization campaigns in India, came under criticism for their disregard of individual rights and their neocolonial imposition of reproductive constraints on some of the world's poorest populations. More broadly, critics asked whether looming scarcity crises and environmental devastation were caused principally by rampant population growth in the developing world or by rampant increases in consumption in the developed world.

By the 1990s, however, most of these controversies had abated. Even though the world population reached six billion in October 1999—double the number of 1960—this event was no longer accompanied by the images of mass starvation and nightmarishly overcrowded spaces it conjured up in the 1960s and 1970s. In part, this is no doubt due to changed growth projections for the future. Although the world population will, according to the most recent UN projections, continue to grow until the middle of the twenty-first century and will add approximately another 40 percent to the 2005 figure of 6.5 billion (the UN forecasts a population of 9.1 billion for 2050), it is now clear that this increase will affect particular regions in very different ways.[1] Whereas a number of industrialized nations, for example Japan, Italy, Germany, the Baltic states, and most of the countries that succeeded the Soviet Union, will face shrinking populations, other countries such as India, Pakistan, China, and several states of sub-Saharan Africa will continue to grow, with the attendant challenges of providing education, jobs, and medical care to an ever-increasing number of people.[2] As far as population figures are concerned, then, the future will be a divided one, with industrialized countries significantly less affected by continued population growth than in the past.

This change in outlook and growth rates—though not in the overall prediction of significant further population increases—has been accompanied by a transformation in the analytical perspective that is usually brought to bear on demographic growth. While earlier approaches tended to emphasize problems of resource shortages and the necessity of "population control," issues of women's rights, access to education, and reproductive health more frequently occupy center stage in discussions of global demographic trends today.[3] Dominant terms of the 1960s and 1970s such as "overpopulation" and "carrying capacity" have receded in importance, giving way to discussions focused more centrally on issues of distributive justice, gender inequality, and uneven resource consumption patterns. This change does not imply that concerns over population growth have disappeared: clearly, any movement toward "sustainable development" cannot leave demographic trends out of consideration. But debates over desirable population sizes tend no longer to be dominated by apocalyptic scenarios; rather, they revolve around how problems of social and gender inequality, migration, or racial discrimination might be mitigated or aggravated by particular population control measures.

Given this fundamental shift, it comes as little surprise that the imagination of the global associated with ever-growing human populations has also undergone substantial change. In the 1960s and 1970s, a wide range of writers and filmmakers translated the idea of environments that were not just mostly human-made but indeed consisted in large part of human bodies themselves into fictional scenarios in which densely crowded urban spaces came to function as a synecdoche for the planet as a whole. By envisioning overpopulation as most centrally a problem of space, and by emphasizing issues of crowding and loss of privacy—sometimes tinged by class-and race-based fears—these texts and films associate demographic growth with broader anxieties about the fate of the individual in mass society that were being forcefully debated at the time. At the same time, midcentury totalitarian dystopias provided powerful templates for envisioning the erasure of the individual under a crushing state apparatus designed to control crowds rather than to support individuals. But occasionally, the focus on metropolitan spaces with their inbuilt heterogeneity also allowed a less dystopian and more cosmopolitan vision of global crowds to emerge. In the novel *Stand on Zanzibar* (1968), by the British author John Brunner, an emphasis on the transforming impact of emergent media technologies and on the encounter with other cultures leads to a more optimistic assessment of how humans might establish a global community. At the same time, Brunner draws on the narrative conventions of the high modernist urban novel in an attempt to reflect on the heterogeneity and disjunctures in such a community as well as on its connectedness, in what amounts to an attempt to translate cosmopolitanism as a vision of the global into narrative form.

Stand on Zanzibar, to some extent, sets the tone for literary texts from the 1980s and 1990s that reengage the issue of population growth against the background of a multitude of interacting political, social, economic, ecological, and technological problems. In this context, far more complex than the totalitarian social structures that tended to prevail in works from the 1960s and 1970s, demographic growth functions as one important variable in the uneven emergence of a new world society. Advanced technologies ranging from genetic engineering to digital computer networks give rise to partly natural and partly engineered bodies and environments, and to a planetary habitat that is part biosphere and part artifact. In these surroundings, the physical crowds of earlier overpopulation novels begin to transmute into virtual crowds of electronic selves in search of new forms of governance and inhabitation. Texts such as David Brin's novel *Earth* and John Cage's poem "Overpopulation and Art" give a deliberately utopian twist to this transformation, at the same time that they, like *Stand on Zanzibar*, seek to cast their cosmopolitan visions into innovative narrative and lyrical forms that combine elements of epic, allegory and collage in their portrayal of societies that rely on both ecological and informational networks for their subsistence.

1. Mr. and Mrs. Everywhere

Concern over global human population growth is neither limited to the post–World War II era nor specifically environmentalist in its roots. At least since Thomas Malthus's *Essay on the Principle of Population* (1798), the rapid growth of humankind has periodically given rise to deep worries and dire predictions about the future. But in the twentieth century, concerns over population growth came to a head in the 1960s and 1970s with the publication of such books as Paul Ehrlich's *The Population Bomb* (1968), the Club of Rome's report *The Limits to Growth* (1972), and Lester Brown's *The Twenty-Ninth Day* (1978), all of which predicted horrendous consequences for the environment, as well as global society, if population growth was not brought under control.[4] At the same time, Garrett Hardin's seminal essay "The Tragedy of the Commons" (1968), which is today mainly remembered for its discussion of the collective use of public resources, really was most centrally concerned with how population growth affects such usage over time.

As a literary topic, overpopulation had begun to make occasional appearances in the 1950s, but it remained limited to isolated short stories, for example Kurt Vonnegut's "Tomorrow and Tomorrow and Tomorrow" (1953), Frederik Pohl's "The Census Takers" (1955), and Cyril Kornbluth's "Shark Ship" (1958). It only became a major theme in science fiction in the 1960s, inspiring a whole series of novels, including Anthony Burgess's *The Wanting Seed* (1962), Lester Del Rey's *Eleventh Commandment* (1962; rev. ed. 1970), Brian Aldiss's *Earthworks* (1965), Harry Harrison's *Make Room! Make Room!* (1966; source for the much inferior film *Soylent Green*, 1973)— Lee Tung's *The Wind Obeys Lama Toru* (1967), James Blish and Norman L. Knight's *A Torrent of Faces* (1967), and John Brunner's *Stand on Zanzibar* (1968). Short stories, for instance J. G. Ballard's "The Concentration City" (1960; first published under the title "Build-Up" in 1957) and "Billennium" (1961), Brian W. Aldiss's "Total Environment" (1968), Kurt Vonnegut's "Welcome to the Monkey House" (1968), Keith Roberts's "Therapy 2000" (1969), James Blish's "Statistician's Day" (1970), and Keith Laumer's "The Lawgiver" (1970), also focused on population growth and its consequences, as did the *Star Trek* episode entitled "The Mark of Gideon," which first aired in early 1969.[5]

In 1971, Ballantine Books copublished a collection of short stories with Zero Population Growth (an organization dedicated to the promotion of population control) under the title *Voyages: Scenarios for a Spaceship Called*

Earth (edited by Rob Sauer), and more novels and short stories followed until the midseventies: Robert Silverberg's *The World Inside* (1971), Maggie Nadler's "The Secret" (1971), Thomas Disch's *334* (1972), Larry Niven and Jerry E. Pournelle's *The Mote in God's Eye* (1974), and John Hersey's *My Petition for More Space* (1974).[6] Michael Campus's film *Zero Population Growth* (1971) also focused on an overpopulated future society, at the same time that reflections on population increase appeared in literary texts whose main concerns lay elsewhere. Thus, Gary Snyder's volume of poetry *Turtle Island* (1974) ends with a prose section, entitled "Four Changes," that addresses central environmental problems and how they might be mitigated, with "Population" as the first one (91–93); Italo Calvino includes among the imaginary cities described in his *Le città invisibili* (Invisible cities) (1974) the city of Procopia, whose population grows so precipitously over the years that by the time of the narrator's last visit, the twenty-six inhabitants of his hotel room turn any movement into an obstacle race (146–47).

Between the early 1960s and the mid-1970s, then, a considerable body of scientific as well as literary works appeared that addressed questions of human population growth and its consequences. Indeed, the two types of approach were not completely separate at the time: on the one hand, Paul Ehrlich illustrated his statistic predictions with three science fiction scenarios in *The Population Bomb*, and he wrote prefaces to Harry Harrison's novel *Make Room! Make Room!*, the *Voyages* anthology, and another collection of ecologically oriented short stories, *Nightmare Age* (1970); on the other hand, Harrison's novel and the short stories in *Voyages* have bibliographical references that include not only literary but also scientific and sociological works on ecological and demographic problems.

The issue was conceptually framed in somewhat different ways in the two genres, however. Scientists and demographers were primarily concerned with what persistent population growth implied for humankind's relationship to its planetary environment, and explored the ecological and social consequences of growth beyond "carrying capacity."[7] They therefore often focused on the developing countries whose population growth rates were highest, even as they emphasized the depletion of natural resources due to Western populations' higher levels of consumption. Novelists and short story writers, by contrast, tended to set their overpopulation scenarios in Western cities and to examine the fate of individuals and communities under conditions of extreme crowding.[8] Burgess's *The Wanting Seed*, Harrison's *Make Room! Make Room!*, Blish and Knight's *A Torrent of Faces*, Brunner's *Stand on Zanzibar*, and Hersey's *My Petition for More Space* all prominently feature descriptions of crowd behavior, while other texts— Vonnegut's "Tomorrow and Tomorrow and Tomorrow," Ballard's "Billennium," Aldiss's "Total Environment," Silverberg's *The World Inside*, and Disch's *334*—comment on the social and psychological transformations that occur in densely populated cities. The literary texts, then, tended to articulate problems of population increase in terms of concerns over the availability and distribution of urban space.

This anxiety about space occasionally also surfaces in the scientific texts. Paul Ehrlich, for example, begins the first chapter of his classic *The Population Bomb* with the following anecdote.

> I have understood the population explosion intellectually for a long time. I came to understand it emotionally one stinking hot night in Delhi a few years ago. My wife and daughter and I were returning to our hotel in an ancient taxi. The seats were hopping with fleas. The only functional gear was third. As we crawled through the city, we entered a crowded slum area. The temperature was well over 100, and the air was a haze of dust and smoke. The streets seemed alive with people. People eating, people washing, people sleeping. People visiting, arguing, and screaming. People thrusting their hands through the taxi window, begging. People defecating and urinating. People clinging to buses. People herding animals. People, people, people, people. As we moved slowly through the mob, hand horn squawking, the dust, noise, heat, and cooking fires gave the scene a hellish aspect. Would we ever get to our hotel? All three of us were, frankly, frightened. It seemed that anything could happen—but, of course, nothing did. Old India hands will laugh at our reaction. We were just some overprivileged tourists, unaccustomed to the sights and sounds of India. Perhaps, but the problems of Delhi and Calcutta are our problems too. (1)

The scenario Ehrlich describes here is meant to prepare the reader for the ensuing argument about demographic statistics by conveying a moment of emotional confrontation rather than rational comprehension.[9] It is intended to give the "feel" rather than the facts of overpopulation, the visceral experience of what are otherwise abstract mathematical figures. Yet most of the details that give the scene its emotional force have little to do with demographic pressures: certainly the heat, a crucial component of the city's "hellish" feel, has no causal relation to it at all, and the fleas, the technical malfunctioning of the cab, the pollution of the air, and the lack of plumbing all seem to have more to do with poverty and underdevelopment than with overpopulation. Not even the sense of a looming threat from dense masses of humans surrounding the individual that culminates in Ehrlich's outcry "People, people, people, people" is exempt from this ambiguity. Is this a genuine experience of overpopulation, or is it the sense of suffocation that can overcome one in the midst of big-city crowds even in countries that are not considered overpopulated? Do we see masses of people in this scene because there are really "too many" of them by some standard, or because poverty has kept them out of the kind of housing that would hide more affluent but no less numerous crowds from public view?[10]

Pointing out the dubious logic that underlies this anecdote does not, of course, imply any challenge to Ehrlich's general argument that the perpetuation of 1960s population growth rates into the future would lead to dire environmental and social consequences. But it does foreground an associative connection typical of many of the neo-Malthusian literary texts of the period: they link the abstract demographic concept of overpopulation to experiences of intense anxiety in urban environments that are described as consisting principally of human bodies, as if physical crowding were the most immediate or the most significant consequence of excessive population growth. From a demographic perspective, of course, "overpopulation" is a far more elusive phenomenon—one that might lead to shortages of water, food, or heating fuel, insufficient resources for education and medical treatment, and the destruction of natural ecosystems, to name just a few—rather than to accumulations of human bodies in one place. Conversely, shortages of living space and crowded conditions can have a wide variety of causes that are unrelated to population growth rates. Nevertheless, the association of overpopulation with urban crowding is persistent in novels and short stories of the 1960s and 1970s.

Typically, the situation such texts focus on and describe with dread is the erasure of individuality under the double pressure of immense human crowds and crushingly anonymous bureaucratic institutions. Sam Poynter, the protagonist of *My Petition for More Space,* perhaps best exemplifies this predicament: the entire novel describes a morning he spends waiting in lines so as to reach a counter where he can submit a petition to have his living space in a communal residence increased from 7 by 11 feet to 8 by 12 feet. The waiting experience is one of unbearable physical and mental claustrophobia, as his body, wedged in between those of others, is constantly scanned by the controlling eyes of strangers ready to denounce him for the slightest misdemeanor. At the same time, he is periodically overcome by a sense of dissolution and vertigo when he envisions the crowd beyond the people with whom he is in actual physical touch:

> My own circle...leaps out to include all those who touch the four who touch me. I must not let myself consider the touchers of those touchers of my touchers, for like flash-fire the sense of contact, of being not a separate entity but a fused line-unit, will carry my selfhood out to the sides of the waitline and crackling along it forward and backward until my perception of myself is wholly lost in crowd-transcendence. In that lost state I will be nothing but an indistinguishable ohm in this vast current of dissatisfaction. (13)

His actual encounter with authority at the end of his wait stands in stark contrast to this sense of fusion, since Poynter cannot even see the official behind the counter but only hears a voice that urges him to present his petition clearly and concisely. His request for more space ends up being denied, as his faltering sense of individuality prevents him from articulating any coherent justification for it.

This portrait of an individual quashed as much by the crushing physical presence of multiple bodies as by oppressive and all-powerful bureaucracies repeats itself in *Make Room! Make Room!* and *The World Inside*, among others. Harrison's novel describes a policeman in turn-of-the-millennium New York who is personally and professionally destroyed by the contradictory demands of his superiors to solve a difficult murder case on the one hand and to be available for crowd control during food riots on the other. Silverberg's characters live in twenty-fifth-century "urban monads"— gigantic skyscrapers inhabited by 800,000 humans each—and are allowed complete reproductive freedom. But they are brainwashed or exterminated without ado if they exhibit any behavior that is considered a threat to social cohesion—for example, a desire to leave the building for a walk in the surrounding landscape. As works of literature, these and quite a few other novels and short stories about overpopulation from the 1960s and 1970s are of limited interest. Often, their vision of cultures to come is heavily indebted to earlier descriptions of totalitarian societies such as Aldous Huxley's *Brave New World* or George Orwell's *1984*, but ignores more contemporary and complex treatments of the individual under authoritarian control as they appear in the novels of, for example, William Burroughs or Thomas Pynchon.[11] Even as they draw on concerns about the fate of the individual in mass society that were widespread in the 1960s,[12] their paranoia about living space is rooted in middle-class fears about the urban experience, as Fredric Jameson has pointed out:

> in the crowded conurbations of the immediate future...the fear is that of proletarianization, of slipping down the ladder, of losing a comfort and a set of privileges which we tend increasingly to think of in spatial terms: privacy, empty rooms, silence, walling other people out, protection against crowds and other bodies. (*Postmodernism* 286)

Overcrowded urban living conditions, in other words, can function as a dystopian image of the future only for a readership that is privileged enough not to have to cope with such conditions in the present.

Most overpopulation dystopias of the period, then, take the modernist metropolis enlarged to planetary size as their matrix for envisioning a global society. In this context, deterritorialization and global connectedness are portrayed as emerging less from individuals' detachment from place than, somewhat paradoxically, from their forcible confinement to the local. In overpopulation novels and films, the individual is squeezed into too tight a place to allow for any attachments to either the local or beyond. Reduced to its most minimal conception, the "local" here encourages fear of intrusion rather than the formation of community, and is presented as cut off from most natural and cultural contexts. Yet in what is unquestionably the most interesting work in this earlier set, British novelist John Brunner turns this usage of the urban matrix upside down so as to approach global space and social systems in quite a different way. In *Stand on Zanzibar* (1968), he moves the emphasis from the portrayal of individuals caught in overcrowded environments to a cosmopolitan panorama of widely divergent social, racial, and national groups, borrowing his narrative procedures from the high modernist urban novels of the 1920s rather than from midcentury dystopias.

By now a science fiction classic, *Stand on Zanzibar* breaks with the genre's convention of linear narrative with clearly defined protagonists. Instead, Brunner presents his future world through a collage of multiple narrative fragments. Party conversations, advertisements, news bulletins, television images, legal texts, statistical data, quotations from books, and a multitude of mini–short stories confront the reader with a far wider range of characters from diverse national, social, racial, ethnic, political, and religious backgrounds than any plot summary could account for. Through this mosaic of perspectives and discourses, the reader gradually comes to know the world in 2010, first in New York and subsequently in a number of other locations around the globe. To the extent that this novel can be said to have protagonists, they are Donald Hogan and Norman House, a white man and an African American man who share an apartment in New York and are sent on political and economic missions to Asia and Africa, respectively. But their individual experiences are subordinated to the more global portrayal of an overpopulated world characterized by densely crowded cities, sudden outbreaks of violence, savage social inequalities and eugenic laws that, varying by region and nation, impose more or less severe restrictions on the reproductive rights of individuals who carry the genes for certain disabilities and diseases. Donald Hogan, at the behest of the government, tracks down a scientist in the fictional Asian nation of Yatakang—an imaginary counterpart to Indonesia—who is rumored to have invented a "gene optimization" procedure that might allow individuals to change their reproductive legal status; news of this procedure causes social unrest around the globe. Norman House travels to the equally fictional African nation of Beninia to initiate a business venture, and by accident discovers an ethnic community with an unusual genetic profile and an unusually peaceful history that by the end of the novel holds out some hope of solving the world's problems of violence. But this plot—rather farfetched in the solution it suggests to the complex problems it outlines—is on the whole far less important for the novel than the portrait of global society that the two men's intercontinental travels open up.

Brunner's unorthodox narrative technique was criticized by some of his first reviewers, while others credited him with the invention of an entirely new kind of science fiction novel. Brunner scoffed at both: "Since . . . sf is a notoriously conservative field in the stylistic sense, it didn't surprise me that a lot of people felt something that was actually a couple of generations old was too much of the *avant garde* to be tolerated" ("Genesis" 36). His models, Brunner explains, were the modernist novels of John Dos Passos such as *Manhattan Transfer*, the USA Trilogy, and especially *Midcentury*, which he refers to as the most immediate influence on *Stand on Zanzibar* (36). In Dos Passos's novels, as in Brunner's, plot is subordinated to the broader portrayal of a contemporary society that presents itself as a collage of heterogeneous discourses. *Midcentury*, the most important model for *Stand on Zanzibar*, gives chapters with such quotations of various discourses the title "Documentary." [13] Analogously, some of the textual fragments that make up *Stand on Zanzibar* are called "context," "the happening world," or "tracking with closeups," in a deliberate attempt to capture political, economic, social, cultural, and ecological developments at different scales. Visual media are as prominent in these fragments as textual ones. Some pages, for example, are split into parallel textual columns that describe images and sound simultaneously and frequently "cut" from one scene to the next. "'Mix a dash of *Ulysses* and a splash of *Brave New World* into a sprawling television script, then attempt to rewrite some of it as a novel,'" one critic characterized the novel ("Genesis" 34), and another observed, "*Stand on Zanzibar* is not a novel; it is a film in book form" (Spinrad 182). Yet Brunner's work is no more coherent or linear considered as a film than as a novel. His mosaic-style accumulation of quotations and stories outlines the functioning of a global media network that itself stands as a metaphor for the complex connectivity of worldwide social and ecological systems.

That a novelist aiming to present his readers with a broad-ranging, multifaceted image of future society would fall back on techniques that were first developed to describe the bewildering heterogeneity of the modern metropolis is not in itself surprising. But it is significant that Brunner chose Dos Passos's work as his model rather than other varieties of the modernist urban novel such as James Joyce's *Ulysses*, Virginia Woolf's *Mrs. Dalloway*, Alfred Döblin's *Berlin Alexanderplatz* (itself influenced by *Manhattan Transfer*), or Robert Musil's *Der Mann ohne Eigenschaften* (The Man without Qualities). All of these novels, even as they paint a comprehensive panorama of the big city, simultaneously affirm the uniqueness of the individual; and all of them, even though they feature a plethora of characters, have clearly identifiable protagonists whose movements through the metropolis the reader is invited to follow. Dos Passos's *Manhattan Transfer*, by contrast, persistently refuses to focus on any one of its several dozen characters in New York City from the 1890s to the 1920s: each character is foregrounded in a short narrative segment, is then abandoned for other characters, and appears again in another story segment further along. Even though Brunner allows two of his characters, Donald Hogan and Norman House, to dominate more of his story than any of the others, they do not compare to Leopold Bloom and Stephen Dedalus, let alone Franz Biberkopf or Mrs. Dalloway in narrative centrality.[14] The narrative structure itself, in other words, is designed in such a way as to turn the reader's attention away from the individual and toward the more general social, economic, and cultural patterns of Brunner's crowded twenty-first-century world.

In the fictional universe of *Stand on Zanzibar,* these crowds are dealt with by means of standardization. One of the advanced technologies that most clearly foregrounds this process is the customized TV set, which, in 2010, allows viewers to insert themselves into the images on the screen, rather than watching other characters perform. Gradually, the novel conveys that this technology is available at different levels of individualization. On TV screens in public places, the characters representing the viewer are standardized by gender, age, race, and body type. For example, when Donald Hogan boards an airplane, the flight attendant immediately switches his TV to the "'white stocky young mature' version of the man" (333), represented in an interior resembling that of the plane. The cheaper TV sets for home use offer the viewer similar choices: Norman House, for example, has chosen an African American male to represent himself, and a Scandinavian woman to stand in for his rapidly changing lovers. But the more expensive units are able to represent an actual viewer in completely individualized fashion. This technology, which allows viewers to project themselves into the virtual world on the screen and to watch *themselves* visiting exotic locations and participating in extraordinary events at varying levels of abstraction from their actual selves, is referred to in the novel as "Mr. and Mrs. Everywhere," the virtual personae who are everywhere and form a part of everything. While Brunner's multiply ironic description of this technology is clearly intended as a critique of a society in which full expression of individuality is restricted to the economic elite (if indeed one can consider participation in premade television scripts an expression of individuality), it also suggests an interesting metaphor for the potential of a cosmopolitan perspective, as it allows individuals to identify themselves with variously defined social groups at different levels of inclusiveness, or to assume virtual selves quite differently situated from their real ones.

Norman House comments on the experience of this new technology when he observes that

> "it's eerie. There's something absolutely unique and indescribable about seeing your own face and hearing your own voice, matted into the basic signal. There you are wearing clothes you've never owned, doing things you've never done in places you've never been, and it has the immediacy of real life because nowadays television *is* the real world. . . . We're aware of the scale of the planet, so we don't ac-

cept that our own circumscribed horizons constitute reality. Much more real is what's relayed to us by the TV." (314) [15]

This confusion between images and the real world carries over into the routine conversations in the novel, in which Mr. and Mrs. Everywhere are frequently alluded to. At a party, for example, one person mentions that "'We were going to spend [our vacation] under the Caribbean, but Mr. and Mrs. Everywhere go there such a lot we're afraid it'll be dreadfully crowded,'" and another comments on a trip to Antarctica by saying, "'I hate the snow but whereinole else is there that Mr. and Mrs. Everywhere haven't been recently? I can't stand all these interchangeable people!'" (234). In conversations such as these, Mr. and Mrs. Everywhere morph from characters on television screens to rhetorical figures referring to the ubiquitous masses in an overcrowded world. The technology that was designed to individualize standard programming ends up standardizing the real world and amalgamating individuals into "interchangeable people." But Brunner does not roundly criticize or reject this technology as other overpopulation novelists no doubt would have; on the contrary, what seems to interest him is the ambiguous status of Mr. and Mrs. Everywhere as at the same time specific individuals, abstract types, and virtual-reality constructs. As the distinction between embodied identities and technologically generated images of the self begins to blur, new possibilities emerge for connecting individual bodies to social collectives and geographical places around the globe.

Brunner's consideration of visual and electronic technologies and the way in which they may come to destabilize the human subject not only eerily prefigures later concerns about the figure of the cyborg and "life on the screen"[16] but also recontextualizes issues of individuality, privacy, violence, and surveillance that dominate other overpopulation novels and films. In a framework of global systems that shape almost every facet of the lives of the novel's numerous characters, their ability to travel not only geographically but virtually to places they have not actually visited transmutes neo-Malthusian claustrophobia into the beginnings of cosmopolitan inhabitation. Brunner does not deliver an unambiguous verdict on this process of social transformation; but through an optimistic ending that makes the genetics as well as the cultural accomplishments of a minority culture available as a partial answer to global problems, he gestures toward such a new kind of community that might arise from this technologically mediated sense of planet. In narrative terms, he configures this sense of the global in terms of a far-flung mosaic of discourses that extends the matrix of the modernist urban novel to the planet as a whole, in an effort to capture both its heterogeneity and its complex connectivity. It is this reactivated collage structure that turns into a template for later literary attempts to consider attachments to the local in the context of an increasingly crowded global society.

2. The Virtual Crowds

By the late 1970s, overpopulation receded from literary texts as a prominent topic, even as environmental problems slowly began to establish themselves as concerns not only in science fiction, but across a wide variety of genres from nature poetry to mainstream novels.[17] When it resurfaces in the literature of the late 1980s and early 1990s, it is no longer presented in the apocalyptic mode of earlier decades. This change in tone is not limited to literary texts: popular scientific approaches to population issues in the 1990s also combine more cautious and complex forecasts with a greater emphasis on how population growth is related to such factors as economic conditions, social inequality, women's reproductive health, and access to education. Donella and Dennis Meadows's *Beyond the Limits* (1992), a follow-up to their 1972 report, emphasized that levels of growth and development were excessive but at the same time gave grounds for cautious optimism. Some of the possible future scenarios they developed by means of computer modeling did not include economic collapse and social decline: therefore, if population growth as well as levels of affluence and consumption were brought under control, they argued, there would still be room for hope. Paul and Anne Ehrlich's two books on population issues, *The Population Explosion* (1990) and *The Stork and the Plow: The Equity Answer to the Human Dilemma* (1995), while they reaffirmed the Ehrlichs' earlier predictions of dire consequences in the absence of comprehensive population planning, presented a more complex view of the problem than Paul Ehrlich's 1968 book. Both works emphasized the importance of equitable social structures and improved conditions, especially for women, in any attempt to come to terms with population growth, a problem that in their view it was not too late to solve. Similarly, Joel Cohen's demographic analysis of the population problem, *How Many People Can the Earth Support?* (1995), gave a much more nuanced and complex assessment of the difficulties of forecasting reproductive behavior and estimating the carrying capacity of different regions than earlier discussions, and thereby made it more difficult to sustain any simple apocalyptic rhetoric. Bill McKibben's *Maybe One* (1998), at the same time, approached the problem from a more personal perspective, exploring the implications of population growth and consumption for affluent Westerners' reproductive decisions.

Literary texts generally share this more cautious approach and tend to approach overpopulation not so much as the dominant theme it was in earlier fiction but as one important dimension among others that shape the world of the future. The novels *Dayworld* (1985), by Philip José Farmer; *The Sea and Summer,* by the Australian George Turner (1987; published in the United States under the title *Drowning Towers*); David Brin's *Earth* (1990); *Das Geheimnis der Krypta* (The Mystery of the Crypt; 1990), by the German Carl Amery; Sheri S. Tepper's *The Family Tree* (1997); and Kim Stanley Robinson's trilogy *Red Mars, Blue Mars,* and *Green Mars* (1992, 1993, 1996), as well as John Cage's poem "Overpopulation and Art" (performed 1992, published 1994), all consider population growth as one factor in a whole complex of environmental, social, and political problems such as pollution, climate change, social inequality, uneven access to power, and international competition and conflict. The mode in which the topic is broached differs fundamentally from texts written twenty or thirty years earlier. Even though bleak background scenarios are taken for granted in many of the later texts, these circumstances are no longer presented in the millennial mode that characterized comparable works of the 1960s. Indeed, quite a few of them cultivate a qualified utopianism; while a sense of horror or apocalypse is still palpable in many of them, it is often displaced from the main plot or the narrative present into a subplot or the narrative past. The two texts I will focus on from this later set, David Brin's *Earth* and John Cage's "Overpopulation and Art," deploy experimental narrative and lyrical forms to reflect on the question of how global ecological and technological systems might be represented, what kinds of human collectivity they enable, and what modes of inhabitation planet-wide communities entail.

David Brin's novel *Earth* (1990) is directly influenced by Brunner's *Stand on Zanzibar* in its narrative technique, but far more resolutely ties the emergence of new global media networks to ecological concerns and the question of what kind of human community might be able to address them. Set in 2038, the novel develops a panoramic vision of world society that pays close attention to social, ecological, and technological developments: among these, the abolition of privacy as a positive cultural value no doubt stands out as one of the most striking consequences of electronic technologies and international legislation, as Brin's characters associate privacy with governmental misdeeds rather than with personal rights. But increasingly aged populations and their conflict with the young in industrial nations, the risks associated with advanced weapons technologies, global warming, rising sea levels, pollution, population pressure, and rampant species extinction equally form part of the picture. For all its ecological bleakness, however, Brin's vision is by no means apocalyptic: rather, the novel again and again stresses how humans continuously struggle with such problems and always seem to find new solutions, though few of them turn out to be long-lasting or definitive. Following Brunner's model in *Stand on Zanzibar,* Brin presents this panoramic vision through a narrative collage that includes a large number of characters and a wide range of episodes, as well as "quotations" from the various media and institutions of the day: news announcements, letters, legal texts, excerpts from electronic books, and online newsgroup discussions establish a complex mosaic of life in the global society of the mid-twenty-first century.

The novel's plot, briefly, revolves around a minuscule black hole that scientists discover deep in the crust of the Earth, whose gradual absorption of more and more mass threatens the existence of the planet. Since the artificial creation of small black holes is one of the more recent branches of science, they at first assume that this lethal threat was created by a state, a group of nations, or a corporation that has lost control over its experiment; they therefore design strategies to remove the hole with the utmost secrecy. But in the course of their investigations, the scientists soon discover that this particular singularity is much older than the human science of "cavitronics," and might be of alien origin. Their attempt to remove it by means of "gravity lasers" causes earthquakes and disasters all over the globe, and soon governments, military organizations, and secret services lock in battle with the scientists over control of the black hole. Inevitably, some information about this struggle leaks into the "Net," where a particularly gifted hacker-environmentalist, Daisy McClennon, has long fought a guerrilla war against those she perceives to be polluters and destroyers of nature. Through her extraordinary abilities to seek out and correlate electronically transmitted information, she discovers and appropriates gravity laser technology, whose destructive power she first turns against its inventors and then diverts to a more gruesome purpose: the systematic extermination of practically all of humankind, whom she has come to consider an ultimately destructive species. Her plan is to leave only ten or twenty thousand hunter-gatherers alive who would pose no threat to natural ecosystems.

But McClennon's genocidal rampage across the globe leads to an unexpected outcome. Due to the constant firing of gravity laser beams through the earth's core from many different locations, more and more electronic currents are activated within the earth itself. When McClennon attacks a station where a Nobel Prize–winning biologist, Jennifer Wolling, is in the process of building a complex model of human cognition on the Net, Wolling's consciousness fuses with the electronic currents that kill her and triggers a spontaneous, quasi-natural expansion of the Net into the currents that crisscross the Earth's core. As McClennon is defeated by one of the natural disasters she herself helped to trigger, this innovative kind of artificial intelligence, an electronic Gaia of sorts, gradually asserts its power to impose a new, more ecologically conscious mode of existence. Excess populations are moved into the areas McClennon had depopulated, and extraction of minerals is shifted from the Earth to asteroids. The planetary artificial intelligence, which Brin describes as a collective consciousness that encompasses a multitude of human voices and minds, does not intervene in ordinary political matters, but sets limits to the exploitation of natural resources that no human government will any longer be able to transcend.

What this utopian ending seeks to portray is nothing less than an existential convergence between the most advanced human technologies and Planet Earth in its most basic materiality. Brin chooses geology as the medium of this fusion, translating it into narrative structure itself. He subdivides the novel's twelve epic chapters into subsections called "spheres," each of which is associated with a particular set of characters. Most of the names of these spheres, such as "core," "crust," "lithosphere," "ionosphere," and "exosphere," designate parts of the Earth's geological and atmospheric structure. Some do not: the term "noosphere," associated with the events surrounding Wolling's transformation into the template for the new Gaian consciousness, is derived from the vocabulary of French theologian and paleontologist Pierre Teilhard de Chardin, who used it to refer to what he saw as a collective human consciousness that would arise from increasing technological connectedness.[18] Even in the architecture of the novel, then, Brin indicates the connection between Earth's physical spatiality and the virtual space created by the most recent technologies. Like Brin's central mythological metaphor, the fusion of Gaia and the Net, the structure of the narrative welds Earth as a physical place and material object together with the abstract, immaterial space of the digital cybermatrix.

More than that, through Brin's narrative technique, the planet itself, understood as both a natural object and a technological construct, becomes to some extent the main character of the narrative. Each of the novel's twelve chapters is preceded by a brief passage in italics, each one summing up a part of the Earth's history from its cosmological origins four billion years ago to the twenty-first century. Some of this cosmological narrative uses the scientific vocabulary of planet formation and geological change, but some of it turns the planet into a person of sorts—to be sure, a cosmological or geological person rather than a normal human individual—who gradually awakens to self-consciousness. These italicized passages are not explicitly integrated into the plot, but they are clearly intended to complement it by offering a long-term cosmological perspective on events that in the main narrative happen in a very short interval of time. This allegorization of the planet as an epic persona contrasts with the high modernist fragmentation of the plot to create an image of a global environment that is both one and multiple, holistic and heterogeneous.

Overpopulation, against this conceptual background, takes on a completely different significance than it did in the novels and films of the 1960s and 1970s. While the numerous ecological and social crises Brin describes would provide more than enough material for an old-style apocalyptic narrative, large-scale catastrophe is instead displaced from the realm of ecology to that of physics. Earth-threatening disaster looms in the form of the quite fantastic plot involving the black hole in Brin's novel, not as a consequence of a far more plausible ecological collapse. As one online book within the text observes, population growth is one of many social, economic, environmental, and technological problems that never quite get solved but never lead to the apocalypses that they were predicted to trigger, either:

> As for starvation, we surely have seen some appalling local episodes.
> Half the world's cropland has been lost, and more is threatened. Still,

the "great die-back" everyone talks about always seems to lie a decade or so in the future, perpetually deferred. Innovations...help us scrape by each near-catastrophe just in the nick of time. (48)

One of *Earth*'s scientists similarly reflects on how mass death as a consequence of overpopulation has so far been avoided, in spite of dire predictions:

Malthusian calamity and the so-called S-curve. On the one hand, utter collapse. And on the other, a chain of last-minute reprieves... like self-fertilizing corn, room-temperature superconductors, and gene-spliced catfish...each arriving just in time for mankind to muddle through another year, eking out a living from one brilliant innovation to the next. (531; Brin's ellipses)

As Brin foregrounds the serious implications of human population growth for the ecological structure of the planet, therefore, he deliberately displaces apocalyptic scenarios of the kind that characterized earlier environmentalist texts into a different plot strand. And even in the black hole plot, it is in the end not so much the concept of global disaster as that of the "singularity," the place and moment where the normal laws of physics are suspended, that enables the emergence of a collective planetary consciousness.

Scenes of physical crowding, accordingly, while they do occasionally occur, are relatively rare in *Earth*. To the extent that the novel does convey a sense of crowding, it is of a very different kind. The density and detail of information about the society of the future that Brin communicates to his readers through a multitude of textual and media sources—statistical surveys, legal documents, newscasts, formal and informal online discussion groups, personal letters—creates the impression of an extremely crowded information space in which billions of voices compete for attention. It is in this context that Brin's vision of a "post–privacy society" in which secrecy in most forms has become illegal assumes part of its significance: if all (or almost all) information is freely shared among ten billion people via advanced global communications technologies, a densely "populated" realm of information exchanges emerges in which competing bits of facts, factoids, details, stories, images, and sounds jostle each other as masses of human bodies did in earlier visions of an overcrowded future.

This does not mean that the problem of large numbers of human bodies simply disappears in the novel. Accumulations of bodies and the concomitant anxieties over space remain a part of the picture, and one can reproach Brin with a double moral in his treatment of this topic. While the character who carries out large-scale exterminations, Daisy McClennon, is vigorously condemned, her atrocities actually become the basis for an at least temporary solution to the population problem, in that they free up space for the relocation of people who were formerly confined to boat settlements on the oceans. Even while he rejects it, Brin is apparently not able to envision a less violent remedy to the problem.[19] Yet the central image of a fusion between Earth and the Net does in fact respond to the concern over space in a very different fashion, since the crowds that dominate in the novel are not really the physical ones of human bodies but the virtual ones of human voices communicating incessantly by means of electronics. Wolling's metamorphosis from an embodied being to an electronic presence is only the most dramatic instance of a process that in more mundane form has become commonplace even for many of the underprivileged in Brin's world. In this transformation, the space anxieties disappear. While the lack of privacy was precisely what made Ballard's billennial city, Harrison's New York, Hersey's New Haven, and Silverberg's urban monads so horrific, the citizens of Brin's global society rejoice in the disappearance of an informational privacy that they have come to regard as nothing more than a protection for the privileges of the affluent (e.g. Swiss bank accounts) or a cloak for the unlawful maneuvers of governmental and corporate institutions. The central narrative response of Brin's novel to overpopulation lies in this metamorphosis of physical into virtual crowds.

It would be easy to argue that such a transformation is nothing more than a metaphor that evades more practical solutions, but the point of Brin's fusion of Earth and Net lies precisely in its metaphoricity. It is an attempt to envision in narrative form a global, utopian space in which fundamental questions of scarce resources, wealth, social class, and place can be reconsidered on the basis of new premises—in other words, it provides an allegory of the rise of global environmental awareness and governance. Brin is at pains to emphasize that the new artificial intelligence, even though it speaks with the voice of Jennifer Wolling, is not one entity, but really an allegorization of the global multiplicity of human voices. It is, in other words, a more condensed version of the multifarious world society that the entire novel describes. Representing global humanity as both multiple *and* connected in narrative form is no easy task, and Brin's choice of a single character as a provisional ordering shape for the global meeting of minds may well be too indebted to totalitarian science fiction clichés of benign overminds that solve humanity's conflicts from the top down.[20] But these shortcomings weigh perhaps less heavily when one considers the ambitious scope of Brin's project: finding a narrative form to articulate a cosmopolitan awareness that links the ecological and the technological across a diversity of cultures, and a utopian kind of human collective that erases neither the individual nor the small community but links both to a global ecological self-awareness, the eco-cosmopolitanism I discussed in chapter 1. If there is a narrative correlative to the environmentalist slogan "Think globally, act locally," Brin's novel is certainly one of the most daring attempts to envision what such a storytelling structure might look like.

The attempt to articulate in literary form how human cultures and communities might be reconceived in their relation to global ecosystems also underlies John Cage's "Overpopulation and Art" (1992), a long poem that, like many of Cage's earlier poetic works, is a hybrid between a lecture of sorts and avant-garde poetry. Cage sees overpopulation as the force for change that will propel humanity into the future by forcing it to break with outdated forms of social organization and communication. The first stanza (ll. 1–20) immediately establishes this link between population growth and communication:

abOut 1948 or 50 the number of people
liVing
all at oncE
equaled the numbeR who had ever lived at any time all added together
the Present as far as numbers
gO
became equal to the Past
we are now in the fUture
it is something eLse
hAs
iT doubled
has It quadrupled
all we nOw
kNow for sure is
the deAd
are iN the minority
they are outnumbereD by us who're living
whAt does this do to
ouR
way of communicaTing

This initial poetic conceit presents the relationship between present and past as a mathematical equation based on population figures, and defines the future as a numerical excess of the present over the accumulated past. It thereby provides an amusing algebraic shorthand for Cage's overarching claim that humanity has undergone a fundamental historical break: the future cannot be symmetrical with the past because economic, demographic, and ecological conditions have changed in such a way that radical new forms of social organization are required. In this context, "ouR / way of communicaTing" refers not only to means of exchanging information such as mail, email, phone, or fax, all of which Cage mentions, but also in a broader sense to forms of organizing community. In the age of overpopulation, increased crowding and scarcity of resources force human communities to break up petrified organizational hierarchies and create "new foRms of living together" (l. 306) so as to confront its principal challenge (ll.483–98):

                    ... the wOrld's prime
                         Vital
                    problEm is how
        to multipy by thRee swiftly safely and satisfyingly
                          Per
                    pOund kilowatt and workhour the overall
                    Performance realizations of the world's
    comprehensive resoUrces this
                    wiLl render those resources
                         Able
                    To support
            100% of humanIty's
            increasing pOpulace at levels
        of physical liviNg
                    fAr above whatever
                has beeN known
                or imagineD

Just how the anarchist society of the future Cage portrays will accomplish
this enormous leap without the dire environmental consequences he de-
plores elsewhere in the poem is, of course, not clear, and could not possibly
be in a text of this sort, which spells out a hope for the future rather than
a full political program.

The concrete suggestions Cage's outline of an anarchist utopia does
include—emphasis on creative unemployment and self-education, the
privileging of use over ownership and profit, the rejection of centralized
bureaucracies and nation-states—are not new to his work. Many of these
ideas had already appeared in his serial poem "Diary: How To Improve the
World (You Will Only Make Matters Worse)" of the 1960s and recurred
later in many other of his works. Much of "Overpopulation and Art" refor-
mulates Cage's anarchist politics and avant-garde aesthetics in the context of rapid population increase. What is particularly interesting about
this reformulation is the role Cage attributes to different communication
media (another long-standing interest of Cage, who was one of the first to
work Marshall McLuhan's media theory into literature and music in the
1960s). Even as he hails new media such as the internet for their capacity
to create a world in which connectedness is more important than conceptual or political borders, he expresses reservations about an unlimited accessibility that makes creative solitude almost impossible (ll. 57–80):

                    enDless
            interpenetrAtion
                togetheR
                    wiTh
                    nOnobstruction
            of what aVail

```
            thEn the use
     of answeRing service
         attemPt
             tO free oneself from
      interruPtion
         solitUde for just a moment regained
      is utterLy
         finAlly
         losT
           fInding 19th
           nOt 21st
           iN 20th century
           Are you
           iN to fax
         anD
   electronic mAil
         aRe you
      in Touch hce
```

"Being in touch" anytime and anyplace is the obligation the new media impose, creating on the one hand a tight web of connected individuals and communities but on the other hand eliminating times and spaces for silence and solitude, two cornerstones of Cage's aesthetic as well as his existential philosophy. His half-resigned and half-amused invocation, at the end of the paragraph, of a character from Joyce's *Finnegans Wake*, H. C. Earwicker—who makes appearances in many of Cage's works—is doubly ironic in this respect, since "hce" also at times stands in for "here comes everybody" in Joyce's text. This reference not only invites a comparison between the artist and the work of art in the early and late twentieth century and their altered position in the media landscape but also evokes a character whose initials make him merge with an inescapable collectivity. "Hce," in a sense, is Cage's counterpart to Brunner's Mr. and Mrs. Everywhere. Yet Cage, even as he mourns the loss of solitude, never expresses the kind of paranoia about the lack of privacy we saw in 1960s texts on overpopulation. On the contrary, the very next stanza celebrates—not unlike Brin's characters—the merging of private space with a global landscape of images: "we live in glass hOuses / our Vitric surroundings / transparEnt / Reflective / Putting images / Outside / in sPace of what's inside / oUr homes / everything's as muLtiplied / As we are" (ll. 82–91). As in Brin, the multiplication of people here begins to shade into the multiplication of signs and images, in a scenario that inspires joy rather than fear: "each momenT / Is magic" (ll. 92–93), Cage exclaims. The vision of a world without conventional boundaries enabled by the new media finally outweighs Cage's fear of constant intrusions on creative silence.

In analogy to the unhierarchical and decentralized social order Cage envisions, he calls for "wOrks of art / in which no Place / is mOre / im-

Portant than another / beaUty / at aLl points" (ll. 105–10), and whose
principal objective is not artistic self-expression but the experimenta-
tion with new forms of aesthetic organization (ll. 122–37). This principle echoes the decentralizing tendency of Brunner's and Brin's novels,
which, as we saw earlier, present the interlaced stories of a whole series
of characters, none of whom is allowed to monopolize the reader's attention. Cage's own poem is structured in terms of a numerical principle
that is derived from the title: the twenty letters of the phrase "overpopulation and art" form the backbone for "mesostics," a kind of acrostic in
which the letters to be read vertically are not placed at the beginning
but in the middle of each line of verse.[21] On the basis of this principle,
stanzas of twenty lines each are created, which are in addition set off by
a capitalized bold letter that precedes the first line of each stanza on the
left margin: these bold letters once again spell "overpopulation and art"
twice over through the total of forty stanzas. Visually, the capitalized mesostic letters in each line of verse do give the poem a center, a backbone of
what are otherwise lines of widely varying lengths. But in oral delivery,
the mesostic letter is indistinguishable from the rest, and a second look
at the typographic layout immediately reveals that if the mesostic runs
down the center of the page, it is not situated at the center of each line:
the mesostic letter is sometimes located near the middle, but it can also
appear at the very beginning or the end of a line. Perhaps more importantly, however, the double mesostic within and across stanzas does not
spell out any hidden or additional dimension of meaning to be read along
with and against the significance of the horizontal lines. Instead, by re-
peating the words of the title and dispersing them over the entire poem,
it serves as a visual reminder that, at least in the poet's intention, no one
line is more important than any other. At the same time, the numerical
structure these words yield emphasizes that the poem is not formally designed to reflect the poet's subjective experience or perceptions, but as a
game that coaxes alternative ordering principles out of the typographical
arrangement of printed language.

Cage certainly did not design these formal strategies specifically to deal
with the topic of overpopulation in poetic form—he had used them before
in many other poems dealing with quite different issues—but it is easy to
see how they work to reinforce the sense that in a world characterized by
physical overcrowding and manifold new "virtual" modes of connection,
the individual is no longer the hub of social or aesthetic forms of organization. Cage celebrates this development with an optimism that has often
been criticized as naïve, and the social, political, and cultural outline he
sketches in "Overpopulation and Art" is certainly open to this charge.
But the least one would have to say in his defense is that this optimism is
programmatic, based on the firm conviction that pessimism and the un-
willingness to imagine utopias merely help to perpetuate outdated sociopolitical structures: "we begin by belieVing / it can bE done / getting Rid /

of Pessimism / blindly clinging tO / oPtimism / in no sense doUbting / the possibiLity of / utopiA" (ll. 566–72).

Most novels and films that have addressed issues of population growth, especially those published in the 1960s and 1970s, focus on the plight of individuals trapped in overcrowded megacities that either extend around the globe or function as a metaphor for a global society that threatens individuality and privacy through space restrictions, reproductive constraints, and opaque, large-scale bureaucracies. In the tiny spaces that define the "local" for these individuals, attachments to either place or larger systems and spaces has become impossible. Formally, these texts tend to build on midcentury dystopian critiques of various kinds of totalitarian states. The three texts I have examined in detail here, however—Brunner's *Stand on Zanzibar*, Brin's *Earth*, and Cage's "Overpopulation and Art"—approach the vision of a crowded planet less as a claustrophobic panorama of oppression than as an opportunity to rethink individual and collective relationships to local places and global systems. All of them attribute crucial importance to emergent networks of information and communications technologies as a new kind of public sphere that functions sometimes as a complement to and sometimes as a metaphor for ecological connectivity. Most explicitly, David Brin allegorizes the emergence of a global, environmentally conscious form of governance as a "singularity" that fuses digital networks with the geological structures of the planet. Less insistently, but not much less optimistically, Brunner and Cage envision communications technologies and networks as opportunities for local individuals and communities to develop an eco-cosmopolitan awareness and presence. In the process, earlier class-coded paranoias about the consequences of omnipresent crowds of humans for the individual transmute into a celebration of physical crowds that merge with or metamorphose into virtual ones, thereby gaining access to a different category of space that is not envisioned as a scarce and unevenly distributed resource. While this transformation opens up new avenues of communication with nature, nature itself is portrayed as irreversibly altered in the process. But part of what this change metaphorizes is really humans' altered understanding of their own identities and places in a global ecological network; if humans' exploitation of nature has been enabled by advanced technologies, these technologies are here also envisioned as a means of remapping global space. In the process, Brunner and Brin redeploy the collage structure of the modernist urban novel to portray global systems that are both heterogeneous and connected—not unlike Klima's installation-based collage—while Cage develops similar strategies of collage in lyrical form. This reconfigured global spatiality becomes the medium for a different kind of encounter between humans, nonhumans, and the natural environment—a cosmopolitanism that reaches for an understanding of both cultural and ecological differences and connectedness.

3

ADVENTURES IN
THE GLOBAL AMAZON

The Amazon rainforest has long functioned as a complex symbol of exotic natural abundance, global ecological connectedness, and environmental crisis in the European and North American
public spheres. Celebrated as the "green lung of the world" for the ability
of its vast forests to absorb carbon dioxide and generate oxygen, the Amazon region has also become a fulcrum of political controversy. While First
World environmentalists over the last few decades have expressed mounting concern about rates of deforestation that might imperil the global atmosphere, South American nations have affirmed their right to determine
on their own the uses of their national resources. The environmental activism of Brazilian rubber tappers Wilson Pinheiro and Chico Mendes in the
1970s and 1980s, however, brought into sharp relief for an international
public just how much even "local" interests diverged. Whereas Pinheiro
and Mendes belonged to a population segment that had used the Amazon
rainforest sustainably, rapidly falling rubber prices had given many local
landowners an incentive to sell their land for unsustainable ranching purposes. The intensifying antagonism between rubber tappers attempting to
salvage their traditional way of life and ranchers intending to convert the
forest to agricultural uses led to the assassinations of Pinheiro in 1980 and
Mendes in 1988; Mendes has remained an international icon of environmental struggle. To this day, periodic media coverage of the dire necessity
that drives the poorest populations, especially of Brazil, to clear rainforest
for agricultural use in spite of its long-term unsuitability for such purposes
presents First World environmentalists with difficult choices between the
urgency of alleviating extreme human misery, at least temporarily, and
the need to preserve one of the most ecologically rich and irreplaceable
natural systems on the planet. Burning swathes of jungle, the felled trunks
of old-growth trees, and the wastelands left behind when the exhaustion

of the rainforest soil forces the rancher to move on to the next plot of forest have become staple images of environmental crisis.

Given its prominent role in international environmental controversies, it is no surprise that writers and artists have chosen the Amazon rainforest as a setting in which to explore the connections between local and global ecology, as well as between local, national and international politics and economy. The two works of art I will examine in this chapter, the experimental nature documentary *Der Ursprung der Nacht (Amazonas-Kosmos)* (The Origin of the Night: Amazon Cosmos, 1973–77) by the German artist Lothar Baumgarten and the novel *Through the Arc of the Rainforest* (1990) by the Japanese American writer Karen Tei Yamashita, both choose the Brazilian jungle as a site with a well-known ecological profile to stage a complex transition to a cosmopolitan reimagination of the natural environment. In both works, the local specificity of the rainforest turns out to be a sort of optical illusion that dissolves when the forest's global connectedness is gradually revealed. Through their experimental narrative techniques, both the film and the novel subtly alienate—or, to use the terminology I discussed in chapter 1, deterritorialize—the Amazon region so that it becomes something other than a site where local ecological authenticity manifests itself. Baumgarten, through a skillfully executed visual and aural deception, forces the reader to think through the connection between the Amazon and the river Rhine in his native Germany, while Yamashita, through narrative strategies borrowed from Latin American magical realism as well as North American ethnic writing, encourages her readers to think across continents and different national traditions of literature as she engages them in a tale of economic globalization. In each of these works, the Amazon turns global, both in its associations with other regions and as a central trope for planetary connectedness, thereby pointing to the difficulty of identifying local ecologies that are not already thoroughly global.

1. The Amazon and the Rhine: *Der Ursprung der Nacht*

Lothar Baumgarten's artistic oeuvre, which by now spans almost four decades, combines a wide variety of media such as photographs, slide projections, objects from the natural world, found objects, and simple words displayed on museum walls in what one is at pains to call anything other than "installation art." Baumgarten himself dislikes this term because of its vagueness (personal communication), yet except for his photographic work, it is difficult to come up with an alternative classification for art that does not fit neatly into categories such as sculpture or painting. The influence of Joseph Beuys is palpable in some of Baumgarten's interest in ordinary items and substances and their reconfiguration into aesthetic objects, but Baumgarten's sustained engagement with the natural world and the names by means of which we categorize and shape it, as well as his concern with the fate of indigenous peoples, their cultures, and their forms of knowledge distinguishes him from his teacher. Baumgarten's works tend to be designed and developed in situ for a particular space and to resist any tendency to make art decorative, portable, and commodifiable (personal communication). In the United States, Baumgarten is perhaps best known for an exhibition in 1993 for which he covered the walls of the Guggenheim Museum in New York with names of dozens of New World indigenous peoples in combination with past participles such as "conquered," "dressed," "researched," and "romanticized." Not only did this cluster of words aim to recall the fate of indigenous cultures without recourse to exoticism or aestheticization but it also served to foreground the fact that many of the names Europeans chose to designate the peoples they encountered in the New World were in fact not the names by which these peoples referred to themselves but quite often those their enemies used. This interest in indigenous cultures recurs in much of Baumgarten's work, and led him to spend a year and a half among the Yanomami between 1978 and 1980.

Indigenous ways of knowing the natural world also frame Baumgarten's only film, *Der Ursprung der Nacht (Amazonas-Kosmos)*. Toward the beginning of the movie, a woman's voice retells in German a myth of the Tupi, a native people of Brazil; in an additional transcultural twist, she follows the version given in anthropologist Claude Lévi-Strauss's work *Du miel aux cendres* (From honey to ashes) (Chang 17; Roberta Smith). "Autrefois la nuit n'existait pas. Il faisait constamment jour. La nuit dormait au fond des eaux. Et les animaux n'existaient pas non plus, car les choses elles-même parlaient," the myth begins, in Lévi-Strauss's rendering (358; "In former times, night did not exist. It was daylight all the time. Night slept beneath the waters. Animals did not exist either, for things themselves had the power of speech"; 416).[1] Interestingly, then, this myth about the origin of the cosmological alternation of night and day also narrates an "origin of species," in which the existence of animals arises through a process of linguistic alienation. This myth, along with Lévi-Strauss's intriguing analysis of the ways it links cosmological, sexual, zoological, and linguistic concerns, forms the backdrop against which the spectator is invited to view Baumgarten's film. At the climax of the Tupi story, disobedient servants of the Great Snake open a nut they were supposed to keep intact, and thereby release the night: "Aussitôt la nuit tomba, et toutes les choses qui étaient dans la forêt se transformèrent en quadrupèdes et en oiseaux, toutes celles qui étaient dans la rivière en canards et en poissons. Le panier se fit jaguar, le pêcheur et sa pirogue devinrent canard: la tête de l'homme fut pourvue d'un bec, la pirogue devint le corps, les rames les pattes" (358–59; "At once night fell and all things that were in the forest changed into quadrupeds and birds; those in the river became ducks and fish. The basket turned into a jaguar, the fisherman and his canoe became a duck: the man's head acquired a beak; the canoe became the body, the oars the feet"; 416–17). As we will see, this mythological ability to metamorphose one thing into another is crucial to the way Baumgarten's documentary deploys particular film techniques, as well as to the connection it postulates between different, geographically far removed locations.

The film's ending returns to the Tupi myth through a male voice that declares "It will never be day again for…" several dozen now extinct indigenous peoples whose names the voice enumerates one by one, an ending that translates the meaning of "night" from its original cosmological context to that of an elegy to the passing of entire cultures. Yet the bulk of the film is less centrally concerned with the fate of indigenous cultures in processes of colonization and modernization than with the emergence, perception, classification, and disappearance of parts of the natural world. The film begins with a screenful of species names in yellow capitals against a black background; while some of these words refer to transparent species or groups of species in German (e.g. "SPECHT," woodpecker; "KÜRBIS," pumpkin; "JAGUAR"; "MANIOK"; "EIDECHSE," lizard), others (e.g. "URUBU," "TONINA," "COATI") remain opaque to the nonspecialist spectator. This enumeration of species is followed by the film's title and then a second screenful of names similar to the first, except that now both familiar and unfamiliar names disappear from the screen one by one until only darkness is left. The night of the title here becomes associated with the extinction of species, just as it is directly linked to the death of entire human cultures at the end of the film.

Yet if this framing might lead one to expect a cinematographic elegy documenting the decline of the natural world and the parallel vanishing of native cultures in the Amazon, the film soon takes its spectators into quite different visual territory. After a brief sequence in which we see the lights of cars speeding by through the night, the camera begins to explore the Amazon landscape: trees, bushes, surfaces of water, clouds, birds, reptiles, and insects in nighttime and daytime, and in various meteorological conditions—sunshine, rain, and thunderstorm. Presenting itself often more as a sequence of still lifes than as a normal motion picture, the film offers images of extraordinary beauty. Surfaces of water reflecting the light, flashes of lightning, constellations of moving clouds, close-ups of tree bark or frog eyes, and rabbits or birds in motion not only strike the viewer through their sheer aesthetic appeal but also constantly call up art historical reminiscences. Certain reflections caught in water begin to remind one of Monet's water lilies, close-ups of logs and leaves or swarms of insects against the sky resemble abstract art, clouds appear like water color paintings, and some of the vegetation seems to be rendered by an impressionist's brush. At one moment, when the camera pans to follow a bird in blurry flight, the result resembles a combination of impressionist color sensibility and brush stroke with futurist Giacomo Balla's attempts to capture the flight of swallows in painting. Nature documentaries of the last few decades, of course, have quite often featured images that almost shock spectators with their beauty and strangeness, as advanced camera technologies along with filmmaker expertise open up perceptual realms beyond normal human capabilities; marine, subterranean, nocturnal, and microscopic domains have opened up to the human eye and ear in ways that were inconceivable with earlier technology. Yet the technique of Baumgarten's film runs against such hyperrealism, indeed against documentary intention in the normal sense. Many sequences are deliberately out of focus or shot so close up that it becomes difficult even to identify what object one is looking at: a bluish vibrating membrane with a knobby texture that appears toward the beginning and end of the film, for example, might be a magnification of a leaf, a toad's skin, or some other substance; an object flecked with yellow and green suggests a chameleon at first but with increasing light reveals itself to be a branch overgrown with moss and speckled by rays of sun. While both the beauty of such images and their hermeneutic puzzle hold the viewer spellbound, they work against the didactic impulse one usually associates with the genre of the nature documentary.

Other visual techniques also lead the spectator to wonder increasingly about the "documentary" nature of the film. The camera often lingers on images—reflections of light on water, branches outlined against sky, river currents, or the neon green of a tree trunk covered with moss—that do not convey any specific information of an ecological or biological sort. Many of the featured animals are shot partially or in such rapid motion—a turtle shell emerging from water, an insect scurrying away behind a tree, part of a snake winding through grass—that it is impossible to identify them with any certainty, quite opposite to nature films, which strenuously attempt to bring even the most elusive creatures into full view. Clearly more interested in visual metamorphosis and suggestive juxtaposition than in providing factual information, the film captures, for example, a group of frogs in water whose vocalizations cause their cheeks to expand into whitish bubbles. During a rain shower a few moments later, the impact of raindrops on the water surface surrounds the frogs with similar bubbles, generating a visually tantalizing metonymy rather than any insight into frog behavior. Even occasional shots of the bright yellow tip of what the spectator presumes to be the camera man's rubber boat assume this metamorphic quality, as they remind the spectator of the fisherman and his boat together transmuting into a duck, according to the Tupi myth narrated at the beginning of the film.

If Baumgarten's cinematographic techniques deliberately undercut documentary conventions, so does the verbal commentary that accompanies the film. Most of this commentary is provided by way of captions that appear alongside certain images; in the second half of the film, some of these are spoken by a male voice rather than displayed visually. Some of the captions seem to provide the names of botanical species or ecological phenomena, though their exact meaning may not be transparent to the average spectator; for instance, "Várzea," "Epiphyten" (epiphytes), "Homarus vulgaris," "Hevea brasiliensis," "Ipecacuahna." But even those uninitiated in biology realize after awhile that the captions only rarely deliver a direct description of what the images show. Some of them might refer to properties or behaviors of the species in question, such as the word "Kulturform" (cultivated variant) alongside a shot of reeds or "Polygamie" (polygamy) accompanying a group of herons. But in other cases, the captions seem metaphorical or curiously detached from the image: "Coca & Kakao" (coca and cocoa) is juxtaposed with a brownish river carrying a boat downstream; the word "Pfeffergericht" (meal prepared with pepper) is superimposed on a close-up of a water puddle of a poisonous orange-red color with lighter-colored pieces of debris strewn into it; "Jagdzauber-pflanzen" (magic hunting plants) accompanies an image of what appears to be a piece of spotted bark or leaf, possibly the skin of a rotting banana which is shown elsewhere lying on the ground; and "antizipierte Gürtel-tiere" (anticipated armadillos) appears in a shot of a tree trunk with no armadillo anywhere in sight. Captions such as "geklopfte Melodie" and "gepfiffene Sprache" (knocked melody, whistled language) might refer to the natural world or to cultural practices of humans inhabiting it, who do not visually appear. The abbreviation "A.L.P." will call up James Joyce's Anna Livia Plurabelle from *Finnegans Wake* for some viewers (Baumgarten, personal communication), and the accompanying Monet-like image of tree trunks in water with golden debris floating on the surface might evoke the washerwomen converted into trees from the novel. But "H.B.K." will remain enigmatic to most; according to Baumgarten, it refers to Humboldt and Bonpland, nineteenth-century explorers of the South American animal and plant world, and to the "Hochschule der Künste" (Academy of Arts) Humboldt was affiliated with (personal communication). Other comments refer more overtly to the colonial history of the Amazon region: "Francisco Orellana" refers to the Spanish conquistador who sailed the entire length of the Amazon in 1542 and named it, while "EL DORADO," ironically combined with a water surface gilded by sunlight, highlights what interested Orellana and other European travelers about the region. Yet other captions, however, are too abstract to allow for such explanations, from "KLIMA" (climate), "GEGEND" (area) or "... ambivalent" to "xi, xi, xi" or the symbols "[___,]" and "[...]" appearing four times scattered across the screen. In part, these enigmatic visual elements derive from Lévi-Strauss' structuralist analysis of indigenous myth: "xi, xi, xi" may well be an allusion to the strange sound inside the nut that prompts the Great Snake's servants to open it and release the night in the Tupi myth, "ten, ten, ten...xi..." (358). Brackets, parentheses, and elaborate diagrams of triangles and circles that Lévi-Strauss uses to illustrate the underlying structure of the myths he analyzes reappear in Baumgarten's film superimposed on certain images, without the explanatory framework that accompanies them in Lévi-Strauss' work. Taken out of context, such symbols seem to parody and cancel out the very convention of the scientific (or anthropological) caption or label to identify species, thereby providing a last clue to the film's metadocumentary design: not to label features of the natural world so much as to ask how such labels shape our perception of nature. Instead of familiarizing viewers with the natural world, the film subtly puts them at a distance from its images and sounds and forces them to reflect on the way these images and sounds themselves might be just as constructed as the captions.

If both Baumgarten's visual techniques and his handling of text produce a certain degree of disorientation over the course of the film's ninety-eight minutes, it is finally the disjunction between its purported content and the actual images that generates the greatest sense of unease. The sound track, with what appear to be unfamiliar animal calls and dull drum rolls, continues to suggest a jungle setting throughout, but the viewer gradually realizes that the landscape just does not look quite like Amazon rainforest. While the vegetation appears strange enough at times, it does not look lush and exuberant enough for a tropical rainforest, and does not exhibit any forms of root or bark that are not familiar from the northern hemisphere (Roberta Smith). By the same token, the animals that we see are made to seem unfamiliar through extreme close-ups or lack of focus, but it is clear enough that most of them are birds such as crows, gallinules or herons, reptiles and amphibians such as turtles, lizards, snakes, and frogs, as well as insects—certainly no icons of tropical exoticism such as monkeys, parrots, jaguars, or alligators. In addition, the film gives more and more clues that the landscape is no untouched wilderness, either; bits of trash and accumulations of debris show up, puddles of water are colored in shades that seem to derive from industrial contamination, airplanes fly overhead with some frequency, knives and a cooking pot are shown hanging from a tree, green pantyhose covers the tip of a plant, brick walls show through behind some trees, and in one scene the camera lingers on a picnic table and four chairs permanently mounted for the enjoyment of visitors. Airplanes, brick walls, and picnic tables in the Amazon rainforest? Clearly, we are a long way from an unspoiled and exotic natural ecosystem.

The growing sense that somehow, in spite of the beauty of the images, this is not really the kind of portrait of the Amazon rainforest that the title, the names of exotic species, and the recital of Tupi myth had led us to expect is confirmed in the film's last caption, "gedreht in den Rhein-Wäldern 1973–77" (filmed in the Rhine forests 1973–77). The film was not made in Brazil at all but in the forests along the Rhine River in Germany, not far from the city of Düsseldorf. Of course, this disclosure lends itself to a whole range of reflections on how the "real" is constituted for us in nature photography, on the way a camera selects and frames images so as to encourage a particular reading, and on the nature of spectatorship. "The distance between the 'civilized' and 'natural' collapses; notions of the exotic and of otherness emerge as necessary fantasies of the mind, especially the Western mind," critic Roberta Smith has commented. But this switch of perspective also changes how we read the environmentalist substance of the film. Clues in the film that this "virgin" forest is in fact inhabited, or at any rate not far from human settlements, seem unremarkable for the Rhine region, and make us revisit our assumption that the Amazon is (or should be) far removed from "civilization." By the same token, images of trash and contamination that one had interpreted earlier in the film as signs of the despoliation of a relatively untouched wild landscape now turn out to be those of a First World, industrialized area. Why are images of a contaminated rainforest so disturbing to us, the film asks, while they seem more acceptable if they are located in a developed nation? It also points to the fact that it *is* to some degree the trash from the Rhine forests that shows up in the Amazon, through the economic and ecological exploitation of the Third at the hands of the First World. Inversely, the revelation that everything that seemed unfamiliar, exotic, and tropical in the film was in fact filmed in Europe forces spectators to reconsider their awareness of local landscapes as well as their imaginative construction of those far away.

The superimposition of Rhine and Amazon that makes spectators move visually and conceptually back and forth from one to the other brings to a climax the multiple visual and verbal metaphors and metamorphoses that the film plays with all along. What this final metamorphosis ultimately suggests is that one can no longer think of the two landscapes as apart from each other, but only as globally connected in multiple ways: through economic exchange and exploitation, through tourism and travel (reaching all the way back to German as well as Spanish and Portuguese exploration and colonization), through environmental pollution, as well as through a natural beauty and strangeness that the film makes appear universal. This sense of connectedness is reinforced by the written and spoken captions that combine Latin and German with Portuguese and indigenous ways of referring to the natural world. Jointly, the superimposed, geographically far-removed ecosystems and the polylingual, often enigmatic captions convey a sense of both Brazilian and German landscapes that are no longer simply authentically themselves but are always alienated from themselves, or in the vocabulary I proposed in chapter 1, globally deterritorialized. Baumgarten's experimental, metadocumentary techniques seduce viewers into believing that they will be acquainted with the details of a particular local ecosystem, only to lead up, in the end, to a sense of the Amazon rainforest as a landscape that is globally connected and embedded in a variety of cultural systems and interactions, both historical and contemporary, without which it would not even be perceptible as such. This connectedness is created through a substitution of ecosystems that gives rise to a variety of juxtaposed perspectives: Europeans gaze at South

America, but in the process become foreigners to their own ecosystems; at the same time, this switch to the perspective of the outside generates a perception of connectedness that Baumgarten, via the originary myth, attributes to a lost indigenous perspective. His camerawork attempts both to recuperate this perspective and to mourn its disappearance, at the same time that it foregrounds just how problematic this attempt to capture a different cultural sensibility through the means of advanced technology must be. Through its invocation of both ecological and cultural connections across continents, and its play on different perspectives and historical moments in the encounter with the natural world, *Der Ursprung der Nacht* gestures toward the eco-cosmopolitan awareness I outlined in chapter 1, at the same time that it anticipates narrative strategies that novelist Karen Tei Yamashita deploys in her approach to the Amazon rainforest a decade and a half later.

2. Local Rock and Global Plastic: *Through the Arc of the Rainforest*

Like Baumgarten's film, Yamashita's *Through the Arc of the Rainforest* appears to focus first and foremost on the Amazon jungle, but its narrative material and storytelling strategies situate it at the intersection of several national and regional literary traditions. Yamashita lived in Brazil for almost a decade, and her second novel, *Brazil-maru* (1992), portrays the country's Japanese immigrant communities; the influence of Latin American fiction in both Portuguese and Spanish is as unmistakable in *Through the Arc of the Rainforest* as it is in her more recent works *Tropic of Orange* (1997) and *Circle K Cycles* (2001). Yamashita's novels weave their story lines around transfers and migrations between the United States, Latin America, and Japan, drawing on North American multicultural writing and Latin American magical realism, as well as, to a lesser extent, on the literary techno-postmodernism that flourished in both the United States and Japan from the 1980s onward. *Through the Arc of the Rainforest*, the work with the clearest focus on ecological issues, is therefore a particularly interesting springboard for a consideration of the connections between ecological and cultural globalism.

The plot of the novel revolves around the discovery of an unknown substance in the Amazon rainforest that forms a very large, rock-like plate of impenetrable material in the soil. First noticed by local residents, this so-called Matacão, or rock-plate, makes it impossible for the community to dig wells and irrigate fields. Since scientists are initially unable to define what the Matacão is or where it came from, divergent theories proliferate, and the strange rock plate soon turns into a point of attraction for various projects and intentions that come to form the core of the narrative. One of these projects involves a São Paulo couple, Batista and Tania Aparecida

Djapan, who run a small business breeding carrier pigeons and choose the Matacão as a site where they can deploy the pigeons effectively for various advertising purposes. A young fisherman, Chico Paco from the Brazilian northeast provinces, becomes the leader of a burgeoning religious revival movement when he turns the Matacão into a main destination point for holy pilgrimages. When the mass media begin to arrive at the Matacão, they discover the rubber tapper and peasant Mané Pena (perhaps an echo of Chico Mendes), who successfully uses bird feathers in healing practices, and they quickly turn him into an international alternative health guru. In addition, the American businessman J. B. Tweep, a notorious over-achiever with three arms, travels to the Matacão to explore its commercial possibilities for his New York–based company. And it is Tweep who even-tually invites the novel's central character to visit the Matacão: Kazumasa Ishimaru, a recent immigrant from Japan who works as an inspector on the Brazilian railroad system and, after winning the lottery, has become one of the major stockholders in Tweep's company. Not unlike the three-armed Tweep, Ishimaru stands out by his physical appearance: from his early childhood, a golf ball–sized sphere of unknown origin has orbited in front of his forehead, spinning on its own axis. As it turns out, this ball has a magnetic attraction to the Matacão and consists of the same mate-rial. As a consequence, Tweep more or less sequesters Ishimaru so as to use him for the discovery of new Matacão fields, and many other parties become interested in the knowledge and potential wealth associated with the mysterious ball.

This convergence of projects at first results in an enormous explosion of commercial and corporate development that soon takes on international dimensions. Chico Paco takes over a radio station and starts to do religious broadcasting, encouraging pilgrimages from across the whole of Brazil. Mané Pena, the illiterate local peasant, becomes an international celeb-rity, the author of several books—his speeches written down and edited by a literate secretary—and watches himself address crowds on TV dubbed into languages that he does not know how to speak. The Djapans, thanks to Tania Aparecida's flair for business, evolve first into a national and then an international corporation that specializes in using pigeons for advertis-ing purposes and later as an alternate postal system. In fact, at the peak of their activity, the global pigeon network turns into an international com-munications network—an internet of sorts, based on bird wings. Tweep, in his turn, brings in teams of scientists and engineers to analyze the Ma-tacão and discovers that it consists of a previously unknown substance with an uncanny versatility similar to that of oil or silicon. Combining strength and malleability, it can be used in an almost infinite range of ap-plications, from housing and construction to body prostheses, clothing, consumer accessories, and even food. In fact, one of the most striking properties of the Matacão is its ability to simulate other objects and sub-stances to perfection: not even Mané Pena can tell the difference between a Matacão feather and a real one. Needless to say, Tweep's company reck-lessly markets this quintessentially Baudrillardesque material, using it to produce everything from fake healing feathers and credit cards to cars.

But as the various businesses that are linked to the Matacão spread na-tionally and globally, a darker side of economic globalization also begins to emerge: the progressive social and emotional isolation of almost all the major characters. Chico Paco finds himself increasingly alienated from the family he left behind in the northeast; Mané Pena's relationship to his family disintegrates as he spends less time with them and more on interna-tional travel, conferences, and TV appearances; Kazumasa Ishimaru, held under house arrest by Tweep and hiding from multiple headhunters, gets separated from his housekeeper, Lourdes, and her two children, whom he has come to love; and Batista Djapan does not get to see his wife for years as she travels around the world expanding their business, and suf-fers terribly from loneliness. Only Tweep finds temporary happiness with a triple-breasted French ornithologist. For all the other male and some of the female characters, global connectivity, whether envisioned through a planetary network of pigeon messengers or through corporate expansion, is accompanied by the inexorable loneliness of the individuals who con-tribute most crucially to establishing it.

At first sight, this story sounds like a rather familiar antiglobalization tale: a valuable natural resource is discovered in a remote Third World locale, multinational corporations and media move in, and as a conse-quence local ecosystems and social communities are laid to waste. Yet the interest of Yamashita's novel lies in the way she evokes this narrative even as she ends up questioning most of its basic assumptions.[2] The Matacão, to begin with, is neither a natural nor a local substance. As Tweep's scientists find out, it is not really genuine rock at all, but a polymer, a kind of plas-tic—hence its surprising transformability. But how did an extremely large plate of plastic come to be located in the subsoil of the Amazon rainforest? The surprising answer to this question is withheld from the reader until almost the end of the novel:

> The Matacão, scientists asserted, had been formed for the most part within the last century, paralleling the development of the more com-mon forms of plastic, polyurethane and styrofoam. Enormous landfills of nonbiodegradable material buried under virtually every populated part of the Earth had undergone tremendous pressure, pushed ever far-ther into the lower layers of the Earth's mantle. The liquid deposits of the molten mass had been squeezed through underground veins to virgin areas of the Earth. The Amazon Forest, being one of the last virgin areas on Earth, got plenty. (202)

The new raw material here turns out to be artificial and a by-product of in-dustrial garbage, though it has been transformed by geological processes in such a way that the very terms "natural" and "artificial" seem no longer to apply; as we saw in chapter 2, a similar fusion between geology and advanced technology occurs at the climax of Brin's novel *Earth*. Moreover, what looked initially like a pristine rainforest locale violated by the advent of multinationals turns out to have been invaded by globalization long before and in a much more insidious fashion, by global plastic masquerading as local rock—global plastic that indeed *is* local rock, since the distinction itself has become meaningless. As the central symbol of the novel, the Matacão signals not only that there is no such thing as pristine wilderness left but more decisively that there is no local geography that is not already fundamentally shaped by global connectivity. The local bedrock that reveals itself to be at the same time global plastic waste functions as a striking trope for the kind of deterritorialization I examined in chapter 1 as a crucial cultural consequence of globalization, the imbrication of the local in the global that leads to the loosening of ties between culture and geography. Like Baumgarten, Yamashita deploys strategies of deterritorialization specifically aimed at the local *natural* environment, which turns out be global and artificial at the same time. A landscape where digging into the soil leads not to rock or roots but polymer makes implausible any return to nature via the immersion into the local. The native soil itself is deterritorialized in Yamashita's vision, turning into a product of human industry and long-distance connections as much as of geological processes in the immediate vicinity.

The sociocultural and economic forms that globalization takes in the novel are no less ambiguous. Tweep's New York–based corporation, GGG, may seem like the epitome of American economic imperialism, aptly symbolized by Tweep's supernumerary arm and his ruthless invasion of Brazil as well as of Ishimaru's personal life. But the fact that a Japanese immigrant to Brazil is a sufficiently important stockholder to be given personal attention by the general manager raises the question of how "American" an enterprise Geoffrey and Georgia Gamble really is. And even as GGG offers one model of the multinational corporation that seems quite familiar to an American reader, Tania and Batista Djapan's company provides another image that fits less comfortably into the stereotype of the greedy, ruthless multinational: growing out of a Third World, home-based mom-and-pop business, this company is run by a woman and eclectically combines the postmodern (advertising, international business travel, global communications networks) with the premodern (international communications conveyed not by radio waves or electronic impulses but by homing pigeons). The flourishing of this company in the novel unsettles the image of the Third World community as helpless victim of American capitalism as much as it raises the question of which forms of economic globalization should be rejected and which ones welcomed.

But perhaps more than any other element, it is the ending of the novel that makes it doubtful whether we should read it only as an antiglobalization story. To be sure, all the globalizing projects and the utopian hopes connected with them fail in a rather spectacular manner: first of all, the Matacão plastic feathers that have come into use as healing devices for everything from the common cold to depression turn out to have a strong hallucinatory effect on some people, who end up committing suicide in the belief that they have acquired the ability to fly. Then a typhus epidemic, transmitted by real bird feathers, spreads rapidly through Brazil and kills hundreds of thousands of people. This epidemic is brought to a halt through the massive use of insecticides, which in turn leads to the exter- mination of all bird species in the Amazon, in scenes clearly reminiscent of Rachel Carson's descriptions of dying birds in her environmental classic *Silent Spring.* Finally, the Matacão itself turns out to be susceptible to a cer- tain type of bacterium that destabilizes it and ultimately turns it to dust; as buildings, body parts, and everyday objects collapse in upon themselves, financial ruin and sometimes death ensue. Many of the major characters are swept away by the catastrophe: Mané Pena and his family succumb to typhus; Chico Paco is killed by headhunters who were really aiming at Ishimaru and his ball; Tweep commits suicide when the ornithologist leaves him, and his corporate empire comes to nothing. Only Ishimaru and Lourdes and Tania and Batista Djapan are reunited at the end and overcome solitude as global connectedness vanishes.

The ironic reversals in this ending are of course multiple, as the non- biodegradable waste turns out to be degradable after all, the rock-hard plastic turns to dust, and the healing feathers kill. One might take these disasters to signal the termination of the globalizing project and the re- turn to a more authentic experience of place. The closing moments of the plot, however, do not lend themselves to so clear a conclusion, but rather remain puzzlingly self-contradictory in the visions of place they offer. On the one hand, the despoliation of nature seems to continue unabated even after the end of the Matacão culture, portrayed in panoramic fashion as a large mourning procession carries Chico Paco's body back across Brazil from the rainforest to the Atlantic coast:

> The procession marched on, day and night, sleeping briefly on the road- side and nourished by the human poverty it encroached upon, continu- ing for weeks through the festering gash of a highway, through a forest that had once been, for perhaps 100 million years, a precious secret.
>
> Retracing Chico Paco's steps, the mourners passed hydroelectric plants, where large dams had flooded and displaced entire towns. They passed mining projects tirelessly exhausting the treasures of iron, man- ganese and bauxite. They passed a gold rush, losing a third of the pro- cession to the greedy furor. They crossed rivers and encountered fishing fleets, nets heavy with their exotic river catch of manatee, *pirarucú, pira- matuba, mapara.* They crowded to the sides of the road to allow passage for trucks and semis bearing timber, Brazil nuts and rubber. They passed burning and charred fields recently cleared and parted for frantic zebu cattle, long horns flailing and stampeding toward new pastures. They

passed black-pepper-tree plantations farmed by immigrant Japanese. They passed surveyors and engineers accompanied by excavators, tractors and power saws of every description. They passed the government's five-year plans and ten-year plans, while all the forest's splendid wealth seemed to be rushing away ahead of them. They passed through the old territorial hideouts of rural guerillas, trampling over unmarked graves and forgotten sites of strife and massacre. And when the rains stopped, they knew they had passed into northeast Brazil's drought-ridden terrain, the sunbaked earth spreading out from smoldering asphalt, weaving erosion through the landscape. (209–10)

There is a certain lyrical beauty to the rhythm of this passage, but the stark panorama of devastation it outlines turns the mourning procession for Chico Paco into a lament for the decline of a relentlessly exploited natural world. While certain forms of destructive globalization may have come to an end with the disintegration of the Matacão, this passage suggests, the national despoliation of nature continues unabated and without any hope of escape.

But the novel does not quite end on this note. Kazumasa Ishimaru's migration to Brazil, his growing love for his adopted home country, and his attachment to Lourdes and her children are all emphatically validated in the novel's happy ending, which shows the interracial nuclear family happily ensconced on

a farm filled with acres and acres of tropical fruit trees and vines and a plantation of pineapple and sugarcane, sweet corn and coffee. [Lourdes' son] Rubens wheeled happily around the guava orchards, and [her daughter] Gislaine sat in the branches of a *jaboticaba* tree, sucking the sweet white flesh of its fruit from their purple-black skins. Kazumasa ran around Lourdes like another child, filling her baskets with miniature bananas, giant avocados and mangos, which seemed to him to reflect the sunset. (211)

For Kazumasa and Lourdes, then, global connectedness leads in the end to a family without solitude and the recuperation of childlike innocence. One may grant that Yamashita here wishes to signal the cultural potential of transnational hybridization even as she rejects some of the political and economic processes that make this hybridization possible. What is more puzzling, though, is how this image of bucolic bliss, of successful reconnection with the rural soil might be compatible not only with the idea of the Matacão as a symbol of the impossibility of such a reconnection but also with the environmental devastation of the Brazilian landscape Yamashita had so eloquently mourned only a page or so earlier. Whatever explanation one might offer for this paradox—that the ending is not to be taken at face value, for example, but rather as a timeless utopia or an imaginary return to a premodern past—it remains that this moment of closure does not quite fit the complexities of the plot. It resolves the problems the plot raises about the experience of place in the global age by a return to pastoral cliché, at the same time shifting the ambiguities of globalism from the physical environment to the family. In other words, it provides a sociocultural solution for a problem that it had earlier articulated in ecological terms, thereby evading the full implications of its own questioning of stereotypes about the relationship of local and global environments. Ecological deterritorialization is contained by cultural reterritorialization, and a reterritorialization of a fairly conventional kind at that: in spite of their divergent national and class origins, Kazumasa Ishimaru and Lourdes end up in a nuclear family of the mom-dad-boy-girl variety that is in some respects as much a cliché as their pastoral refuge from the global.

Yet Yamashita's engagement with the question of place experience does not limit itself to the narrative plot. It also emerges through her subtle reworkings of two earlier novels, both of which portray the condition of Latin America through the spatial configurations their protagonists encounter: Gabriel García Márquez's *Cien años de soledad* (One hundred years of solitude; 1967) and Mário de Andrade's Brazilian classic *Macunaíma: O herói sem nenhum caráter* (Macunaíma: The hero without any character; 1928). Perhaps most obviously, the term "Matacão" echoes both García Márquez's fictional village of Macondo and Andrade's protagonist Macunaíma, and many of Yamashita's characters fall prey to longings and loneliness similar to those suffered by García Márquez's Buendía family and Andrade's "hero without character." More indirectly, Yamashita converts García Márquez's chronicle of a remote Latin American town that only gradually establishes contact with the rest of the world into a story of an equally remote rainforest location that is all too easily invaded by economic and cultural forces from outside, and she translates Andrade's tale of supernatural metamorphoses into one of ecological adaptations, albeit with a slightly futuristic twist. The question she foregrounds through these transformations is no longer so much that of Latin American regional and national identity but one of local identity in an age when lasting attachments to a specific environment have become difficult to sustain.[3]

Yamashita's indebtedness to García Márquez's *Cien años de soledad* is easily visible in some of the basic narrative materials of her novel. The characters with unusual body attachments or extra limbs echo the Buendías' fear of having a descendant with a pig's tail, for example, and events such as the rain of feathers from exterminated birds evoke the rain of small yellow flowers at the death of the first José Arcadio Buendía. The catastrophic disintegration of the Matacão, in addition, takes the reader back to the apocalyptic destruction of Macondo at the end of *Cien años*. But more prominently, it is the motif of a pervasive "soledad" that connects the two novels. García Márquez's protagonists are afflicted with a loneliness that appears almost genetic in nature; over a hundred-year period, generation after generation of the Buendía family suffers from its inability to establish genuine love relationships with those outside the family and a tendency to develop erotic and often illicit attractions inside it. This long genealogy of relationship shortfalls symbolically replicates some of the challenges that face the Buendías' community, the gradually developing village of Macondo. Macondo is initially isolated geographically from the rest of the Latin American continent as well as from the world at large. Its founding moment and early history are marked by a series of geographical misprisions and erroneous mappings. José Arcadio Buendía and his followers set out from the older town of Riohacha to search for an access route to the ocean, but fail to find one: "al cabo de veintiséis meses desistieron de la empresa y fundaron a Macondo para no tener que emprender el camino de regreso" (after 26 months, they gave up their plan and founded Macondo so as not to have to undertake the return trip; 20).[4] In its early years, Macondo's only contact with the outside world occurs through the periodic visits of a group of gypsies that bring them news of the latest scientific insights and technological inventions, kindling a desperate desire in José Arcadio Buendía to break away from Macondo's isolation: "'En el mundo están ocurriendo cosas increíbles,' le decía a Úrsula. 'Ahí mismo, al otro lado del río, hay toda clase de aparatos mágicos, mientras nosotros seguimos viviendo como los burros'" ("'Incredible things are happening in the world,' he said to [his wife] Úrsula. 'Right there, on the other side of the river, there are all kind of magical contraptions, while we go on living like donkeys'"; 17). He organizes an expedition "para abrir una trocha que pusiera a Macondo en contacto con los grandes inventos" (to open up a path that would put Macondo in contact with the great inventions; 19), but instead of access to the world of scientific discovery, he ends up finding the route to the ocean he had missed on his earlier expedition. Deeply disappointed, he draws up an erroneous map that depicts Macondo as located on a peninsula, surrounded by water on three sides and cut off from the rest of the world, and proposes to relocate the entire town. Only his wife's ironclad resistance to the move allows Macondo to remain in its founding location.

The novel traces Macondo's gradually intensifying connections with national and global space, from the visits of the globetrotting gypsies and a mail service on donkeyback to the construction of a train line, the town's entanglements in interminable civil wars, and the invasion of a United States–based banana company.[5] Many of the Buendía children of various generations leave Macondo in search of adventure, education, or erotic relationships, or are sent away by their parents as a consequence of some misbehavior; but many of them eventually return to their hometown, and the family's endogamous tendencies often catch up with them even after they have traveled around the globe. Indeed, it is often in the intimacy of the familial house that they succumb to the most intense forms of loneliness. Spatially, the novel frequently plays on the dialectic between enclosed domestic spaces—especially a small room in the Buendía house to which generation after generation of the men withdraw to do scientific experiments, create gold ornaments, or study the unintelligible scriptures left behind by the gypsy Melquíades—and the far-flung global destinations to which some family members travel. The narrative usually does not follow the travelers but tends to remain behind in Macondo and to focus on family members who in various ways seem obsessed with confining and enclosing themselves in extremely limited spaces.

This dialectic is foregrounded again with the last Aureliano Buendía, who after a long period of childhood confinement inside the family house and an unfailing dedication to the decipherment of Melquíades' writings hooks up with a group of friends with similarly bookish tastes. But while these friends end up dispersing over various continents, as one moves to Barcelona, another relocates to Paris, and yet another goes off on a journey to the United States, Aureliano stays behind in Macondo. His sedentarism, however, is at least partially compensated for by an encyclopedic and supernaturally detailed knowledge about life in faraway places (his uncle José Arcadio, recently returned from Rome, is amazed to discover that Aureliano knows such details as the prices of particular items in that city even though he has never set foot outside Macondo). When his aunt Amaranta Úrsula returns from her studies in Belgium with a husband who dreams of starting an airplane company, Aureliano falls in love with her, and it is this final attraction between the European-bred cosmopolitan and her sedentary, domestic nephew that generates the feared descendant with a pig's tail and brings about the end of the Buendía family line, as well as of Macondo. For the Buendías, then, global travel almost always ends up being temporary; attracted to their town of origin like homing pigeons to their roost, they end up returning and falling prey to the overwhelming solitude of the local.

Yamashita translates this narrative matrix to a Latin America that is no longer either geographically or economically isolated. Multinational corporations, transcontinental migrants, and environmental pollution all penetrate to the core of the Latin American continent without much difficulty in her novel, and the heterogeneous social and geographical origins of her central characters put them at the opposite extreme of the self-enclosed Buendía family. Only one of these characters, Mané Pena, was originally born in the Matacão region, while the reader follows all the other characters on their journeys from far-flung places of origin to the rainforest. Through this narrative procedure, the novel inverts the spatial organization of *Cien años de soledad,* whose focus remains persistently on one village: while Macondo is a place of roots, return, and residence, the Matacão is primarily a destination. Under these circumstances, the question of how identity is tied to rootedness in place obviously presents itself in somewhat different form; Yamashita's characters cannot easily return to a place that is "naturally" their home.

By the same token, the solitude the characters of both novels share differs quite sharply, in that the Buendías' loneliness seems almost an inherited, genetic property that prompts them often to reject fulfilling relationships even when opportunities for them happen to present themselves. By contrast, Yamashita's protagonists do have close ties to partners and families but are thrown into solitude as they become entangled in the dispersive projects of globalization. This loneliness arises not only from the protagonists' separation from their families and their native soil, but more profoundly from the fact that the very notion of "native soil" loses its meaning in a world where the bedrock of one's hometown can turn out to be the accumulated garbage of faraway countries. The solitude Yamashita portrays is therefore not just the psychological, social, and cultural condition that it is in *Cien años de soledad*; it is also an ecological condition, an index of the deterritorialization individuals and communities experience even in relation to their most immediate natural surroundings.

The question of what relationship to nature might be possible in a context of globalization also undergirds Yamashita's reworking of Mário de Andrade's *Macunaíma*. Andrade's novel describes the adventures three brothers, Macunaíma, Jiguê, and Maanape, have on their journey from their native village in the Amazon to the metropolis of São Paulo and back again to the jungle. During the first part of this journey, Macunaíma meets and then loses the woman he most loves, the Amazon queen Ci, Mother of the Forest, who turns into a constellation of stars after their baby dies at a very young age. Macunaíma longs to return to her throughout the rest of the novel, much of whose plot revolves around his efforts to recapture a lost amulet Ci gave him as a gift that remains his only souvenir of her. Andrade refers to his state of mind as "saudade," the nostalgic longing that has for a long time been stereotypically associated with Brazilian national character, but which is here given a specific motivation all the way to the end of the novel, when Macunaíma himself turns into an astral constellation. Alluding both to the general cultural stereotype and to *Macunaíma*, Yamashita translates "saudade" into the age of globalization through the solitary longings her characters experience as the international projects associated with the discovery of the Matacão take shape. Batista and Tania Aparecida (nicknamed "Cidinha") Djapan are perhaps the most obvious counterparts of Macunaíma and Ci in *Through the Arc of the Rainforest:* the Amazon queen who turns into a constellation has become the CEO of a multinational business enterprise who travels around the globe so much that, as far as Batista is concerned, she might as well be in outer space,[6] and the flocks of wild birds that become Macunaíma's retinue once he is recognized as Ci's partner are ironically echoed in the scores of homing pigeons that surround Batista.[7] That the Djapans breed birds who are able to find their way home no matter where they are released provides another ironic comment on the humans' inability to locate themselves culturally and emotionally in their global surroundings.

Through the Arc of the Rainforest inverts the basic spatial trajectory of *Macunaíma*, in that several of the central characters—Kazumasa Ishimaru, Lourdes, and the Djapans—travel from São Paulo to the Amazon.[8] Andrade uses his characters' journeys in *Macunaíma* to portray the Brazilian landscape as a panorama of diversity and abundance, always subject to sudden and unforeseen metamorphoses. Indeed, Andrade delights in extended chase scenes that take his characters across vast stretches of Brazil and sometimes into adjacent countries at supernatural speed, where they encounter panoramas of national geography and history that are described with the exuberance and humor that are characteristic of the novel as a whole. *Macunaíma* includes an abundance of epic catalogs that enumerate features of the natural landscape, plants, or animals. (Interestingly, they do not replicate these features realistically: while the locations Andrade's characters travel through can be traced on a map of Brazil, the plants and animals are often placed in regions or combined in ways that blur differences between specific locales so as to reinforce the national allegory, as Andrade himself has admitted.)[9] In *Through the Arc of the Rainforest*, these journeys resonate in, for example, the description of the mourning procession quoted earlier, which also travels across vast landscapes of Brazil; but in this case, as the landscape yields up its mineral, botanical, and zoological riches, its abundance turns into devastation.

But what is perhaps most remarkable about the way Andrade presents Brazilian landscapes and the human and nonhuman beings that inhabit them is their enormous capability for metamorphosis. A little boy transforms himself into an adult man, into a leaf-cutting ant, or into an annatto bush; a dead body or a bit of thrown-up food can turn into a hill, a dune, or an island of floating weeds; persons as well as animals can ascend to the sky and metamorphose into constellations of stars, and dead bodies, even hideously mutilated ones, can be restored to life and health by the appropriate magical procedures. Not even the realm of modern technology is exempt from these constant processes of transmutation: a louse can turn into a key, a jaguar into an automobile, a stork into an airplane, and when Macunaíma needs to make a call during his stay in São Paulo, he simply converts his brother Jiguê into a temporary telephone. Neither living beings nor objects, in other words, seem to have any essential properties or modes of being in *Macunaíma:* both the natural and the technological worlds are at any moment subject to sudden and unpredictable transformations.

A somewhat modified sense of this infinite mutability of the physical world also pervades Yamashita's *Through the Arc of the Rainforest*—as it does Baumgarten's *Ursprung der Nacht.* Indeed, her title is derived from a saying that foregrounds precisely this transformability, as one of her epigraphs indicates: "I have heard Brazilian children say that whatever passes through the arc of a rainbow becomes its opposite. But what is the opposite of a bird? Or for that matter, a human being? And what then, in the great rain forest, where, in its season, the rain never ceases and the rainbows are myriad?" One of the ways Yamashita translates this magic into realism is in her emphasis on adaptation as an ecological mechanism that transforms bodies as well as landscapes. Her description of an abandoned junkyard in the Amazon jungle that has turned into an open-air laboratory of biological adaptation moves along the borderline between ecological science and Andradean magic:

> There was...discovered in one region, about seventy-two kilometers outside the Matacão, an area which resembled an enormous parking lot, filled with aircraft and vehicles of every sort of description. The planes and cars had been abandoned for several decades, and the undergrowth and overgrowth of the criss-crossing lianas had completely engulfed everything....What was most interesting about the discovery of the rain forest parking lot was the way in which nature had moved to accommodate and make use of it. The entomologists were shocked to discover that their rare butterfly only nested in the vinyl seats of Fords and Chevrolets and that their exquisite reddish coloring was actually due to a steady diet of hydrated ferric oxide, or rusty water. There was also discovered a new species of mice, with prehensile tails, that burrowed in the exhaust pipes of all the vehicles. These mice had developed suction caps on their feet that allowed them to crawl up the slippery sides and bottoms of the aircraft and cars...the females sported a splotchy green-and-brown coat, while the males wore shiny coats of chartreuse, silver and taxi yellow....[A] new breed of bird, a cross between a vulture and a condor...nested on propellers and pounced on the mice as they scurried out of exhaust pipes. Finally, there was a new form of air plant, or epiphyte, which attached itself to the decaying vehicles....Meantime, back on the Matacão, human life was adapting itself to the vast plastic mantle in ways as unexpected as those found in the rain forest parking lot and as expected as the great decaying and rejuvenating ecology of the Amazon Forest itself. (99–101)

In this passage, Yamashita exaggerates basically plausible processes of adaptation just enough to turn them into a fantastic ecology that begins to suggest the transformability of biological species and their partly natural, partly technological environments. This junkyard ecosystem echoes the more drastic ecological mutation in the novel, that of waste and rock into plastic, whose more radical fusion of natural and technological substances begins to approach Andrade's magical metamorphoses.

If Yamashita's ecologically transformed junkyard in the midst of the rainforest already suggests something of the way the specifics of "place" can emerge from entirely alien elements, the Matacão itself signals how the very bedrock of the local is reshaped by the global: while Andrade's magical realism serves mainly to outline some of Brazil's distinctive national character, Yamashita's is designed specifically to highlight the way conceptions of the local and national are bound up with global processes.[10] This interconnection is foregrounded not only through the Matacão's origins in the First World but also through some of the uses to which it is put once its properties as an industrial raw material have been discovered. One of the most fanciful projects it serves to complete is a Disneyland-like amusement park, Chicolándia, that the newly minted televangelist Chico Paco builds for his young friend Gilberto as a realization of Gilberto's film- and TV-based fantasies:

> Everything in Chicolándia was being made of Matacão plastic, from the roller coasters to the giant palms, the drooping orchids and the build- ings, whose interiors and exteriors were designed to imitate scenes from Gilberto's favorite movies.... The animated animals, also constructed in the revolutionary plastic, were mistaken for real animals.... Ele- phants, lions, kangaroos, zebras, anteaters, camels, sloths, buffaloes, panda bears, vultures, penguins and crocodiles—to mention only a few in an enormous variety of thudding, crawling, creeping, hanging and flying fauna—would soon create a bizarre ecology as they tramped through a projected maze of magnificent scenes: Babylonian towers on a desert oasis, the Taj Mahal, the docks of Amsterdam, Times Square in New York City, the Miami International Airport, the French Riviera, the Las Vegas strip, Patagonia, the California gold rush, Egyptian and Peruvian pyramids, Indonesian temples, medieval castles, the *Titanic*, ancient Rome, mythical Greece, and the moon. Gilberto's imagination and memory of television were endless. The former invalid, who had never known any place other than his birthplace on the multicolored dunes [of Brazil's northeastern coast], and now the Matacão, could soon be suddenly anywhere both in time and space. (168)

Even more than in the account of its remote origins, the Matacão here re- veals itself to be an allegory of the global, evoking the simultaneous pres- ence of natural ecosystems, cultures, and histories from across the world in one location in the Brazilian rainforest.[11] The double mediation of global sites through their representation in film and television images that serve as the basis for plastic reproductions—with the added irony, in the case of the Las Vegas strip, that the original is itself already a simulation of other places and periods—does nothing to diminish the force of their pres- ence in the local; on the contrary, it helps to foreground how much global space reshapes the lives of even those like the handicapped Gilberto, who have only minimal geographical mobility. By alluding at the same time to Andrade's magic transformations of Brazilian identity and the U.S. idea of the "magic kingdom," Yamashita ingeniously blends different cultural traditions of the Americas so as to create a narrative scenario that is both natural and artificial, both local and global. Her reworking of fictional materials and strategies that derive from two classical treatments of Latin American places and identities into a story of the global age inscribes the deterritorialization of the local into the basic organization of her novel.

Just how complex that deterritorialization is, however, becomes clear only when one turns to the novel's very last page, which concludes the story of Kazumasa and Lourdes with the laconic sentence "But all this happened a long time ago" (212) and returns us to the narrative frame and the narrator's own present. Or, more precisely and more paradoxically, the narrator's own future, for the narrator no longer exists at this end point of the story; in fact, he no longer existed even at the novel's beginning, where he appeared as the invocation of a memory from the past during a Candomblé ritual. Neither is it accurate to refer to the narrator as "he" or "she," for the instance that narrates *Through the Arc of the Rainforest* is not human at all. As the reader finds out toward the beginning of the novel, the "I" that tells the story is the sphere that attached itself to Kazumasa Ishimaru's forehead during his childhood and has accompanied him ever since, spinning on its own axis like a "tiny satellite" (8) or a "tiny impudent planet" (5). This sphere, consisting of the Matacão substance, to which it is magnetically attracted, functions rather obviously as a miniature replica of the Earth itself, the voice that emerges from the depths of geology. Even as Yamashita clearly gestures toward an ecocentric narrative stance through her extraordinary choice of narrator, however, this stance must inevitably remain as ambiguous as the Matacão itself. The planet that here conveys the narrative is strangely transformed, half plastic and half rock, half waste and half raw material, and it orbits around a human head as if to signal the inevitability of anthropocentrism in even so fantastic a narrative strategy.

This choice of narrative perspective also has important implications for the way the novel approaches the relationship between local place and global space. What looks at first sight like a magical realist version of Lovelock's Gaia here attaches itself to a specific character who migrates from East Asia to Latin America. Yamashita thereby associates her vision of global connectedness with a specific human and local situation, but not one that defines itself in terms of an innate or essentialist attachment to place: Ishimaru only gradually comes to love the new home country that he crisscrosses on the railroad day after day. Rootedness in a particular place, for Ishimaru, arises precisely through his mobility, as he travels from Japan to Brazil and then across Brazil again and again. As the sphere accompanies Ishimaru on his journeys, it comments repeatedly on its own role as an observer, noting that sometimes it is able to foresee future events (8–9, 28), to perceive more that its human counterpart (111), or to anticipate Ishimaru's emotions before he has had time to become aware of them himself (35), while it confesses that at other times it is not entirely capable of understanding human feelings. As Caroline Rody has shrewdly observed, the ball functions as "a parodic literalization of narratorial omniscience itself" (629). In its ambiguous status in between an omniscient first person narrator and a third person narrator associated with one character, Yamashita's mini-Earth narratologically models a vision of place that is committed to both the specificities of the local and the broader horizon of the global.[12]

If such a perspective might appear tenuous, its fragility—or more precisely, its biodegradability!—is confirmed when the sphere disintegrates along with the rest of the Matacão substance under the onslaught of adverse bacteria. The only reason it can even function as a narrator after its demise is that in the narrative frame, it is brought back as part of a ritual of collective memory; the narrator declares at the beginning:

> By a strange quirk of fate, I was brought back by a memory....That I should have been reborn like any other dead spirit in the Afro-Brazilian syncretistic religious rite of Candomblé is humorous to me...brought back by a memory, I have become a memory, and as such, am commissioned to become for you a memory. (3)

At the very end, it reaffirms, "Now the memory is complete, and I bid you farewell. Whose memory you are asking? Whose indeed" (212). With these last words, Yamashita's text reaches beyond its own boundaries to include the reader in the ritual, since the sphere and its story have now become part of the reader's memory as well.[13] By locating the story of the Matacão at the same time in a slightly science fiction–tinged future and in the narrator's and readers' memories, Yamashita portrays it as a sort of *futur antérieur:*

> On the distant horizon, you can see the crumbling remains of once modern high-rises and office buildings, everything covered in rust and mold, twisted and poisonous lianas winding over sinking balconies, trees arching through windows, a cloud of perpetual rain and mist and evasive color hovering over everything. The old forest has returned once again, secreting its digestive juices, slowly breaking everything into edible absorbent components, pursuing the lost perfection of an organism in which digestion and secretion were once one and the same. But it will never be the same again. (212)

This final vista of the Matacão echoes that of the junkyard in the jungle earlier, and reaffirms the power of ecological forces even as it points to inexorable change. On the ruins of Matacão modernism, Yamashita describes the regrowth of a jungle that is itself bound to become a mere memory for the reader in just another three sentences, seen through the eyes of a narrator that is itself nothing more than a memory at the time of its speaking.

This temporal displacement of the narrating instance, which speaks its memories even as it has itself become memory, compounds the spatial deterritorializations around which much of the novel revolves. As readers, we rely on the narrator's voice to give us access to the story, yet the story tells us about the disintegration of the narrator, just as much of the narrative plot hinges on globalization processes whose failures are in the end as crucial to the novel as its successes. Since the narrator is only "present" at the beginning and end of the novel in a very mitigated sense, the narrative frame does not offer us any firm grounding for the story the novel tells but merely points to yet another framing device, the future Candomblé ritual by means of which the narrator's memory is evoked. About this ritual, however, we are told very little, and nothing at all about the community that performs it or the world and time it inhabits. Yamashita's novel, in other words, tells a somewhat futuristic story embedded in a narrative frame that refers to this story as long past, without offering any further information about its own even more distant future. The only aspect of the future environment that is foregrounded is the continuing presence of a rainforest that has preserved its endless capability for metamorphosis in the midst of the irrevocable transformations imposed on it by humans. Even in this final scenario, then, nature in its local manifestation does not appear as a stable ground in which human identities can be firmly rooted but as a dynamic force of constant transformation.

The challenge that both *Der Ursprung der Nacht* and *Through the Arc of the Rainforest* hold out to environmentalist conceptions of place, therefore, is to imagine local environments less as foundations for an unalienated existence than as habitats that are ceaselessly being reshaped by the encroachments of the global as well as by their own inherent dynamism. With such a deterritorialized sense of place, the environmentalist's task would not so much be to preserve pristine, authentic ecosystems as to ensure their continued ability to change and evolve. But of course, even as this vision of place offers at first sight an attractive alternative to more static notions of "rootedness," it comes with its own set of vexed theoretical questions. For an environmental perspective, it raises the difficult question of how an endorsement of constant transformation and change would allow one to discriminate between the inherently dynamic evolution of ecosystems and the kinds of disruptive change that might ultimately lead to serious ecosystemic problems and failures. Baumgarten's film and Yamashita's novel, both of which invest a great deal of narrative capital in the blurring of the boundaries between biology and technology, and between naturally grown and humanly manufactured objects, cannot really provide an answer to this question. Neither would it be fair, perhaps, to expect works of fiction to deliver detailed solutions to such complex theoretical problems.

By forcing us to look at a particular regional ecology with the gaze we normally reserve for a quite different continent, and by reworking allegories of national and regional identity into a story of ecological deterritorialization, however, both *Der Ursprung der Nacht* and *Through the Arc of the Rainforest* challenge us to reimagine our attachments to an environment whose very "nature" may be global rather than local. Baumgarten's film and Yamashita's novel ask how the environmentalist imagination might mobilize the cognitive and affective charges that are associated with the local in favor of a cosmopolitan attachment to the global. As I have pointed out, *Der Ursprung der Nacht* responds to this challenge by forcibly dislocating the viewer's ecological perspective, while *Through the Arc of the Rainfor-est* answers it more obliquely through Kazumasa Ishimaru's adoption of a new country and family, as well as through the emergence of a nonhuman narrative voice. The cognitive and perceptual adjustments that these experimental strategies require on the part of the viewer and reader stand as aesthetic analogues of the kind of cultural and political reorientation that an environmental approach to the global might involve.

PART II

Planet at Risk

4

NARRATIVE IN THE
WORLD RISK SOCIETY

Academic concepts, at times, take on a life of their own in figures of speech, everyday habits, or market commodities, while
their intellectual merit and implications are still being discussed among the
experts. Many of the terms associated with postmodern culture, such as
"deconstruction" and "hyper-reality," trickled down in this way. But when
German sociologist Ulrich Beck coined the term "risk society" in the mid-
1980s as an alternative to the notion of "postmodern" social structures, he
could not have anticipated that the idea of a society reconfigured by pervasive ecological and technological risk scenarios would one day translate
into the commodified cuteness that characterizes certain sectors of the child
and youth entertainment industry. Yet precisely this kind of translation underlies a whole series of recent toy figures marketed by UNKL, a division of
the design company big-giant. Founded by Derek Welch and Jason Bacon
in 2000, UNKL designs toys and apparel for a hip and urban youth culture.
One of their series of toy figures (and related T-shirts) is called HazMaPo,
most likely an abbreviation of "Hazardous Materials Police," and consists
of about a dozen different vinyl figures in various kinds of gas masks and
protection suits. Offered in a variety of colors from translucent white, pastel
blue, and green to neon red, orange, and black, these figures combine the
ominous look of gas masks, breathing tubes, oxygen tanks, helmets, and
full-body suits with the quaint charm of robot tin toys and the neotenic
cuteness of Japanese toys such as Hello Kitty, Badtz-Maru, the innumerable Pokémon characters or the enduringly popular Tamagotchi (fig. 4.1).
Welch and Bacon explain on their website:

> In creating the HazMaPo figures, the concept was to take two things
> representing opposite points of view and combine them together form-
> ing something both familiar and fresh. We took a friendly, simplified
> figure and juxtaposed it with the ominous implications of hazmat suits

Figure 4.1. UNKL's line of HazMaPo toy figures. Reproduced by permission of UNKL.

and gas masks. They're cute, in a sinister sort of way. (www.unklbrand. com/stories_detail.php?ID=7)

The disconcerting idea of an adorable toy figure with little pink and white hearts on her hazmat suit and oxygen tank, in one HazMaPo version, may at first sight seem to derive from nothing more than the slightly cynical imagination of two artists turned youth culture marketeers. Yet an entirely mainstream German toy manufacturer such as Playmobil also now includes a "HAZMAT Crew" among its toy figurine sets, outfitted with green protective suits, helmets, rubber boots, gloves, shop vac, and a barrel of toxic material lovingly detailed down to the yellow warning label with skull and bones on the side (fig. 4.2). As opposed to UNKL's, Playmobil's website betrays no sense of any incongruence in offering such a scenario to children from the age of four. And perhaps it should not, given that toy figures and vehicles even for young children have long included police cars, ambulances, and fire trucks. Yet the fact that toxic cleanup crews have now become as routine a part of children's playworlds as fire trucks foregrounds that the contaminated environment Rachel Carson decried at the inception of the environmental movement in the 1960s is now fully integrated into the ordinariness of everyday life. Some awareness of technological and ecological as well as other risk scenarios, these toys indicate, from carcinogens in food to toxic spills and global warming

Figure 4.2. Playmobil's toy set "HAZMAT Crew."

has, consciously or unconsciously, become an inescapable component of daily routines.

Increasingly, such risk awareness has also come to reshape the imagination of the global in its environmentalist as well as other dimensions. To some extent, one could argue that translocal risk perceptions reveal the dark side of the cosmopolitanism I outlined in chapter 1, in that an awareness of ecological and cultural connectedness implies a knowledge of the kinds of risk that are generated by such connectivity: the introduction of nonnative organisms into local ecosystems, for example, the impact of global markets on local natural resources or farming practices, pollution of oceans, acid rain, radioactive fallout, or global warming. But to leave it at that would be to ignore the ways risk perceptions, and a particular understanding of the relationship of certain risk scenarios to modern societies, have galvanized the environmentalist movement from its beginnings and continue to do so, in various forms, to this day. Risk has also become an important theoretical lens with which to envision the emergence of new social movements and structures, foregrounding cosmopolitan forms of awareness and inhabitation on the basis of shared risk. This is the gist of much of the environmental justice movement's work (which admittedly tends not to frame its objectives in terms of risk, for reasons I will discuss shortly) as well as of Ulrich Beck's "Cosmopolitan Manifesto," which predicts the rise of new kinds of transnational communities and politics from the "world risk society." Considerations of risk and of local and global forms of belonging, therefore, are imbricated in each other in complex ways that cannot be summed up in any simple dichotomy of utopian versus dystopian visions.

But while the concept of a contemporary "risk society" has gained currency in the academic circles of Europe, North America, and beyond, Beck's work has often been received in a rather superficial way in literary and cultural studies, where it tends to be invoked without much attention to its details or internal tensions. The relation of Beck's theory to other analyses of risk perceptions and of the connections between risk and modernization are hardly ever mentioned, and indeed the entire field of risk theory, an important interdisciplinary area in the social sciences, is for the most part unknown to literary and cultural scholars, including, most importantly for my purposes, to many ecocritics. In the first section of this chapter, I will therefore briefly survey studies of risk perceptions, as one of the most important areas of risk analysis over the last four decades, and the major theoretical frameworks on which they are based. Even though such studies gained importance in part because of the public's increased awareness of ecological and technological risk scenarios since the 1960s, they have been received warily by environmentalists, who since the 1980s have objected to both the general usage of the term "risk" and specific dimensions of risk theory. Such objections, I will argue, were based in part on misunderstandings of the theory and in part on resistance to early antienvironmentalist biases in risk perception studies that have since been questioned and reversed in the field itself. Investigations of risk perceptions, therefore, have become an extremely important resource for the cultural study of contemporary societies' relation to the natural environment. Section 2 elaborates on such concerns that are shared between risk theory and literary study by highlighting the ways perceptions of ecological and technological risk scenarios are shaped by and filtered through narrative templates that manifest themselves in both visual and verbal artifacts. Apocalyptic narrative, with its portrayal of an entire planet on the brink of ecological collapse and human populations threatened in their very survival, has been one of the most influential forms of risk communication in the modern environmental movement, especially since it has often implicitly or explicitly relied on pastoral as the template for alternative scenarios. Both apocalypse and pastoral have been controversially debated among ecocritics; while many consider both genres at best ambivalent tools in the current state of environmental discourse, they nevertheless feel uncomfortable with what they perceive to be the impact of risk discourse on these rhetorical templates, especially since risk analyses, which can easily accommodate apocalyptic and "toxic discourses," are more difficult to compatibilize with lingering pastoral impulses. As I showed in chapter 1, such pastoral residues manifest themselves variously in longings for a return to premodern ways of life, "detoxified" bodies, and holistic, small-scale communities. To explore more generally what kinds of narrative risk analysis has relied on and how they relate to environmentalist story templates, section 3 turns to theoretical approaches that address the relationship of contemporary hazards to processes of modernization and technosocial innovation, including Beck's hypothesis of an emergent "risk society." Such theories partly diverge from and partly dovetail with the environmental justice movement in their conception of the connection between risk scenarios and the transformation of basic social structures, including modes of spatial belonging and deterritorialization. This particular concern is elaborated further in section 4, which explores the impact of technological and ecological risk scenarios on ways of inhabiting local, national, and global spaces and systems. As risk scenarios, especially those that transcend the local, form part of the complex processes of deterritorialization that I analyzed in chapter 1, they both disrupt existing ties to place and create alternative networks of cultural practices at various scales and across national and regional borders, in a process that transforms some of the trivialities of everyday life as much as some of the large-scale workings of international politics. Beck's "Cosmopolitan Manifesto" articulates the possibility of new, transnational communities arising from shared risk experiences. But Beck's somewhat simplistic understanding of the relationship between shared risk and shared cultural assumptions needs to be tempered by the more complex accounts of power differentials and cultural conflict even in the face of shared political struggles in the writings of environmental justice advocates and political scientists. Both the risk society and the environmental justice models, I will suggest, stand to benefit from the more nuanced analyses of crosscultural literacy in cultural scholars' approaches to cosmopolitanism that I discussed in chapter 1. Understanding global risks as shared environmental realities that are nevertheless shaped by and filtered through a range of different cultural frameworks, including local forms of inhabitation, forms part of the environmentally oriented cosmopolitanism I outlined in that chapter.

Chapters 5 and 6 will tie these theoretical considerations back into the analysis of literary texts; chapter 5 focuses on two American novels that prominently feature incidents of local chemical exposure, Don DeLillo's *White Noise* and Richard Powers's *Gain*, while chapter 6 examines two German novels, Christa Wolf's *Störfall: Nachrichten eines Tages* (Accident: A day's news) and Gabriele Wohmann's *Der Flötenton* (The sound of the flute), which revolve around the international risk scenario that unfolded after the nuclear reactor explosion at Chernobyl, Ukraine, in 1986. All of these texts reflect on the way individuals and communities renegotiate the relationship between local, national and international networks of culture and economics in light of their exposure to risk, at the same time that they explore what narrative shape such a reconfigured relationship might take.

1. Theories of Risk Perception:
Science, Culture, Narrative

Seen from an anthropological perspective, human cultures have engaged with risk scenarios of widely varying kinds throughout their history. But more formal studies of risk have only emerged more recently. The study of medical and economic risks reaches back at least to the eighteenth century, while investigations of technological hazards and natural disasters began in the early twentieth century (Golding 25). Analyses of technological and ecological risk scenarios emerged as a separate area of study in the social sciences in the late 1960s and early 1970s. In 1969, a seminal article by the engineer Chauncey Starr that set out to measure social benefits and technological risks in relation to each other opened up the problem of risk assessment to systematic research, at a time when the public had become increasingly aware of and concerned about chemical, nuclear, and other environmental dangers.[1] In the following decades, risk theory developed in an interdisciplinary matrix involving mainly cognitive psychology, sociology, and anthropology; especially from the 1990s onward, political scientists and economists have also become increasingly interested in the field.[2] Over time, a range of different theories have evolved in the field that focus on somewhat different objects of study and base themselves on divergent methodological assumptions. The most empirically oriented part of the field, which is also the one that has to date generated the greatest bulk of research, focuses on the ways risks are perceived and evaluated by different population segments, and attempts to identify the sociological, psychological, or other factors that might explain these risk assessments. Some of the basic theoretical paradigms that have been proposed in this part of the field will be discussed in this section, while section 3 will focus on theories that address the underlying causes of technological risk, their relation to modernization processes, and their impact on social structures.

In the late 1970s, risk analysis was dominated by the so-called psychometric paradigm. Empirical studies, often carried out by cognitive psychologists, sought to determine how the public perceives a wide range of different types of risks and what reasoning leads to these assessments. Psychometric studies usually assume that the reasons for particular risk assessments combine certain characteristics of the risks themselves with individuals' cognitive behavior, and therefore explore such assessments in terms of theories of heuristics and cognitive biases, that is, decision-making rules and selective information processing. Different groups of individuals, it emerged, use different cognitive models in assessing risks. One of the most salient differences that psychometric research highlighted was the one between expert and lay perceptions. Experts such as scientists, doctors, statisticians, or engineers often tend to evaluate and prioritize risks quite differently from the way the general public does. Statistical considerations, usually the probability of a particular adverse event multiplied by the magnitude of its consequences, tend to shape expert opinions, while the public's view quite often defies such numerical calculation. The risks associated with nuclear power plants provide an obvious example: based on the very limited number of actual accidents and deaths nuclear plants have so far caused, experts tend to rate their risks as relatively low, while nonexperts, regardless of the low statistics, assess them as much more hazardous than, say, coal mines or highways, which cause a much larger number of fatalities annually.

Psychometrically oriented research has discovered a number of variables that shape such divergences, not only between experts and the general public but also between different segments of the public itself. Regardless of the magnitude of the risk involved, voluntarily selected risks tend to be assessed as less hazardous than those that are involuntarily imposed, for example, leading some people to worry about secondhand smoke even as they underestimate the health effects of bad nutrition. The protagonist of Art Spiegelman's graphic novel *In the Shadow of No Towers*, a chain-smoker, humorously foregrounds this discrepancy when he fulminates against what he believes to be the authorities' cover-up of dangerous air pollution in lower Manhattan in the aftermath of the attack on the World Trade Center: "I'm not even sure I'll live long enough for cigarettes to kill me," he sums up his dual risk perception with characteristic self-irony (3). Similarly, dangers that are imperceptible to the average person tend to appear greater than those that are directly observable; new risks appear greater than old ones and unfamiliar ones more hazardous than well-known ones; risks that entail delayed effects tend to be perceived as greater than those whose effects manifest themselves immediately; risks with controllable or nonfatal consequences are perceived as smaller than those that entail uncontrollable or fatal ones. The geographical scope of a potential hazard also affects perceptions of its magnitude, with local ones appearing less risky than regional or global ones, as do the benefits that are thought to accrue from incurring a particular risk scenario. At times, these kinds of variables in risk perception do not operate in isolation but correlate with each other in individuals' perceptions through an underlying evaluative perspective that statisticians uncover by means of the technique called "principal component analysis." One of these factors is "dread," an almost intuitive fear of some risks that may be less dangerous than other, nondreaded ones: nuclear technology and radioactivity as well as cancer, for example, tend to evoke such dread, while flu epidemics, heart disease, or diabetes do not. Some of these distinctions may strike an outside observer as more rational than others: it seems reasonable, for example, to rate a risk with potentially fatal consequences higher than one with nonfatal ones, whereas assessing risks differently in terms of their perceptibility or imperceptibility, or their immediate or delayed consequences, may seem understandable but illogical. However one rates the validity of such variables that shape risk perceptions, the fact is that they point to complex evaluative models that go far beyond any simple algorithmic calculation of probability and magnitude (Fischhoff et al., *Acceptable Risk*, chaps. 4–7; Fischhoff, Slovic, and Lichtenstein, "Lay Foibles and Expert Fables"; Slovic, "Perception of Risk").[3]

Differences of gender and race turned out to be other dimensions affecting risk assessments, with women often rating risks as greater and more threatening than men (Spigner, Hawkins, and Loren; Steger and Witte; Stern, Dietz, and Kalof). In a large study carried out by James Flynn et al. in 1994, nonwhite respondents tended to express greater concern about a variety of risks than white ones, and risk assessments were greater among those with lower incomes and education levels. When the results of this survey were analyzed according to four groups, white females, nonwhite females, white males, and nonwhite males, however, it turned out that it was white males who rated risks far lower than the other groups; closer analysis revealed that it was only about 30 percent of the white males that skewed the results through much lower risk assessments, while the rest corresponded roughly to the other groups. Paul Slovic summarizes the questions and directions these results point toward:

> Why do a substantial percentage of white males see the world as so much less risky than everyone else sees it? . . . Perhaps white males see less risk in the world because they create, manage, control and benefit from many of the major technologies and activities. Perhaps women and non-white men see the world as more dangerous because in many ways they are more vulnerable, because they benefit less from many of its technologies and institutions, and because they have less power and control over what happens in their communities and their lives. Although the survey conducted by Flynn et al was not designed to test these alternative explanations, the race and gender differences in perceptions and attitudes point toward the role of power, status, alienation, trust, perceived government responsiveness and other sociopolitical factors in determining perception and acceptance of risk. ("Trust" 402)

As these comments already indicate, and as psychometric research has more broadly documented, some risk perceptions have less to do with the public's view of the risk in and of itself than with trust in the institutions in charge of managing it. Sociologist Allan Mazur's detailed study of the Love Canal crisis has shown, for example, that the neighborhood residents' perception of their own endangerment by the toxic waste deposit under the local school was exacerbated by their growing sense that they were being left in the lurch by the New York state health commissioner, which led them shrewdly to enlist the help of the media instead (67–113, 162–93). Trust, in turn, in some cases depends on whether the public perceives the authorities as sharing its salient values (Cvetkovich and Winter 288–89).[4] As Brian Wynne has argued, it is also inflected by the risk bearers' sense of their sometimes inevitable dependency on the social institutions that manage risk, which by their way of defining and managing it force risk bearers to identify themselves in relation to the knowledge embodied by these institutions ("Sheep" 54–60). Risk perceptions, therefore, cannot be analyzed in isolation from the social and institutional structures that situate individuals, and through which dangers are communicated and administered.

In the late 1970s, psychometrically oriented research assumed on the one hand that lay risk perceptions respond to certain qualitative properties of the risks themselves, and on the other hand that expert assessments, with what was believed to be their clearer grasp of the scenarios, established the accurate and objective scale of a particular risk. Lay perceptions that diverged from this view, it was thought, needed to be explained in social scientific terms and ultimately corrected. In the course of the 1980s, however, these and other assumptions behind the psychometric paradigm came increasingly into question with the rise of "cultural theory" (not to be confused with the meaning of this phrase in the context of cultural studies). Pioneered by anthropologist Mary Douglas and sociologist Aaron Wildavsky's highly controversial book *Risk and Culture: An Essay on the Selection of Technological and Environmental Dangers* (1982), cultural theory in its initial phase built on Douglas's earlier work on taboo in premodern societies. Douglas and Wildavsky started from the observation that any community, whether modern or premodern, is affected by a wide range of risks, but only some of these are selected for conscious awareness and given particular social and cultural significance. The cognitive models of individuals are far less important in explaining this awareness and significance, according to Douglas and Wildavsky, than the question what a particular risk perception accomplishes for the values and ultimately the perpetuation of the social structure that shapes it. From this theoretical perspective, individuals do not make risk assessments on a case-by-case basis; rather, their risk assessments can be predicted in broad outline in terms of their association with certain types of social structures (Douglas and Wildavsky; Wildavsky and Dake).

At first glance, this mode of theorizing may appear more familiar and persuasive to scholars in literary and cultural studies than the highly empirical and statistical procedures of the psychometric paradigm. After all, the attempt to explain individual risk perceptions in terms of their function for the self-perpetuation of certain social structures—in other words, in terms of what in literary studies would probably be called their "political implications"—seems to rely on a theoretical gesture that is quite common in studies of culture over the last three decades, in that it exposes risk perceptions as, more or less, forms of ideology. Yet Douglas and Wildavsky are not strict social constructivists where risk is concerned, nor does their concluding analysis in *Risk and Culture* resemble anything one would be tempted to call "politically correct." Douglas, in this book as well as in her later publications on risk, portrays risks as undoubtedly real, but sees their selection and meaning as culturally conditioned (see Lupton 39). This selection is shaped by social structures that are defined through a "group" variable (that is, the degree to which individuals are bound into a social entity) and a "grid" variable (that is, the way these social bonds are structured by means of particular categories such as hierarchy, gender, kinship, and so on). While this basic grid-group framework can be used to analyze a wide variety of social forms of organization, its particular relevance for Douglas and Wildavsky's argument lies in the way it can predict the shape risk perceptions are likely to take, specifying, for example, what kinds of individuals are most likely to see the greatest risk in economic crises, in international relations and conflicts, or in technological scenarios, respectively.

For someone trained in literary and cultural studies, which have in recent decades stressed the way cultural dispositions and worldviews are shaped by social categories such as race, ethnicity, class, gender, nationality, and religious affiliation, the idea that "the perceiver [of risk] is not an individual, but an institution or organization that is driven by organizational imperatives to select risks for management attention or to suppress them from view" (Rayner 86) has a great deal of intuitive plausibility. In very crude form, a similar basic assumption seems to underlie a novel such as Michael Crichton's notorious *State of Fear*, which aims to expose global warming as a scam with a shrewd mix of action-thriller plotting and references to scientific literature. In the chapter that gives the novel its title, Crichton's spokesperson, a professor specializing in the "ecology of thought," proposes to the protagonist Peter Evans that risk scenarios, including fear of climate change, are systematically generated and maintained by what he calls the "PLM," the "politico-legal-media complex":

"Western nations are fabulously safe. Yet people do not feel they are, because of the PLM. And the PLM is powerful and stable, precisely because it unites so many institutions of society. Politicians need fears to control the population. Lawyers need dangers to litigate, and make money. The media need scare stories to capture an audience. Together, these three estates are so compelling that they can go about their business even if the scare is totally groundless." (456)

Environmental risk perceptions, in this perspective, are just one in a series of socially generated fears designed to keep the population in check, and lawyers and journalists in business:

"For fifty years, Western nations had maintained their citizens in a state of perpetual fear. Fear of the other side. Fear of nuclear war. The Communist menace. The Iron Curtain. The Evil Empire. And within the Communist countries, the same in reverse. Fear of us. Then, suddenly, in the fall of 1989, it was all finished.... The fall of the Berlin Wall created a vacuum of fear.... Something had to fill it.

Evans frowned. "You're saying that environmental crises took the place of the Cold War?"

"That is what the evidence shows.... The point is, although the specific cause of our fear may change, we are never without the fear itself. Fear pervades society in all its aspects. Perpetually." (454–55)

Lest one be tempted to dismiss this claim as nothing but right-wing propaganda—though that is undoubtedly the way it is used in this novel—it may be well to remember that left-wing writer and filmmaker Michael Moore makes a very similar argument toward the end of his documentary *Fahrenheit 9/11*, when he suggests that fear of terrorism is largely the fabrication of a right-wing government in conjunction with certain class and religious interests, intended to keep the more disenfranchised segments of the U.S. population in check. Whatever political coloration this idea takes, in other words, the assumption in both cases is that some of the risk scenarios that have dominated public debate in the United States over the last few decades are shaped by well-defined institutional interests and social organizations.

One might expect that Douglas and Wildavsky's "cultural" approach to risk would translate into a more sophisticated and detailed investigation than Crichton's or Moore's of how particular social institutions generate or contribute to risk perceptions, as well as how they intermesh with more individual preferences and biases. While some such research has been undertaken—some of it more strongly influenced by Foucault than by Douglas and Wildavsky, however, as I will explain shortly—most cultural theorists have developed the paradigm in a quite different manner. They have analyzed how certain types of grid-group formations tend to generate worldviews that can be characterized broadly as, for example, "fatalism," "hierarchy," "individualism," "egalitarianism," or "technological enthusiasm," which in turn tend to be accompanied by specific patterns of risk perception. This type of research had to grapple with methodological difficulties such as the question of how to operationalize the grid-group schema into empirically testable research hypotheses, how to theorize the coexistence and interaction of these different structures at various scales of social organization, and how to account for individuals' varying engagements with different kinds of social structures (Rayner 96–98, 104–6; Lupton 51–57).[5] Nevertheless, it clearly emerged that such basic worldviews or dispositions do play a role in shaping the risk perceptions of individuals. But while Douglas and Wildavsky, in their own study, had much to say about the way environmental organizations inflect the risk perceptions of certain parts of the U.S. population, detailed analyses of the functioning of other institutions—schools, universities, political parties, professional organizations, churches, clubs and associations, or particular media—have remained far fewer in number than more general surveys of the public.

The use of such survey data in cultural-theoretical research facilitated integration of some of its findings into psychometric research, which has not adopted cultural-theoretical assumptions wholesale, but has nevertheless worked to incorporate a wide variety of cultural factors into its analyses. Psychometric analyses have taken over from cultural theorists the insight that worldviews, understood broadly as "general social, cultural and political attitudes" inflect perceptions of risk, and that they seem to do so more for some risk scenarios than others (Slovic, "Trust" 402). One study, for example, showed that attitudes toward nuclear power were particularly strongly correlated to such general worldviews (Peters and Slovic). The same study, as well as a series of others, also demonstrated the important role of positive and negative affect in people's judgments of risk; according to these studies, mental representations of particular phenomena or events are associated with varying degrees of affect, and individuals refer consciously or unconsciously to such emotional tags when they make judgments or decisions, using what some researchers call an "affect heuristic" (Finucane et al., Peters and Slovic). Recent psychometric research, then, by integrating variables such as worldviews, cultural biases, and affect into its basic models, has moved far beyond its original framework of the 1970s.

Another dimension of risk research that at times tends to blur the distinction between psychometric and cultural approaches involves the social mechanisms and institutions whereby risk perceptions are generated, altered, and disseminated. The mass media, schools, universities, and churches play an obvious role in this process, but also less formal networks of family, friends, private organizations, internet chat groups, and so forth. In the mid-1980s, Roger Kasperson et al. proposed the concept of the "social amplification of risk" to describe the mediating processes and institutions that shape the social experience of risk, which they later expanded to encompass both "social amplification" and "social attenuation" of risk (Flynn et al., *Risk, Media and Stigma*; Kasperson, "The Social Amplification of Risk: Progress"; Kasperson et al., "Introduction" 35–39; Kasperson et al., "The Social Amplification of Risk"). This concept has remained extremely important to the field today, and to the extent that most individuals only find out about the risks that immediately concern them through one or another social network or institution, it points to an important dimension of knowledge about risk.[6] But obviously, studies of how risk perceptions are socially transmitted must also take into account the institutional interests that shape these mediation processes, and thereby the broader questions about the role played by social entities and organizations that cultural theory tends to focus on. While some basic differences between the psychometric and cultural approaches persist, then, the distinctions between them are no longer as clear-cut as they were in the early stages of cultural theory in the 1980s.

Consideration of risk perceptions as they are generated and shaped by institutions also links the psychometric and cultural paradigms to a third approach that crucially relies on Michel Foucault's concept of "governmentality." Following the lines of argument established by Foucault's research on sexuality, madness, criminality, and discipline, theorists especially in Britain and Australia investigate how governments, insurance companies, and other social institutions establish categories of people at risk that ultimately serve purposes of social surveillance and control (see Castel; Ewald, "Insurance and Risk" and "Two Infinities"; O'Malley). Risk insurance practices that arose in the nineteenth century provide a rich field of historical investigation in this respect, but Foucaultian researchers also take an interest in how less formal but nevertheless pervasive categories operate. Deborah Lupton, for example, has studied how contemporary societies envision pregnant women and young children as categories of people particularly at risk, and what formal and informal regimes of advice and constraint follow from this perception (88–90).[7]

Some recent work on risk perception has questioned the validity especially of the psychometric and the cultural-theory paradigms. Swedish psychologist Lennart Sjöberg has pointed out that the kinds of factors these paradigms tend to investigate in surveys often only explain a small part of the variance in the responses ("Risk Perception Models"). In his own research on the European public's attitudes toward genetically modified foods, he found that perceived "interference with nature" as well as New Age beliefs and moral persuasions exerted a greater influence on risk assessments than novelty or dread, factors typically associated with the psychometric approach, or the worldviews dominant in cultural theory. In view of such variables that are not adequately accounted for in the existing models, Sjöberg calls for the development of new paradigms to explain existing risk perceptions ("Principles" S49–S51).

Research on risk perceptions, therefore, is constantly evolving, even as the theoretical frameworks by means of which it should be organized continue to be debated. As even my brief survey here shows, these discussions take place at an intersection of science, society, and culture that defines "risk" as a concept that encompasses far more than its technical or actuarial definitions to include complex cognitive, affective, social, and cultural processes without which it cannot be conceived, defined, or investigated. In the debates over how risk should be theoretically understood, empirically studied, and politically managed, questions over the "objective" or "socially constructed" nature of risks have persistently surfaced, as have questions about their social mediation ("amplification" and "attenuation"). Like other research areas at the intersection of science and culture, risk analysis is marked by conflicts between realist and various kinds of constructivist approaches that cut across the different theoretical paradigms. As I have shown, risk analysis moved from the predominantly realist assumptions of the psychometric paradigm in the 1970s to increasingly nuanced analyses of the social and cultural frameworks that shape nonexpert risk assessments, in a process that ended up undermining neat distinctions between expert and lay perceptions. As risk theorists attempted to model the different kinds of rationalities that go into such assessments, the question was no longer only which risk perceptions might be the most rational or realistic but also what criteria should be used to gauge degrees of rationality or realism.

Raising this question has led some theorists to a more radical perspective that emphasizes the difficulty of positing any unequivocal boundary between objective and subjective judgments about risk. In this view, the assessments of experts are not exempt from bias, specific interests, and underlying value structures, and the concept of "objective risk" really makes no sense. Any debate about risk includes participants who have widely varying values and priorities, and their definitions of risk as well as their assessments of what constitutes acceptability or the magnitude of a particular risk will depend on these values; being an expert or nonexpert is only one variable in this priority structure. Any decision about risks is therefore at bottom political. This argument comes in several different versions, with some theorists willing to accept some distinction between different degrees of objectivity (if not between absolute objectivity and subjectivity), while others dismiss the notion of objectivity completely and associate their rejection with a more general constructivist critique of science as a privileged mode of knowledge (Otway; Wynne, "Institutional Mythologies").

Needless to say, these controversies are far from mere academic quibbles. Risk assessment is a large applied field in industry and government today, and sometimes comes loaded with political charges. Controversies in these areas are often deeply embedded in conflicts over cultural values and the question of who has the right to make decisions over how technologies are implemented—conflicts that lie at the heart of many environmental struggles around the globe. These struggles have carried over into the academic investigation of risk perceptions, especially since such conflicts are often experienced as confrontations between local knowledge and abstract scientific or administrative expertise, between traditional and modern or global ways of life, and between the different ways risk scenarios are understood and managed in these frameworks. The question of environmentalist perspectives, therefore, has been a crucial dimension of debates over risk in political terms since the 1960s, and in theoretical terms since the 1980s.

Struggles around environmentalist perceptions of present and future dangers began to reshape the political scene in the 1960s and continued throughout the 1970s and 1980s, including Rachel Carson's warnings regarding pesticide overuse, Paul Ehrlich's cautions about rapid demographic growth, the Meadows's projections of resource shortages, confrontations over nuclear technology, and incidents involving industrial accidents and spillages around the world: for example, the mercury poisoning discovered in Minamata, Japan, in 1956 that caused investigation and litigation until the early 1970s and gave rise to the eloquent writings of Michiko Ishimure; the dioxin release at the disaster in Seveso, Italy, in 1976; the Love Canal crisis of 1978–80; the Three Mile Island incident in 1979; the chemical explosion in Bhopal, India, in 1984; the dioxin scare that led to the evacuation of Times Beach, Missouri, in 1985; and the nuclear explosion in Chernobyl in 1986, to name only a few of the most prominent crises. In this context, as risk analysis gradually transmuted from a fairly specialized area of research and professional practice into a prominent object of public awareness and debate, some environmentalists resisted adopting usage of the term "risk" instead of alternative concepts such as "danger," "hazard," or "threat." As political science professor Langdon Winner, for example, argued at the time, even using the term "risk" implied ceding territory to the enemy:

> Employing this word to talk about any situation declares our willingness to compare expected gain with possible harm. We generally do not define a practice as a risk unless there is an anticipated advantage somehow associated with that practice. In contrast, this disposition to weigh and compare is not invoked by concepts that might be employed as alternatives to "risk"—"danger," "peril," "hazard," and "threat." Such terms do not presuppose that the source of possible injury is also a source of benefits. From the outset, then, those who might wish to propose limits upon any particular industrial or technological application are placed at a disadvantage by selecting "risk" as the focus of their concerns. (149)

From this perspective, Winner argues categorically that "the risk debate is one that certain kinds of social interests can expect to lose by the very act of entering" (148). He is certainly right in highlighting the way a change of terminology such as the one from "hazard" to "risk" can alter the terms of social debate and problem solving. Yet Winner overstates the difference between these particular terms. As Douglas and Lupton have both pointed out, the term "risk" today is associated with overwhelmingly negative connotations for most people in most contexts (Douglas, *Risk and Blame* 24; Lupton 8). At the same time, Winner understates the practical complications that attach to the terms he proposes as alternatives. "Fortunately, many issues talked about as risks can be legitimately described in other ways.... A toxic waste disposal site placed in your neighborhood need not be defined as a risk; it might appropriately be defined as a problem of toxic waste," Winner argues (151). True enough—but choosing this seemingly more straightforward terminology does not exempt environmental activists, decision-makers, or the public from complex and often comparative calculations of which dangers are the most urgent to prevent or remediate, how public funds should be allocated to prevent or clean up a variety of different hazards, or how the interests of different institutions and population groups should be negotiated in the process. In other words, finding a solution to "a problem of toxic waste" will inevitably involve many of the considerations—from statistical calculation to institutional interests, cultural predispositions, affective heuristics, worldviews, and so on—that risk theory has investigated.

A somewhat different but related objection came from environmentalists who understood risk analysis essentially as the setting of "acceptable" levels of certain risks, a procedure that in their view obscured the cost in human health and lives as well as in environmental quality that such acceptability might entail. Physician Joseph Regna, for example, insisting on the "unacceptability of acceptable risk," argued that "the 'no' option—no victims, having zero discharges—never enters the hermetically sealed world of risk assessment" (14). Many other environmentalists have similarly advocated what has come to be called the "precautionary principle," according to which actions whose consequences in the future cannot be determined with scientific certainty should be eschewed in the interest of preventing the emergence of new risk scenarios. "Here is one possible benchmark: if a chemical is not safe for a six-week-old [human] embryo, it is not safe and should not be allowed into the environment," Sandra Steingraber argues in her study of environmental carcinogens (278). This argument makes sense especially in the case of environmental toxins, where specific substances can often be replaced by alternative, less toxic ones, and where industry has often used risk assessment to obscure the dangers that derive from the use of a particular chemical. In other cases, however, the precautionary principle is clearly more difficult to apply. The disposal of existing nuclear waste, for example, affords no "no-option," and advocacy for the discontinuation of nuclear energy has to weigh competing risks associated with the increased burning of fossil fuels. While Regna, Steingraber, and many other critics of the chemical industry in particular may therefore be right in insisting on the application of the precautionary principle wherever possible, this principle cannot generally be extended to all ecological and technological risk scenarios.

"Risk assessment" in the narrow sense in which Regna uses the term—that is, the statistical setting of acceptability levels for chemical substances—is at any rate not identical with risk analysis and theory. Steingraber, who explicitly rejects "risk assessment" (284), nevertheless deploys the vocabulary of "risk factors" and "risk perceptions" throughout her study, in the broader sense of clinical analyses of factors that contribute to disease, and cultural investigations of certain discourses about risk. Academic work in risk analysis, at any rate, is not so much concerned with establishing acceptable levels of safety and risk in various contexts as with examining precisely why and how limits of safety and risk are established in particular social, cultural, historical, and political contexts—including both the rhetoric of "acceptable risk" and that of "zero risk."

Winner, Regna, and other environmentalists, therefore, took a somewhat reductive view of risk analysis, even considering that they published their critiques in the 1980s, when the field was still in its early stages of development. Nonetheless, they sensed correctly that some of these earlier forms of risk analysis suffered from an in-built antienvironmentalist bias. The psychometric approach, one could argue, manifested such a bias indirectly in its initial tendency to privilege expert rationality over other kinds of cultural logic, without acknowledging that expert opinions might be based on cultural assumptions of their own. Since environmentalist risk assessments often relied on dimensions that were hard to quantify—the sanctity of nature, long-term futures, uncertain consequences—and experts often tended to rate quantifiable risks lower than environmentalists, an imbalance ensued that was only corrected when the psychometric approach increasingly integrated social and cultural factors into its analyses in the 1980s and 1990s. But antienvironmentalist bias is much more obvious in Douglas and Wildavsky's early formulation of cultural theory in *Risk and Culture*. While they started out by using the relatively complex grid-group model of social analysis to characterize different social formations and the worldviews that typically accompany them, they applied their own framework to the United States by postulating a simple dichotomy between social hierarchy and the market at the "center" of American society and egalitarian movements at the "border," which according to their argument generated most technological and ecological risk perceptions. To make things worse, they denigrated environmentalist risk perceptions as "sectarian" while failing to apply any critical analysis to the risk perceptions of corporations or governmental institutions.

Environmentalists were no doubt justified in rejecting an approach that so simplistically and summarily dismissed their perspective. Yet in taking Douglas and Wildavsky's early formulation to be representative of risk analysis as a whole, they overlooked not only alternative theoretical approaches but also the ways Douglas and Wildavsky's theory itself contradicts the logic of some of their antienvironmentalist conclusions, and the ways this theory might in fact be useful for an environmental perspective. Social scientists such as Dorothy Nelkin were quick to point out that Douglas and Wildavsky's analysis of the "egalitarian" bent of the environmentalist movement ignored the broad spectrum of organizations environmentalism had come to encompass by the 1980s, many of which functioned exactly like other highly hierarchical political or corporate organizations (Nelkin). Subsequent cultural theorists have argued that Douglas and Wildavsky's misguided judgment of environmentalism does not logically invalidate their basic suggestion that in order to understand risk perceptions, we need to examine sociocultural institutions, their value systems, and their modes of operation rather than just individuals' views. This basic assumption logically leads to a critical examination of corporate, governmental, and generally antienvironmentalist risk assessments just as much as of environmentalist ones, as the theory insists on "the inherently cultural nature of any group or community's perceptions and judgments about risk" (Lupton 57). For this reason, Douglas and Wildavsky's antienvironmentalist bias is often seen as clashing with the implications of the theory itself by later cultural theorists, whose work tends to be far more balanced. The core of cultural theory, in other words, is not logically related to and indeed contradicts the antienvironmentalist uses to which Douglas and Wildavsky initially put it.

Almost a quarter century later, the suspicion that risk theory might be inherently antienvironmentalist may itself seem dated, given both the maturation and diversity in the field and the widespread use of risk concepts in public debates. Yet my point is not merely that debates about risks are here to stay but that an acquaintance with the theoretical assumptions and empirical findings in the field are useful and indeed indispensable for environmentalist thinking generally and ecocritical analysis in particular. If environmentalism as a form of social activism aspires to change people's perceptions of the natural world and the threats that emanate from certain activities both for human health and the sustained functioning of ecosystems, it is crucial to understand why and how individuals and communities arrive at such risk judgments. If these assessments are often based on a multiplicity of factors outside of factual information, as risk analysis has shown, environmentalists need to take these factors into account in their own thinking rather than assume that better information will in and of itself lead to a more environmentally oriented perspective. Ecocritics, who have made it their principal task to investigate the cultural practices and artifacts that evolve out of particular conceptions of the relationship between nature and human societies, have a vested interest in the findings of risk theory as an essential part of such conceptions. Not only is risk theorists' exploration of the ways cultural worldviews and institutions shape risk perceptions fundamental background knowledge for anyone interested in the forms that environmental art and writing have taken at different historical moments and in various cultural communities, but inversely, literary critics' detailed analyses of cultural practices stand to enrich and expand the body of data that an interdisciplinary risk theory can build on.

2. Risk and Narrative

If the field of technological and ecological risk analysis put its major emphasis on scientific and statistical assessments in the 1970s, it has increasingly come to investigate cultural contexts, dispositions, institutions, and

processes in its attempts to account for both the complexities of risk perceptions and the relationship between risk and modernization. This approach
to risk as constituted from within specific sociocultural fields links risk
analysis to social studies of science on the one hand and to the concerns
of cultural and literary studies on the other. But while the work of Sheila
Jasanoff, Brian Wynne, and other scholars has successfully established
bridges between social studies of science and risk theory, the interface between risk analysis and literary and cultural studies has so far been less
frequently addressed. Risk theorists have paid relatively little attention to
the role that particular metaphors, narrative patterns, or visual representations might play in the formation of risk judgments.[8] If Lennart Sjöberg
is right in arguing that "interference with nature" acts as a powerful explanatory variable in public perceptions of gene technology, for example,
the question immediately arises what exactly "nature" means for the individuals who invoke this term, and to what extent it might be shaped by
the narrative template of the Frankenstein story (in both its book and film
versions). As historian Jon Turney has argued in *Frankenstein's Footsteps*,
this seminal story exerts a powerful influence on current discourses about
genetic engineering. In general, literary and cultural scholars have produced a vast amount of research on the ways basic concepts such as nature, landscape, self and other, and the functioning of the human body in
health and illness have been popularly envisioned by means of particular
metaphors and stories in different cultures and at different historical moments. It stands to reason that such conceptualizations, which tend to be
far more available to the general public than scientific information, play
an important role in the selection and evaluation of risks.

Along similar lines, a culturally inflected study of risk perceptions
stands to gain from closer attention to the way certain visual images
come to function as shorthands for particular dangers and crises. Television viewers have become well familiarized with images of so-called
charismatic megafauna—panda bears, mountain gorillas, or whales, for
example—that synecdochically evoke the beauty and value of entire ecosystems such as tropical forests or oceans at risk.[9] The oil-covered seabird,
as Andrew Ross has pointed out, has come to function as a general icon
of environmental crisis (chap. 3, esp. 166, 171–72). Novelist Ron Sukenick
foregrounds the power but also the danger of such visual shorthands in his
Mosaic Man, a novel that ends around the time of the first Gulf War, during
which two of the protagonists watch coverage of the war on TV:

> Also we see that the Iraqis are releasing oil into the Red Sea, creating
> an ecological disaster dwarfing the Alaska oil spill. Once again pictures
> of oil mucked critters dying their slow deaths. Painted in oil, art brute.
> Totalling our totems. Why is it that it's the exceptional animal that isn't
> beautiful, especially among the wild ones? SCREEN OFF.

+

Later it turns out that that image of the doomed cormorant trying to escape a pool of oil, played over and over again, is from stock footage. So that even the imagery of truth is deceptive. And what about the images we aren't shown? (252–53)

Sukenick here alludes to the way visual synecdoches can make risk perceptions portable, easy to transfer from one specific context to another, but also to the way they can occlude an understanding of a particular risk scenario as it is being interpreted in terms of images derived from another one. Such issues of representation, to the extent that they are raised by mass media and likely to affect public opinion, deserve to be studied in greater detail.

More situation-specific images sometimes derive from the shaping influence of narrative traditions. In a detailed and very perceptive study, Ferreira, Boholm, and Löfstedt examine the images that accompanied television coverage of toxic leakage from a tunnel construction project in southern Sweden, emphasizing how these image sequences deliberately created the sense of a pristine agricultural landscape polluted by the spill (285–96). In particular, they foreground how images of milk that had to be poured out because of the contamination conveyed symbolic meanings of innocence and purity that were being undermined by the presence of the toxins. Curiously, however, these authors never once mention the genre of pastoral, which is precisely what gives these images a large part of their communicative power: it is because Western cultures have long traditions of looking upon the countryside as a peaceful, nature-bound, and harmonious counterweight to the corruptions of urban life that evocations of poisoned meadows and milk so powerfully convey a sense of disaster. Narrative genres, as this example suggests, provide important cultural tools for organizing information about risks into intelligible and meaningful stories. But to the extent that such genre templates have a cultural power that can make them override alternative stories that fit less well into existing narrative patterns, they can also shape, filter, and rearrange such information in ways that are not always politically or ecologically benign. Narrative analysis should therefore play an important role in examining the ways risk perceptions are generated by and manifest themselves through various forms of representation, from documentaries and journalism to fiction and poetry.

The study of narrative and metaphorical mediations of risk also contributes to an understanding of important parts of environmentalist discourse itself as a form of risk communication that raises similar questions. To what extent does environmentalist rhetoric translate new technological and ecological risk scenarios into already existing narrative templates, and how does this affect their evaluation? To what extent are existing templates altered or new ones formulated? Lawrence Buell has addressed some of these issues in his analysis of a type of environmental rhetoric that he labels "toxic discourse," defined as "expressed anxiety arising from perceived threat of environmental hazard due to chemical modification by human agency" (*Writing* 31). According to Buell, this kind of discourse about a specific kind of risk, chemical contamination, surfaces in the bourgeois and mostly white, middle-class environmentalist movement as well as in the environmental justice movement, which tends to focus on the poor, minorities, and urban populations. Buell diagnoses four major rhetorical components in toxic discourse: a rhetoric of disrupted pastoral that he describes eloquently as a "mythography of betrayed Edens" (*Writing* 37), often accompanied by an individual's awakening consciousness to the way a pristine environment (or one retrospectively perceived as such) has been contaminated; totalizing images of an entirely polluted world that leaves no escape from the toxins; the moral passion of the weak and politically repressed against those perceived to be strong and politically powerful that is mobilized through a "David vs. Goliath" scenario; and gothic elements that surface in descriptions of deformed bodies and polluted landscapes, especially Virgilian descents to the "underworld" of pollution victims (*Writing* 43–44). As Buell traces some elements of this rhetoric back to nineteenth-century writings about urban blight and others to more remote literary sources, he makes it clear that even the dimensions of toxic discourse that strike one as most realistic have in fact emerged from long traditions of cultural risk representation. But his purpose is not so much to relativize environmental rhetoric by foregrounding its "social constructedness" as to show that it is precisely through these traditions that some stories acquire the power to represent risk in terms that we understand as realistic. The question how such rhetorical traditions filter and shape information about risk so as to postulate certain causal sequences, to make some scenarios plausible and others less so, to make some appear more threatening than others, and to outline likely future courses of events is clearly crucial for both risk theorists and ecocritics.

Buell's analysis of toxic discourse points the way toward a broader analysis of the rhetoric of environmental and technological risk. Implicitly or explicitly, accounts of risk tend to invoke different genre models, for example the detective story—in the evaluation of clues and eyewitness accounts, and in the discovery and exposure of the criminal; pastoral—in the portrayal of rural, unspoiled landscapes violated by the advent of technology; the gothic—in the evocation of hellish landscapes or grotesquely deformed bodies as a consequence of pollution; the *Bildungsroman*—in the victim's gradually deepening realization of the danger to which she or he is exposed; tragedy—through the fateful occurrence of events that individuals are only partially able to control; and epic—in the attempt to grasp the planetary implications of some risks. Along with the selection of such templates that make risk scenarios intelligible to the reader or viewer in a particular way, narrators have to make choices about which individuals or institutions are cast as protagonists or antagonists in technological controversies, about where and how to conclude their stories, and about how to characterize their own relationship to their story material (for example, as eyewitness, victim, scientific expert, or journalist).

Buell's study of toxic discourse as a particular form of environmentalist rhetoric also alludes to the question of how risk narratives construct the relationship between particular places and the planet at large. Fear of chemical contamination at a specific site, in many of the writings he analyzes, is linked to a sometimes paranoid vision of an entire world infested by poisons that no human being can escape or protect herself against. He traces this totalizing toxic consciousness back to its most obvious source, Rachel Carson's *Silent Spring*, and beyond that to George Perkins Marsh's *Man and Nature* (1864) and the writings of European colonial officials in the seventeenth and eighteenth centuries who had the chance to observe threatened island ecosystems firsthand (*Writing* 39). This vision of global pollution, Buell notes, ends up functioning as a countermodel to the better-known environmentalist conception of the planet as a holistic, Gaian-style system of harmonies and balances:

> Toxic discourse calls for a way of imagining physical environments that fuses social constructivist with environmental restorationist perspectives....[T]he nature that toxic discourse recognizes as the physical environment humans inhabit is *not* a holistic spiritual or biotic economy but a network or networks within which, on the one hand, humans are biotically imbricated (like it or not), and within which, on the other hand, first nature has been greatly modified (like it or not) by *techne*. (*Writing* 45)

This fascinating observation seems to suggest that the kind of environmentalist rhetoric Buell here analyzes has turned its back on the fundamentally pastoral vision of ecology I discussed in chapter 1, a vision that understands ecological systems as harmonious and balanced networks and that sees nature as self-regenerating if left on its own. Yet I am less confident than Buell that the longing for a return to precisely such a naturally balanced world does not inform many of these descriptions of exploited, deformed, and polluted landscapes and bodies as an imaginary countermodel. Calls for "risk-free" environments, undisturbed communities and neighborhoods, pure and "detoxified" bodies, and in some cases, premodern ways of life, in tandem with calls for grassroots democracy, self-sufficiency, and respect for indigenous forms of knowledge that are often articulated in this context seem to spell out a pastoral countermodel to the toxic world. Viewed from this angle, the vision of a terminally polluted planet appears less as an alternative to Lovelockean holism than as a subgenre of apocalyptic narrative, which has played an important role in modern environmentalism from the 1960s onward.

Apocalyptic narrative, by definition, addresses the fate of the world as a whole: it is a particular form of imagining the global. As it was deployed by environmentalist writers in the 1960s and 1970s, it paints dire pictures of a world on the brink of destruction as a means of calling for social and political reforms that might avert such ruination. Unlike biblical apocalypse, in other words, it assumes that the End of the World can in fact be prevented (Garrard, *Ecocriticism* 99), and the destructive intensity of its scenarios is not so much an attempt at accurate prediction as an indicator of the urgency of its call for social change (Killingsworth and Palmer 41). Apocalyptic narrative, in this secular sense, can appropriately be understood as a form of risk perception. Yet to the extent that such narrative, even in its secular version, articulates quite clear-cut distinctions between good and evil, desirable and undesirable futures, it indeed relies on a different mode of projecting the future than theories of risk, which tend to emphasize persistent uncertainties, unintended consequences, and necessary trade-offs. To put it somewhat differently, environmental apocalypses include an ideal socioecological countermodel—often a pastoral one—that discourses about risk typically lack (although Beck's rather idiosyncratic version of risk theory does contain a utopian element that I will discuss shortly).

Since environmental apocalyptic discourse was often dismissed when its predictions did not come true (although, as environmentalists are quick to point out, one reason that they did not come true may well be precisely the fact that these end-of-the-world stories kindled public awareness and galvanized political action) and the rhetoric of risk has become more widespread in public debate, ecocritics have assessed its current relevance in rather divergent terms. Michael Killingsworth and Jacqueline Palmer, in their analysis of "millennial ecology," have traced the genre from 1960s scenarios of nuclear annihilation, pollution, overpopulation, and mass starvation forward to the 1980s, when they see it as reemerging in journalistic as well as scientific warnings about the greenhouse effect. Environmentalist writers at that moment, they argue, were aware that some of the specific predictions of earlier end-of-the-world scenarios had not come true and had thereby put the credibility of environmentalist prognoses in question. They therefore revived the genre with greater caution, and eschewed forecasting anything more than broad trends; nevertheless, global warming has led to a revival and continuation of the genre in their view. Frederick Buell, by contrast, has argued in his tellingly entitled study *From Apocalypse to Way of Life* that the millennial expectation of future crises that prevailed in environmentalist thought and writing in the 1960s and 1970s has given way to the cultural integration of crisis and risk into the experience of the present from the 1980s onward. People no longer fear environmental disasters in the future so much as they "dwell in crisis," as he puts it: that is, they live with an awareness that certain limits in the exploitation of nature have already been exceeded, that past warnings were not heeded, and that slowly evolving risk scenarios surround them on a daily basis.

Frederick Buell is clearly ambivalent about this shift. On the one hand, he recognizes that a steady drumbeat of gloom-and-doom rhetoric is liable to discourage and alienate individuals more than it incites them to action. On the other hand, he is obviously worried that too much normalization of crisis might lead to an implicit acquiescence to the environmental status quo. Instead of such a "domestication within crisis," he calls for "a way of dwelling actively within rather than accommodating oneself to environmental crisis" (205, 206). What exactly this means in practical terms is not really clear in his account, and he himself notes that precisely the novels that describe the contemporary "dwelling in crisis" without unduly apocalyptic or utopian overtones offer no way out of crisis (322).[10] But his diagnosis of the demise of environmental apocalypse is nevertheless perceptive in its analytical insight. It contrasts with Killingsworth and Palmer's persuasion that apocalypse is alive and well as an environmental genre, and more importantly, it suggests that apocalyptic scenarios differ from risk scenarios in the way they construe the relation between present, future, and crisis. In the apocalyptic perspective, utter destruction lies ahead but can be averted and replaced by an alternative future society; in the risk perspective, crises are already underway all around, and while their consequences can be mitigated, a future without their impact has become impossible to envision.

It is worth emphasizing that this difference does not amount to any fundamental dichotomy. Apocalyptic scenarios are and remain a particular narrativization of risk perceptions, and analyses of risk certainly sometimes include panoramas of large-scale upheaval or disaster: some forecasts of the consequences of current global warming trends are a case in point. The more important difference, I would argue, lies in the way many (though not all) environmental apocalypses continue to hold up, implicitly or explicitly, ideals of naturally self-regenerating ecosystems and holistic communities in harmony with their surroundings as a countermodel to the visions of exploitation and devastation they describe, while perspectives grounded in risk analysis tend to outline more or less desirable consequences and futures of certain courses of action, but by definition none that are completely exempt from risk. In a certain sense, the futures that risk analysis tends to project correspond to typically high modernist patterns of narrative in literary analysis in their (implicit or explicit) emphasis on indeterminacy, uncertainty, and the possibility of a variety of different outcomes. This emphasis, however, does not imply that risk theorists necessarily remain noncommittal with regard to specific programs of risk management and mitigation. On the contrary, it is precisely theorists who understand the complexity and uncertainty of risk scenarios as an inherent dimension of modern societies and their technologies whose agendas in the end turn out to be conceptually closest to those of environmentalists.

3. Risk, Complexity, and Modernization

Studies of risk perceptions only rarely invoke the broader sociological and historical theories that focus on the relationship of certain types of risks and risk perceptions to processes of modernization and globalization; conversely, these broader theories tend not to incorporate empirical research on risk perceptions, so that the two fields of inquiry have remained somewhat disjointed. One of the studies that has exerted influence in both arenas, however, is Charles Perrow's seminal analysis of "system accidents." In his by now classic study *Normal Accidents: Living with High-Risk Technologies* (1984), Perrow investigates a variety of contemporary technological systems, from dams and mines to marine and air traffic, space exploration, weapons systems, and biotechnology. The most serious risks, Perrow argues, stem from technological systems with such a degree of complexity that even experts cannot understand all the connections and feedback loops they contain, and therefore cannot predict some of their most dangerous failures. System accidents occur when several different and sometimes minor failures in independent but coupled subsystems interact in such a way as to produce failures in the system as a whole. This interaction produces risks that could not have been anticipated by an analysis of the system's normal functioning or of individual subsystem failures. Perrow emphasizes that

> if interactive complexity and tight coupling—system characteristics—inevitably will produce an accident, I believe we are justified in calling it a *normal accident*, or a *system accident*. The odd term *normal accident* is meant to signal that, given the system characteristics, multiple and unexpected interactions of failures are inevitable. This is an expression of an integral characteristic of the system, not a statement of frequency. (*Normal Accidents* 5)

Improved designs or better operator training, therefore, will not lead to increased safety, because the complexity of the technology itself will always defeat them.

System complexity and coupling lead from small, unimportant failures—"the banality and triviality behind most catastrophes" (*Normal Accidents* 9)—to large-scale disasters and characterize, according to Perrow, several technologies that were only introduced in the course of the twentieth century but now pose the greatest and most unpredictable hazards for contemporary society. In part, this is because complex systems are designed in such a way that the banal beginnings of a major accident are often not immediately observable. "In complex industrial, space, and military systems, the normal accident generally (not always) means that the interactions are not only unexpected, but are *incomprehensible* for some critical period of time. In part this is because in these human-machine systems the interactions literally cannot be seen" (*Normal Accidents* 9). Nuclear energy is such a complex and tightly coupled technology prone to system accidents, as Perrow demonstrates in a detailed analysis of the Three Mile Island accident that is, like most of his other case studies, as suspenseful and surprising as many a novel. Complexity and tight coupling are also the factors that generally make nuclear power plants and weapons, in Perrow's view, unacceptable in terms of their risk;[11] marine transport and biotechnology acceptable, with major investments in reducing their risks; and other technologies including chemical plants, air traffic, mining, fossil fuel plants, highways and automobiles acceptable, with relatively minor improvements (*Normal Accidents* 304–5).

Perrow is aware that this evaluation puts him at odds with the usual perspective of risk assessors: "Current risk assessment theory suggests that what I worry about most (nuclear power and weapons) has done almost no harm to people, while what I would leave to minor corrections (such as fossil fuel plants, auto safety, and mining) has done a great deal of harm" (*Normal Accidents* 305).[12] But it is precisely his focus on the structure and functioning of technological systems, he argues, rather than on the consequences of their past performance, that allows a more realistic assessment of their future potential for harm. From this perspective, he concludes, the dimension of "dread" that psychometric investigators of risk perceptions in the 1970s had discovered with respect to certain technologies, and that had seemed to them to derive merely from the public's ignorance and emotionality, actually turns out to have some foundation in reality, since many of the technologies with a "dread risk" factor also rely on interactively complex and tightly coupled systems. In this respect, Perrow points out, his classification meshes more closely with public perceptions of risk than with technical assessments by governmental, corporate, and academic experts (*Normal Accidents* 327–28).

If Perrow here suggests a different lens for the psychometric study of certain kinds of public risk perceptions, his analysis also implies a different approach to the historicity of risk. While theorists with an anthropological approach, including Douglas and Wildavsky, tend to focus more on the mechanisms by means of which cultures select risks for attention than on the nature of the risks themselves, Perrow proposes that with industrialization and, even more markedly, with the technological innovations of the twentieth century, new kinds of risk scenarios have come into being. Qualitatively different kinds of risks, in other words, arise as a consequence of economic and technological modernization processes that cannot simply be equated with risks from, say, the plague, warfare, or natural disasters in earlier times. The central question for Perrow, therefore, is the development of technological risk scenarios and only secondarily their social construction and perception.

A somewhat broader but related analysis about why risk has become so all-encompassing in contemporary culture emerges from the work of the historian of technology Thomas Hughes. What has transformed modern society, and American society in particular, Hughes argues, is not so much the invention of individual technological principles and devices—such as electricity, the telephone, or the automobile—as the creation of large-scale and extremely complex techno-economic systems by means of which these devices are produced, distributed, and managed. For Hughes, the invention and implementation of these complex technological and organizational networks is the unique contribution of the United States to modern culture. The technological hardware is only one part of such networks, which also include transportation, communications, and information systems, as well as people and institutions with all their organizational, legal, social, and economic structures. Though Hughes does not explicitly frame his argument through theories of risk, he refers to Perrow to argue that these large-scale systems in which technologies are embedded have become so complex that they can no longer be easily understood or controlled, and therefore give rise to risks whose origins and outcomes are extremely difficult to trace and manage (443–72). As chapter 5 will show, this idea forms the narrative nucleus of Richard Powers's novel *Gain*, which portrays in great detail the growth of a chemical corporation as a complex system that ends up distributing toxic products around the globe.

British sociologist Anthony Giddens, whose concept of "disembedding" I discussed in chapter 1, analyzes risk even more broadly in the context of the social transformations that characterize modernization processes. By creating institutions, networks of exchange and expertise that reach far beyond the local, Giddens argues, disembedding mechanisms generate security for vast areas and populations, for example through steady and safe supplies of food, water, and electricity, shared legal conventions, and insurance practices. But they also generate new kinds of risks with sometimes global reach:

> All disembedding mechanisms take things out of the hands of any specific individuals or groups; and the more such mechanisms are of global scope, the more this tends to be so. Despite the high levels of security which globalised mechanisms can provide, the other side of the coin is that novel risks come into being: resources or services are no longer under local control and therefore cannot be locally refocused to meet unexpected contingencies, and there is a risk that the mechanism as a whole can falter, thus affecting everyone who characteristically makes use of it. Thus someone who has oil-fired central heating and no fireplaces is particularly vulnerable to changes in the price of oil. In circumstances such as the "oil crisis" of 1973, produced as a result of the

actions of the OPEC cartel, all consumers of petroleum products are affected. (*Consequences* 126–27)

The fact that the disembedding mechanisms characteristic of modernization create networks of both safety and risk also affects the social trust that in Giddens's theory is fundamental for the functioning of modern societies. Trust in the continuous proper functioning of invisible networks of law, expertise, and exchange is the fuel on which the large-scale social systems of modern societies run. Risk scenarios, exceptionally serious or far-reaching ones in particular, put this foundation of trust to the test, since modern networks of information and communication also give rise to widespread awareness of a host of different risks, as well as of the limits of expertise in dealing with them. In addition, modern societies typically do not offer their members easy ways of converting such limits of knowledge or management ability into the certainties of magical or religious conviction (*Consequences* 125). The change in both the kind of risk scenarios that disembedding mechanisms create and the type of risk awareness they give rise to, therefore, leads Giddens to refer to late modernity as a "risk culture" (*Modernity and Self-Identity* 3).

Giddens's writings on risk and trust are clearly influenced by the work of Ulrich Beck, who links the concept of risk even more resolutely to broader theorizations of modernization and globalization. Like Giddens and Scott Lash, Beck postulates that modern societies have entered a phase of "reflexive modernization" in which modernizing processes transform not traditional social structures, but those created by earlier waves of modernization.[13] According to Beck, the hazards that are characteristic of this new era can be defined by two criteria: they are themselves the effects of modernizing processes, thereby reflexively confronting modern societies with the results of their own modernization; and some of these risks, such as global warming and the thinning of the ozone layer, are for the first time truly planetary in scope. In his most famous, far-reaching, and speculative claim of the mid-1980s, Beck proposed that risks such as these will lead to a new stage in the evolution of modernity—not to a "postmodern" but instead to a "risk society." While social distinctions and conflicts at an earlier stage of modernity were centrally articulated around the production and distribution of wealth, Beck argues, "in advanced modernity, the social production of *wealth* is systematically associated with the social production of *risks.* Accordingly, the distribution problems and conflicts of the scarcity society are superseded by the problems and conflicts that originate in the production, definition and distribution of techno-scientifically generated risks" (*Risikogesellschaft* 25).[14] Such new risks reach across existing stratifications to create a new kind of social structure. "Poverty is hierarchical, smog is democratic," Beck sums up his argument in one of the most frequently quoted aphorisms from *Risikogesellschaft* (48).

What he means by this is that the technological development of modern society has reached a stage where it has become unable to protect itself against the unintended "side effects" of its own technologies, which, formerly latent and invisible, are now emerging into full public view. Even as the socially privileged attempt to export such side effects to the less empowered, in the end they cannot prevent these effects from returning to harm them. Ecological crisis, in Beck's view, is a case in point, as it ends up undermining the means by which any population sustains itself—including those who might have originally profited from ecological exploitation (*Risikogesellschaft* 48–50). Excessive pesticide provides an easy example, in Beck's perspective, as it is exported to countries with lax environmental regulations that in turn export their pesticide-contaminated harvests back to the countries who meant to avoid just these chemicals, in a global cycle he calls the "boomerang effect." Of course, buying organic produce may offer a temporary release from this cycle for the affluent; but when soil, air, and drinking water are polluted, even the socially privileged are increasingly impacted by risks that affect the foundations of life. And if some risks are deliberately moved across national borders, others travel around the globe without anyone's conscious intention: even the remote lakes of Canada turn acidic, and the forests of northernmost Scandinavia die from acid rain. An atomic bomb is, in Beck's view, the clearest example of a risk that makes no distinction at all between rich and poor; the ecological crisis, according to him, works in a more gradual and delayed fashion, but ultimately has a similar effect (*Risikogesellschaft* 50).

All this does not imply that Beck denies the increased risk exposure that material disadvantage entails at the present moment. He frequently emphasizes, in what may seem like a contradiction to his quip about the "democracy of smog," that "there is a systematic 'force of attraction' between extreme poverty and extreme risks" (*Risikogesellschaft* 55). This is because he does not see the risk society as a fully established social pattern, but as an emergent one that at the moment overlaps with the structures of the modernist scarcity society. His point, in other words, is not that the increased number and scope of modern risk scenarios have already overridden existing social inequalities, nor that they will lead to an egalitarian society, but that they will eventually lead to a rearticulation of inequalities on a different basis. "One thing is clear. Endemic uncertainty is what will mark the lifeworld and the basic existence of most people—including the apparently affluent middle classes—in the years that lie ahead" (*World Risk Society* 12). In this context, he highlights the ambivalence of what he calls the "individualization" of life stories, that is, the idea that the course of people's lives is becoming increasingly less predictable in terms of their social origins; while this individualization (which, he emphasizes, is identical neither with "individuation" nor with "individualism") may have emancipatory implications in some respects, "the expression 'precarious freedoms' denotes a basic ambivalence between the cultural script of individual self-fulfilment and the new political economy of uncertainty and risk. All too swiftly, the 'elective,' 'reflexive' or 'do-it-yourself' biography can become the breakdown biography" (*World Risk Society* 12). This nuance is worth bearing in mind: rather than arguing that people from different social strata will be equally affected by particular risks (though that may be the case in some contexts) or that current social structures will give way to a determinate new social architecture, Beck's main point is precisely the unpredictability of current risk scenarios, and as a consequence, the idea that social status will not in the future function as a reliable indicator of risk exposure. As I will argue in chapter 5, it is possible to read Don DeLillo's novel *White Noise* as a fictional engagement with precisely the realization that risk scenarios are becoming unmoored from conventional class distinctions.

While Beck's book gained enormous popularity in western Europe in the late 1980s and in the United States throughout the 1990s, it also came under attack for a variety of reasons, including its conceptualization of modern "reflexivity" and its neglect of risk taking as a positively valued and sometimes pleasurable experience. Most importantly, sociologists have pointed out that little empirical evidence exists to support Beck's claim that social categorizations are indeed in the process of being rearticulated around issues of risk. But even some of his critics admit that the interest of Beck's argument may be polemical rather than descriptive: it is not really necessary to accept wholesale his theory of a fundamental social shift to see the force of his argument that risk is becoming one important area of sociocultural concern and conflict.[15]

For an environmental perspective, Beck's theory presents curiously ambivalent challenges. On the one hand, Beck radicalizes environmentalist claims about technological and ecological risk by turning them into a set of ineluctable global conditions and making them the very principles on the basis of which societies around the globe will have to reconfigure themselves. Lawrence Buell has highlighted this dimension of Beck's work by labeling him "the Rachel Carson of contemporary social theory" (*Future* 5). But in a sense, Beck's is an even more extreme vision of the impact of ecological crisis on social structure than many of the scenarios proposed by the apocalyptically minded environmentalists of the 1960s and early 1970s, in that it predicts the advent of a new kind of society that cannot really be averted. Even if one takes this claim somewhat less than literally, as I mentioned, the concept of a world risk society bolsters environmentalist claims about the increasing social importance of technological and ecological risk scenarios. Beck's criticism of the role scientists have sometimes played in ignoring or covering up such dangers, as well as his diagnosis of the general failure of established social and political mechanisms to deal with some of the new risks, concurs with environmentalist views.

On the other hand, Beck's most fundamental claim, that modern so-cial structures shaped by conflicts over the distribution of wealth will be replaced by stratifications originating in differential vulnerability to risk, does run counter to the perspectives that have been formulated around the concept of "environmental justice." In the view of environmental justice advocates, technological and ecological risk scenarios superimpose them-selves on and help to reinforce existing structures of social inequality, in that the world's poor and racial or ethnic minorities tend to be dispropor-tionately exposed to risk, as well as, in quite a few cases, women. The sta-tus of the disenfranchised in the international economy—their places of residence and types of work—the argument runs, typically exposes them to hazards from which the more affluent mainstream has better means of sheltering itself. From the location of dangerous industries and toxic waste disposals all the way to the quality of building materials and foodstuffs they have access to, the poor and underprivileged receive a greater portion of the risks and a smaller share of the benefits than the more privileged so-cial strata. Indeed, as Guha and Martínez-Alier have emphasized in their studies of environmentalist movements in India and Latin America, poor and indigenous communities often confront the risk of seeing their own, sustainable ways of exploiting local ecosystems displaced by the unsus-tainable practices of large corporations that sometimes operate with gov-ernment support (6–11). Beck's aphorism "Poverty is hierarchical, smog is democratic" is anathema from this perspective. And even if a particular threat presented itself similarly to two socially different populations, their means of mitigating its impact would still set them apart: Bangladesh and the Netherlands may, by virtue of their topographical characteristics, be exposed to similar hazards from rising sea levels, but their socioeconomic means of countering this threat differ significantly.

One might be tempted to diffuse this difference by pointing precisely to some of the passages I quoted earlier in which Beck highlights the at-traction between poverty and risk. But doing so would obscure what is, in my view, a genuine and deep-seated difference of social vision between the two approaches. Environmental justice advocates tend to see the cur-rent global ecological crisis in its manifold manifestations as a logical consequence and exacerbation of a socioeconomic organization based on capitalism, and of an approach to knowledge shaped by the rationalism of the Enlightenment; only a genuine social revolution against these exist-ing structures, in their perspective, will remove the underlying causes for the destruction of the natural environment. Beck, by contrast, sees in the same ecological crisis a sign of the disintegration of the capitalist class so-ciety and of modernist approaches to knowledge. Far from intensifying ex-isting social inequalities, global risk scenarios will gradually undermine them. In this view, the revolution is already underway, though in a very different fashion than the one usually envisioned in socialist politics.

This contradiction seems to me difficult to resolve if we take Beck's claims *au pied de la lettre:* while the diagnosis of the status quo overlaps in the two approaches, the underlying social analyses differ significantly. If one takes Beck's analysis somewhat less literally as highlighting the important role that risk scenarios have begun to play in social conflicts, however, the tension diminishes. Indeed, one could argue that the rise of the environmental justice movement is itself evidence of just this role. And when one considers just how the transition to something like a "risk society" might actually occur, the struggles carried out by the environmental justice movement may well turn out to be one crucial part of such a shift. Risk theorists who currently study global environmental hazards, at any rate, address issues of environmental justice as a crucial part of their investigation, and have begun to develop the concept of "vulnerability," defined broadly as "'differential susceptibility to loss from a given insult'" as a hinge term in their analyses (Kasperson et al., "Introduction" 24).[16] By the same token, Beck's own cosmopolitan vision of new social communities arising from transnational risk scenarios, to which I will turn next, has a great deal of affinity with the increasing internationalism of the environmental justice movement.

4. Risk, Globalization, and the Cosmopolitan Imaginary

The theories of the relation between risk and modernity proposed by Perrow, Hughes, Giddens, and Beck, among others, foreground how experiences of risk are imbricated in far-flung ecological, technological, economic, and social systems that operate across a variety of scales from the local to the planetary. Beck's concept of the "world risk society," indeed, represents one of the most important recent ways of imagining the global from an environmentalist perspective. Lawrence Buell has gone so far as to envision Beck as the latter-day counterpart of James Lovelock, in that Beck turns Lovelock's theory of Planet Earth as a self-sustaining, harmoniously balanced feedback system upside down into a theory of a world thrown permanently off-balance by the unintended and uncontrollable consequences of technological development (*Future* 90). Considering the lasting influence of the Gaia hypothesis on environmentalist thought and culture, one would expect such an inversion of global vision to have similar reverberations in the realm of the local and the everyday.

Indeed, in what for a cultural critic may well be one of the most intriguing facets of his theory, Beck examines the awareness of pervasive risk in its impact on modes of everyday reasoning. Some contemporary risk scenarios, unlike those of earlier ages, he claims, challenge conventional modes of perception and experience through their "mediatedness" or "second-handness" (or what other risk theorists would call "social amplification and attenuation"). Most individuals, even many scientists and engineers, cannot identify and analyze such scenarios on their own, in a process he calls "expropriation of the senses": given the complexity and specificity of contemporary technological hazards, only highly specialized experts can examine them, while the majority of scientists are as non-expert as laypersons. In Beck's view, the fact that knowledge about risks comes in such highly mediated form to the overwhelming majority of individuals leads gradually to a transformation in the logic that structures everyday experience:

> In order to perceive risks as risks and to make them a reference point for one's own thought and action, one has to *believe* in fundamentally invisible causal connections between conditions that are often substantively, temporally and geographically far removed from each other, as well as in more or less speculative projections....But that means: the invisible, more than that: that which as a matter of principle cannot be perceived, that which is only theoretically connected and calculated becomes...an unproblematic component of personal thought, perception, experience. The "experiential logic" of everyday thought is, so to speak, turned upside down. One no longer only induces general judgments from one's own experiences, but instead general knowledge that is not based on any experience becomes the determining center of one's own. Chemical formulae and reactions, invisible toxins, biological circuits and causal chains must dominate vision and thought to lead to active fighting against risks. In this sense, risk awareness is not based on "second-hand experience," but on "second-hand *non*-experience." Even more pointedly: ultimately *no one* can know of risks if knowing means having consciously experienced them. (*Risikogesellschaft* 96)

As opposed to, say, epidemics of contagious diseases, with which human societies have been familiar for millennia, modernization and globalization create risk scenarios with no known precedents in Beck's analysis. No one can forecast with certainty, for example, what the cumulative health effects might be of dozens of different toxic substances in our daily surroundings, each one at a level officially considered acceptable, but never assessed in combination. Neither is it easy, even for experts, to predict the long-term consequences of large-scale risk scenarios such as climate change or loss of biodiversity. Yet all of us, Beck points out, have come to live with a daily awareness and indeed expectation that these types of risks form part of our ordinary environment; toys of the kind I described at the beginning of this chapter, representing people in protective suits and gas masks that have come to form part of children's normal inventory of toys, indicate one of the earliest stages of initiation into daily life in the risk society.[17]

Obviously, this logic of "secondhand experience" and "secondhand nonexperience" can also be expected fundamentally to transform modes of spatial belonging and inhabitation. Indeed, the change in experiential logic that Beck describes, in which insights and incidents from other places and facets of expert knowledge come to reshape everyday reasoning, can be understood as one form of deterritorialization as I discussed it in chapter 1. Deterritorialization, as I pointed out, involves the detachment of cultural practices from their anchoring in place and their reconfiguration in relation to other places as well as other scales of spatial experience. Some of this transformation brings about alienation, social uprooting, economic displacement, cultural unease, or psychological discomfort, but some of it may also entail welcome new forms of connectivity, new choices, and a general broadening of existential horizons. Risk scenarios, especially those that do not originate locally but at the national, regional, or global scale, contribute to deterritorialization processes as they prompt individuals and communities to reconfigure their practices of inhabitation in relation to these larger sociospatial scales.

Such reconfigurations come in a wide variety of changes and adjustments that have been examined across vast portions of the social scientific literature on environmental impacts. Most obviously, risk perceptions can either intensify or break individuals' and communities' bonds to a local place. In the first case, the desire to protect an area from danger may deepen residents' affective attachments to it, or victims of a local hazard may pull together to eliminate it or defend themselves against its consequences by a variety of means (including, of course, the well known tendency of early environmentalism toward NIMBYism that sought to ward off risks from one's own backyard without close attention to the risk scenarios this displacement might generate in other communities). Conversely, the perception of danger can break inhabitants' bonds with a place and prompt them to move away, or stigmatize a site to such a degree that its material as well as aesthetic and cultural value decreases.[18] More indirectly, risk perceptions affect ways of inhabiting, using, or enjoying a place through transformations of daily habits or social customs. Local inhabitation is sometimes consciously and sometimes unconsciously, sometimes subtly and sometimes manifestly shaped by risk perceptions relating to a variety of concerns, including food sources or ways of cultivating land that are chosen with pressures from ecological depletion or market demands in mind; patterns of mobility that are shaped by perceptions of what people and places are dangerous or safe; distinctions that are drawn between activities and products that are "clean" or "dirty," "pure" or "polluted"; and processes and institutions of governance and surveillance that are designed to prevent or manage particular dangers.

Some of these adaptations to risk are short-lived responses to a temporary threat, as when food scares involving bovine spongiform encephalopathy in Britain or avian flu in Germany over the last decade prompted people to change their diets or seek out different food providers, or when news about severe acute respiratory syndrome in 2003 led tens of thousands of travelers to cancel travel plans to East Asia and Canada. Others involve more permanent changes in ways of life, such as the switch from trawling to more sustainable kinds of fishing in some parts of the world due to fears of fish stock depletion, or changes in building, heating, or waste disposal practices in view of risks from resource exhaustion or contamination. One would expect the more permanent changes to be associated with more deep-seated cultural transformations; yet temporary crises and disasters of the kind I mentioned earlier, even if they are quickly resolved, sometimes propitiate more long-lasting conceptual and cultural changes, as I will show in more detail in chapter 6.

A similar multivectoral causality characterizes local and translocal risk scenarios in their impact on forms of inhabitation. Strictly local hazards can at times resonate culturally and politically far beyond their limited geographical domain, according to the logic of "secondhand experience," as in the case of Love Canal, which led to community activism against toxic waste disposals in many other regions of the United States and beyond. Regional and global risk scenarios fall into at least two distinct categories that involve local perception and experience in quite different ways. In Turner et al.'s useful distinction, *systemic risks* such as climate change or the depletion of the ozone layer arise from systems that are global in scale, so that if they undergo change anywhere, the system as a whole is affected. *Cumulative risks*, by contrast, derive from the planet-wide summation of local changes that end up affecting large portions or even the totality of a global environmental phenomenon or resource. Cumulative risks result either from their global distribution, as in the case of groundwater depletion or biodiversity loss, or from the magnitude of their impact on a global resource, for example in the case of agricultural soil depletion or deforestation. Systemic risks can result from human activities that are not themselves global, while cumulative risks do tend to derive from very widespread processes ("Two Types" 15–16). For the purposes of my discussion here, this distinction matters because cumulative global risk scenarios tend to be perceptible at the local scale in a way that systemic ones are not, or only with a far longer delay. As a consequence, the perceptual, cognitive, and ultimately cultural mechanisms by means of which such systemic risks are addressed can be expected to differ substantially from those pertaining to cumulative ones.

It might seem intuitively plausible that in the case of cumulative risks, locally perceptible signals of environmental change—shortages of water, erosion of arable soil—would make it easier to conceive of regional and global risks that result from the multiplication of such changes. A form of inhabitation attuned to local changes in nature, in other words, might seem to offer an obvious gateway to the understanding of larger-scale risk scenarios—and that is indeed, as I showed in chapter 1, the basis for many environmentalist calls for a return to the local. Yet even in the case of cumulative risks, cultural awareness does not always follow such a direct trajectory. Tim Gallagher, in the description of his long quest for the extinct ivory-billed woodpecker that finally led to the rediscovery of one specimen in 2004, provides an interesting example of local awareness actually blocking the perception of more large-scale risk. Gallagher mentions his repeated visits to old-growth cypress forests resembling those of the southern United States in the nineteenth century, the preferred habitat of the ivory-bill, and dwells on his feelings of mourning and loss over the massive logging that eliminated most of this landscape. One of his sources, an elderly man from Louisiana, remembers asking loggers about the almost inconceivable magnitude of this forest destruction in his youth:

> When Greg was young, he talked to every old logger he could find and asked them about the old days there. Many times they would say, "You should have seen it when the big trees were here." And he would get frustrated and ask them, "Why did you cut them down if you liked them so much?" The answer was complicated. Most of the loggers were isolated, with no connection to any other group. Times were hard, the money was good, and there were thousands and thousands of trees. How could it ever end?
>
> The loggers seemed to have no idea that dozens, if not hundreds, of other crews were out there cutting away. Many came from other states—Mississippi, Arkansas, Texas—to take part in the harvest. And the logging continued right up till the end of the 1920s. "They were surprised when there were no more trees to cut," said Greg. "So that was that." (138)

This account is an intriguing example of a case in which detailed local knowledge apparently not only failed to lead to any awareness of the cumulative regional risk scenario but in fact prevented such awareness in the absence of more mediated information about the larger context. Beck's claim about the crucial importance of highly mediated information for the understanding of modern risk scenarios here confirms itself in a somewhat unexpected way; in this case, it is not so much that mediated information provides knowledge that cannot be obtained on the evidence of the senses as that it establishes the connection between perfectly perceptible evidence and the more elusive ecological systems to which it points.

The texts I will analyze in chapters 5 and 6 negotiate this question of how an awareness of risks at different scales of the local, regional, and global transforms ordinary modes of language, narrative, and thought through their novelistic scenarios. DeLillo's protagonist Jack Gladney provides an example of an individual confronting a perceptible local risk scenario with imperceptible consequences for his health and life expectancy. Powers's Laura Bodey encounters a less tangible local risk that ramifies into a global one in ways that are not quite captured by the distinction between systemic and cumulative risks, as the pesticide that perhaps caused her cancer turns out to be produced by a multinational chemical corporation with branches around the globe. The protagonists of Wolf's and

Wohmann's novels, situated in post-Chernobyl East and West Germany, experience the more subtle forms of deterritorialization that a large-scale regional disaster imposes on them. All of these novels are concerned with distinctively modern risk scenarios (though they have not always been interpreted in this way) and explore how cultural practices of inhabitation are transformed through risk scenarios that link the local in various ways to risks and institutions encompassing large regions or the planet as a whole. In the process, they also experiment with the different ways such risk experiences might be translated into narrative form and arrive, as I will show, at quite different conclusions.

The distinction between systemic and cumulative risks not only raises the question what purchase local experience has on global ecological systems but also how such a distinction relates to social networks based on risk. Many of the nonfictional texts on individuals and places exposed to ecological and technological threats, as well as quite a few of the fictional ones, centrally rely on the assumption that the experience of risk is detrimental to social cohesion; at the same time, risk in these texts sometimes brings about a collective social impulse that leads to political action as well as to a more deeply experienced local community. As Lawrence Buell has pointed out, environmental justice discourse in particular tends both to presuppose the existence of tightly knit historical communities with long traditions, and to fashion communities that seem to have coherence only in the face of risk, such as the residents of a certain ZIP code (*Writing* 41). Especially in the last two decades, the environmental justice movement has also increasingly attempted to forge international alliances between communities at risk, in the hope of creating global coalitions that might be able to resist the power of multinational corporations and, in some cases, institutions of international governance such as the World Bank or the International Monetary Fund.

From a different political perspective, the assumption that risk-sharing can generate new forms of community and political agency has led Beck to postulate the rise of what he calls a new kind of cosmopolitanism:

> *Risk-sharing* or a "*socialization of risk*"...can...become a powerful basis for community, one which has both territorial and non-territorial aspects....Post-national communities could thus be constructed and reconstructed as communities of risk. Cultural definitions of appropriate types or degrees of risk define the community, in effect, as those who share the relevant assumptions. "Risk-sharing" further involves the taking of responsibility, which again implies conventions and boundaries around a "risk community" that shares the burden. And in our high-tech world, many risk communities are potentially political communities in a new sense—because they have to live with the risks that others take. There is a basic power structure within world risk society, dividing those who produce and profit from risks and the many who are afflicted with the same risks. (*World Risk Society* 16)

This argument is not in essence so different from some claims of the environmental justice movement, except that Beck is less interested in the idea of already existing communities and their confrontation with risk than in the possibility of emergent communities and political agents that he envisions as explicitly transnational. In his perspective, such risk collectives hold the promise of transcending NIMBYist tendencies, not just through temporary action coalitions but also by becoming the building blocks of a new cosmopolitan culture, quite different from the official institutions of cosmopolitan democracy on which political scientist David Held and others have based their theories of global citizenship. This risk-based cultural solidarity, which Beck takes to be more important than bureaucratic processes and institutions, ultimately harkens back to Marx and Engels's vision of an international working class:

> Without a politically strong cosmopolitan consciousness, and without corresponding institutions of global civil society and public opinion, cosmopolitan democracy remains, for all the institutional fantasy, no more than a necessary utopia. The decisive question is whether and how a consciousness of cosmopolitan solidarity can develop. The *Communist Manifesto* was published a hundred and fifty years ago. Today, at the beginning of a new millennium, it is time for a Cosmopolitan Manifesto. The *Communist Manifesto* was about class conflict. The Cosmopolitan Manifesto is about transnational-national conflict and dialogue which has to be opened up and organized.... The key idea for a Cosmopolitan Manifesto is that there is a new dialectic of global and local questions which do not fit into national politics. (*World Risk Society* 14–15)

In his writings during the 1990s, Beck saw these questions taking shape in what he called a global "subpolitics" that unfolds both above and below the scale of the nation-state, involving actors such as nongovernmental organizations and a variety of institutions and citizens' initiatives whose role he perceives as increasingly important in the coming world risk society. In his more recent work, the idea that interdependencies arising from risks related to ecology, economy, and terrorism enforce the shaping of a cosmopolitan political order moves center stage; rather than "subpolitics," global risks in this perspective reconfigure mainstream politics itself. *Der kosmopolitische Blick* (The cosmopolitan perspective; 2004) explores the consequences of this shift both for politics and for sociological methodology.

As my main concern here is with the cultural articulations of cosmopolitanism, I cannot delve deeply into the political models that such an approach to cosmopolitanism might generate. Yet Australian political scientist Robyn Eckersley, in an original and lucid account, has explored in far greater detail than Beck what political structures an ecological democracy that thinks beyond national boundaries might aim to build, and her approach is at least worth mentioning here. Eckersley's concept of "transnationally oriented green states" (202) situates itself in between

two models of transnational democracy: Jürgen Habermas's model of supranational communities and institutions modeled on the nation-state,
whose democratic structures rely on the "communitarian" principle of be-
longingness or membership, and David Held's model of global democratic
structures based on the "cosmopolitan" principle of affectedness, according to which individuals should not be ruled by norms to which they have
not given their consent (Eckersley 173).[19] Eckersley pursues a model

> that remain[s] mindful of the insights of communitarians while also
> moving practically toward the ideals of cosmopolitans. Without knowl-
> edge of and attachment to particular persons or particular places and
> species, it is hard to understand how one might be moved to defend the
> interests of persons, places, and species in general. Local social and eco-
> logical attachments provide the basis for sympathetic solidarity with
> others; they are ontologically prior to any ethical and political struggle
> for universal environmental justice. Most environmental activists in-
> tuitively understand this and work from the premise of our unavoidable
> social and ecological embeddedness in particular places and communi-
> ties. Yet it is impossible to arrest the growing gap between those who
> generate ecological problems and those who suffer the consequences,
> along with the increasing dis-embeddedness brought about by the
> processes of economic globalization, without developing sympathetic
> solidarity with environmental victims wherever they may be located.
> The transnationally oriented green state takes the next step and offers
> practical democratic procedures for ecological citizenship within and
> beyond the state. (190)

In her exploration of what political procedures and structures might enable such a transition from an ethic of proximity to an eco-cosmopolitan
ethic (in the vocabulary I suggested in chapter 1),[20] Eckersley proposes that
instead of projecting comprehensive transnational political institutions
and structures,

> it is quite possible and feasible to transnationalize democracy in piece-
> meal, experimental, consensual, and domain-relative ways. Such an ap-
> proach would enable the practical negotiation of principles in response
> to particular transnational problems, rather than a priori. Formal
> democratic space-time coordinates would still need to come into play
> for the proper enactment of legal norms and for the substantive enjoy-
> ment of ecological citizenship rights in transboundary environmental
> domains, but these coordinates would not necessarily be the same for
> all domains. . . . Such a project would thus entail building upon, qualify-
> ing, and supplementing (rather than replacing) the principle of belong-
> ingness with the principle of affectedness. (192–93)

Eckersley here provides a general outline, filled in with more detail elsewhere in her discussion, of how transnational risk scenarios (as well as

other ecological conflicts) might become the points of departure for new forms of democracy.

Beck's vision of an international risk-based solidarity, by comparison, hovers on the border between the descriptive and the normative, between a realistic account of current political conflicts and the projection of an ideal development that is itself based on more than a little utopian thinking. Yet to the extent that one is willing to concede the usefulness of utopian models, this tendency may be less problematic than Beck's simplistic assumptions about the relationship between risk and culture. From much of the risk-theoretical work that I have surveyed in this chapter, Beck takes the important insight that the experience of risk only takes on meaning within particular cultural contexts and assumptions. But from this general insight he seems to infer that shared risk automatically implies enough cultural commonality to serve as the basis for new kinds of communities. The experiences of environmental justice advocates who have actually tried to forge such alliances, however, tell a more complex story that highlights "barriers such as differences in language, culture, education, class, and access to resources" (Kiefer and Benjamin 233). Risk communities in the developing world, as Kiefer and Benjamin show, often retain vivid memories of colonialism and neocolonialism and therefore sometimes react with wariness or suspicion to the overtures of environmental groups in the developed world. At the same time, differences in basic cultural habits such as how to advance a conversation, what kinds of knowledge to rely on, or how to act politically exacerbate the difficulties in creating effective action coalitions, let alone more long-lasting transnational communities of risk (234–35). Shared risk, in other words, remains only a first stepping-stone, so long as it is not accompanied by a more comprehensive cultural literacy that allows the members of one community to grasp what sociocultural significance the risk scenario has for the members of another.[21]

Beck's vision of a cosmopolitan consciousness and an alternative global culture that might arise from the politics of shared risk, then, needs to be complemented by the more acute sense of sociocultural differences that emerge in stark relief from the fieldwork of environmental justice activists. Yet it is also true that the environmental justice movement has often focused primarily on the urgencies of political action, mobilization, and coalition-building, with no in-depth attention to the shaping influence of different cultural frameworks of understanding. While the movement has sometimes drawn on the insights of feminist, postcolonial, and critical race theory, it has done so mostly by reconfirming central assumptions of these bodies of theory rather than showing how the context of communities exposed to ecological, economic, and technological endangerment might transform some of these foundations. As environmental justice scholar T. V. Reed has argued, "the environmental justice movement, as currently constituted, has often worked with a rather thin sense of culture and has not utilized cultural workers as much as it might" (153).

Rather than a sophisticated theoretical framework for approaching questions of crosscultural understanding and misunderstanding in an ecological context, the accounts of environmental justice fieldwork offer a rich inventory on which such a theory needs to draw in order to elaborate Beck's approach to the relationship of risk and the emergence of cosmopolitan forms of solidarity. By contrast, the attempts of anthropologists, sociologists, philosophers, and literary critics to reenvision cosmopolitanism as an effort at crosscultural literacy, which I discussed in chapter 1, do offer such a more nuanced account. These recuperations of cosmopolitanism consciously situate themselves in the unequal political and economic playing fields created by various types of globalization, though they do not, for the most part, concern themselves either with the nonhuman world or the global environmental risk scenarios I have been chiefly concerned with here. As I proposed earlier, an environmentally inflected cosmopolitanism needs to combine sustained familiarity and fluency in more than one culture with a systemic understanding of global ecology that goes beyond environmentalist clichés regarding universal connectedness and the pastoral understanding of ecology that informed earlier kinds of modern environmentalist thinking. The merit of environmental justice activism along with Beck's more sweeping vision of new forms of solidarity emerging out of global risk scenarios is their analysis of how such an eco-cosmopolitanism might link experiences of local endangerment to a sense of planet that encompasses both human and nonhuman worlds.

5

TOXIC BODIES,
CORPORATE POISONS

Local Risks and Global Systems

As has often been noted, the modern environmental movement in the United States received one of its crucial initial impulses from the publication of Rachel Carson's *Silent Spring* (1962), a book that focused on the adverse effects of excessive pesticide and herbicide use in American agriculture and households. By comparing the dangers of environmental chemicals to those of nuclear radiation, a hazard that by the early 1960s was associated with an ample body of stories and images, Carson was able to alert a population and politicians who knew little about chemical exposure in a way that other books presenting similar information did not—for example, *Our Synthetic Environment*, by Lewis Herbert (aka Murray Bookchin), which was published six months before *Silent Spring*, or Robert L. Rudd's *Pesticides and the Living Landscape*, which appeared in 1964. Exposure to environmental chemicals has remained a dominant topic in the environmental literature of the United States to this day. In the late 1970s, the Love Canal crisis, which propelled Lois Gibbs to the forefront of citizen activism against toxic waste, brought the topic back into public discussion, and gave rise to a number of studies, including Gibbs's own account, *Love Canal: My Story* (1982). The 1990s and early 2000s saw an abundance of films and books on the topic, both fictional and nonfictional: Todd Haynes's film *Safe* (1995), Theo Colborn's book *Our Stolen Future* (1996), Sandra Steingraber's nonfiction account *Living Downstream* (1997), Stephen Zaillian's film *A Civil Action* (1999), Steven Soderbergh's movie *Erin Brockovich* (2000), and Susanne Antonetta's memoir *Body Toxic* (2001), to name only a few of the best-known works, all engage with scenarios of toxic contamination and their consequences. At the same time, the burgeoning environmental justice movement in the United States drew public attention to increased risks to minority and poor communities located near dangerous industries or waste disposals.

Yet it would be a mistake to assume that this intense interest in the effect of chemicals on the human body is limited to the environmental movement. The dual nature of chemicals as toxins and medicines and the attendant fascination with altered physical and psychological states of various kinds has been a recurrent issue in American literature and culture of the last forty years. The American counterculture of the 1960s, more than its analogues in other regions, was fascinated with hallucinogenic drugs, with their ambivalent symbolic role as an instrument of liberation and a tool of addiction and subjugation, as the literature of the period, including the writings of Allen Ginsberg, William Burroughs, and Thomas Pynchon, testifies. Mainstream medical culture with its concern to develop pharmaceutical remedies for all kinds of physical and psychological conditions, as well as the New Age counterculture's attempt to both counter and replicate this regime through allegedly "natural," "herbal," and "detoxifying" remedies all bear witness to an enduring obsession to heal, alter, or improve the human body and mind by chemical means, as well as with persistent fears that such intervention might itself turn to poison (see Ross, *Strange Weather*, 15–74).

Lawrence Buell, therefore, is justified in focusing his analysis of risk perceptions in environmental literature on chemical contamination.[1] Chemical pollution is indeed a central issue for American environmentalism, at the same time that it functions as a crucial trope by means of which writers and filmmakers explore the porous boundaries between body and environment, public and domestic space, and harmful and beneficial technologies. My analysis here focuses on two novels that are not specifically environmentalist but nevertheless explore the danger of chemical contamination as part of a larger investigation of the risks to which citizens of modern societies are exposed, and of the way risk scenarios form part of the texture of contemporary sociotechnological structures. Don DeLillo's postmodern classic *White Noise* (1985) and Richard Powers's *Gain* (1998) both engage with questions of risk perception and its cultural framing in portraying a "risk society" in Beck's sense. DeLillo's *White Noise* explores a local risk scenario by means of satire and thereby raises complex questions about the role of realism and hyperbole in risk perception and representation. Richard Powers's *Gain*, by contrast, examines risk in the context of complex global systems so as to investigate how such systems might be effectively captured in narrative. Building on and modifying Lawrence Buell's analysis of "toxic discourse," this chapter foregrounds the connections between ecocriticism, risk theory, and narrative to suggest on the one hand that a focus on the notion of risk as a literary theme can substantially sharpen and shift standard interpretations of some contemporary texts, and on the other hand that a consideration of risk and the kind of narrative articulation it requires has potentially important implications for the analysis of narrative form.

1. "Unreliable Menace": Don DeLillo's *White Noise*

DeLillo's *White Noise* was published in January of 1985, only a little over a month after a toxic gas accident at a Union Carbide plant in Bhopal, India, killed at least two thousand people and injured several thousand more. The coincidence was not lost on the novel's first reviewers, who pointed out the eerie echoes between the Bhopal accident and the toxic gas incident that occurs in the novel's middle chapter.[2] This "airborne toxic event," as the media euphemistically call it, occurs in the midwestern college town of Blacksmith, where Jack Gladney, a professor of Hitler studies, lives with his wife and family. After an accident at a train depot, the gas Nyodene Derivative, a byproduct of pesticide manufacture, leaks from one of the wagons and forms a large cloud over Blacksmith, whose inhabitants receive the order to evacuate. En route to the evacuation camp, Gladney is briefly exposed to the toxic gas. When the evacuees' health data are recorded at the camp, Gladney realizes that even this short exposure might have potentially serious consequences for his health. During his interview with one of the health technicians, the following conversation unfolds:

> "Am I going to die?"
> "Not as such," [the technician] said.
> "What do you mean?"
> "Not in so many words."
> "How many words does it take?"
> "It's not a question of words. It's a question of years. We'll know more in fifteen years. In the meantime we definitely have a situation."
> "What will we know in fifteen years?"
> "If you're still alive at the time, we'll know that much more than we do now. Nyodene D. has a life span of thirty years. You'll have made it halfway through."
> "I thought it was forty years."
> "Forty years in the soil. Thirty years in the human body."
> "So, to outlive this substance, I will have to make it into my eighties. Then I can begin to relax."
> "Knowing what we know at this time."
> "But the general consensus seems to be that we don't know enough at this time to be sure of anything."
> "Let me answer like so. If I was a rat I wouldn't want to be anywhere within a two hundred mile radius of the airborne event."
> "What if you were a human?"
> He looked at me carefully....
> "I wouldn't worry about what I can't see or feel," he said. "I'd go ahead and live my life. Get married, settle down, have kids...."
> "But you said we have a situation."

"I didn't say it. The computer did. The whole system says it. It's what we call a massive data-base tally. Gladney, J.A.K. I punch in the name, the substance, the exposure time and then I tap into your computer history. Your genetics, your personals, your medicals, your psychologicals, your police-and-hospitals. It comes back pulsing stars. This doesn't mean anything is going to happen to you as such, at least not today or tomorrow. It just means you are the sum total of your data. No man escapes that." (140–41)

This conversation and others like it have generated a good deal of critical comment that focuses on how it makes death appear both real and completely vague, and how Gladney's existential concern is transformed, not without a considerable amount of humor, into a simulacrum of computer data.[3] Such a transformation is hardly surprising, many critics would argue, in a novel in which even the starkest realities seem to disappear behind layers and layers of representations and simulations. In *White Noise,* disaster victims feel unable to relate to their own situation unless it is amply covered by the media, Adolf Hitler and Elvis Presley appear side by side in an academic lecture on their relationship to their mothers, and the Nyodene D. accident turns into a mere prelude to the simulated evacuations rehearsed by Advanced Disaster Management, a company relying on the philosophy that such simulations not only prepare for but actually prevent real disasters. Gladney discovers his own nine-year-old daughter impersonating a victim in one of these simulations and remarks to the manager, perhaps sarcastically, perhaps seriously, "'Are you people sure you're ready for a simulation? You may want to wait for one more massive spill. Get your timing down'" (204). The abundance of Baudrillardesque scenes such as these has led many critics to interpret *White Noise* as a narrative showcase of the postmodern culture of the simulacrum, a novel in which simulation systematically takes precedence over whatever might be left of the real.[4]

DeLillo's undeniable emphasis on representation as reality has led critics to dismiss the novel in terms of its engagement with the problem of technological risk. A. O. Scott, for example, claims that "DeLillo's 'airborne toxic event' is freighted with symbolism: it's a projection of the ambient dread that pervades the social and emotional lives of his characters, and its source as a physical occurrence is thus irrelevant to the novel's purposes" (41).[5] Even as eminent an ecocritic as Lawrence Buell has argued that "*White Noise*'s framing of th[e] toxic event as, chiefly, a postmodern symbol of inauthenticity" reduces it "to the status of catalyst to the unfolding of the [protagonist's] culturally symptomatic vacuousness" (*Writing* 51). Hence, in Buell's view, any other disaster with no ecological implications would have served the plot just as well. Such arguments, however, have validity only if one isolates the Nyodene D. incident from the rest of the novel as the only point of engagement with technological risk scenarios. As I will argue, a diametrically opposed picture emerges when one traces

White Noise's thematic engagement with risk more systematically, and when one pursues some of the implications of risk theory for its narrative form.[6]

As a thematic motif, the Nyodene D. spillage is far from the only risk scenario the Gladney family is involved in. On the contrary, the novel abounds in pointed or casual references to the multiple technologically generated risks that the average American family encounters in daily life. Early on in the novel, for example, the Gladney children's school has to be evacuated because of toxic fumes, possibly caused, as the reader is told, by the "ventilating system, the paint or varnish, the foam insulation, the electrical insulation, the cafeteria food, the rays emitted by microcomputers, the asbestos fireproofing, the adhesive on shipping containers, the fumes from the chlorinated pool, or perhaps something deeper, finer-grained, more closely woven into the basic state of things" (35), an enumeration that—not unlike the toy figures I discussed at the beginning of chapter 4—balances humor with horror in highlighting so many potential sources of risk in the ordinary surroundings of children. Whatever their origin, these fumes are lethal enough to kill one member of the school inspection team (40). Gladney, at another point, worries over his son Heinrich, who is beginning to lose hair even though he is only fourteen, and Gladney wonders whether this might be caused by exposure to chemical waste or polluted air (22). The father of Gladney's stepdaughter, Denise, drops by on his way to a fundraiser for the Nuclear Accident Readiness Foundation, which he refers to as a "just in case kind of thing" (56). And not only the adults are aware of risks; Heinrich details the dangers of electromagnetic radiation emanating from electrical wires and appliances: "'The real issue is the kind of radiation that surrounds us every day. Your radio, your TV, your microwave oven, your power lines just outside the door, your radar speed-trap on the highway....Forget spills, fallouts, leakages. It's the things around you in your own house that'll get you sooner or later'" (174–75). Less eloquently, daughter Steffie points out the carcinogenic additives in chewing gum to her mother, Babette (41–43), and daughter Denise insists that Babette use sunscreen during her runs so as to avoid skin cancer (264).

In fact, the children at times appear to take risk more seriously than the adults. "'Every day on the news there's another toxic spill. Cancerous solvents from storage tanks, arsenic from smokestacks, radioactive water from power plants. How serious can it be if it happens all the time? Isn't the definition of a serious event based on the fact that it's not an everyday occurrence?'" Babette asks at one point (174), outlining an entire "riskscape" surrounding the family even as she denies its dangers.[7] At another point, she similarly dismisses a radio injunction to boil water before consuming it as just another fad (34). But her perception that such occurrences are frequent, at any rate, seems to be accurate: several months after the poison gas incident, Blacksmith is once again overwhelmed by airborne substances, this time in the form of chemical smells drifting into town from across the river (270–71). Along somewhat different lines, risks associated with car accidents and plane crashes are mentioned frequently in the novel, and I will comment presently on those associated with pharmaceutical products. These examples show that the "airborne toxic event" at the center of the plot is by no means an exceptional type of event, but simply one that is (or appears to be) much larger in magnitude than other hazards in the Gladneys' universe, where environmental risks ranging from the trivial to the deadly surround the average citizen. DeLillo's novel, then, is not so much about an ordinary family's encounter with one exceptionally dangerous technological accident as about the portrayal of life in the kind of "risk society" I outlined in chapter 4.[8]

From the beginning, Jack Gladney's experience of risk is intertwined with his self-perception as a member of the middle class. In the novel's first scene, he observes the students as their parents bring them back to campus at the beginning of the academic year: the fathers are "content to measure out the time, distant but ungrudging, accomplished in parenthood, something about them suggesting massive insurance coverage" (3). The bourgeois establishment, in his view, is defined by its possession of time and insurance against risk—two assets that Gladney no longer has, or thinks he no longer has, after the poison gas accident. But at the beginning of the Nyodene D. crisis, Gladney still seems to believe that being a member of the middle class is a sort of insurance against risk. When his family expresses increasing concern that they might be affected by the gas, Gladney claims:

"These things happen to poor people who live in exposed areas. Society is set up in such a way that it's the poor and the uneducated who suffer the main impact of natural and man-made disasters. People in low-lying areas get the floods, people in shanties get the hurricanes and tornados. I'm a college professor. Did you ever see a college professor rowing a boat down his own street in one of those TV floods? We live in a neat and pleasant town near a college with a quaint name. These things don't happen in places like Blacksmith." (114)

Whether Gladney himself believes this statement or primarily wants to reassure his family, he relies on the conviction that exposure to risk follows established lines of social stratification. As discussed in chapter 4, Beck argues precisely the opposite, namely, that new kinds of risk will create new types of social structure that are characteristic of a different form of modernity. In Beck's terms, Gladney here attempts to portray his own position in the risk society by means of categories that derive from the scarcity society of an earlier phase of modernity; significantly enough, he bases his argument on natural disasters such as floods and hurricanes, not on humanmade crises like the one he is already immersed in. That his assertions about the relationship between class and risk are at that moment part of a rather obvious denial strategy lends support to the claim that in *White Noise*, DeLillo is concerned with the way new kinds of risk have invaded the lives of even those citizens who might earlier have had reason to believe themselves safe from their most dire consequences.

Lawrence Buell argues that the Gladneys' death obsession, which the novel's final chapter focuses on, is "no more than tenuously linked" to the poison gas accident, for him further evidence that this event is nonessential to the plot, a mere "supporting metaphor" (*Writing* 51). In "Dylarama," the last chapter, Gladney discovers that Babette has obtained an experimental drug called Dylar that is designed to suppress fear of death in exchange for sexual favors to one of the psychopharmaceutical company's representatives. He becomes obsessed with finding and killing this man, as well as with obtaining a supply of the pills to fight his own chronic fear of dying. What he finds, however, is a man devastated by the side effects of an overdose of the medication. Gladney first attacks and injures him, but then, in a complete reversal of his plan, rescues him by taking him to a hospital. Critics other than Buell have also argued that this sequence of events does not entirely seem to make sense as a narrative plot.[9] But if *White Noise* is understood as a portrayal of the technological risk society, the plot is not as incoherent as it seems. The Gladneys' desperate hunt for a drug that might alleviate their existential fear, regardless of its experimental status and unknown side effects, is simply the narrative inversion of the risk scenario that was portrayed in the previous chapter. While the description of the poison gas accident revolves around an individual's involuntary exposure to potentially lethal risk from a chemical substance, "Dylarama" portrays the same character's voluntary acceptance of risk from another chemical substance that he hopes will counteract the effects of the first one.

That Nyodene D. and Dylar are meant to point to the complementary sides of exposure to powerful chemicals is marked quite clearly in the text. Nyodene D. forces people out of their homes, and Gladney is exposed to it outdoors, while Dylar foregrounds the penetration of chemicals into the domestic sphere. For this reason, the health technician's advice to Gladney to ignore his health prospects and "get married, settle down and have kids" is doubly ironic (141): not only is this piece of advice offered by a young man to a college professor in his fifties who has been married four times with three children and two stepchildren, it also projects the domestic sphere as a way out of the uncertainties of chemical risk assessment. As it turns out, however, the family home exposes the individual to its own array of chemical hazards. When Gladney casually remarks, early in the novel, that he regularly takes "blood pressure pills, stress pills, allergy pills, eye drops, aspirin. Run of the mill.... Everybody takes something" (62), he gives a first glimpse of the multiple therapeutic chemicals that form part of daily domestic routine. The question that surfaces in this early scene as to what side effects such drug combinations might have only unfolds in its full significance later, when Gladney discovers the nature of the new pills his wife has been taking. But even at this early moment in the novel, it becomes clear that the family homestead offers no refuge from chemical exposure. If Nyodene D. threatens the community and the public sphere, Dylar signals the presence of chemical hazards in the privacy of the domestic realm.

Both substances, moreover, have effects on the human body that are only partially known but potentially lethal. "'In powder form [Nyodene D.]'s colorless, odorless and very dangerous, except no one seems to know exactly what it causes in humans or in the offspring of humans. They tested for years and either they don't know for sure or they know and aren't saying,'" Heinrich comments during the evacuation (131). Similarly, Babette explains, official tests of the drug Dylar were suspended because the company considered them too fraught with risk: "'I could die. I could live but my brain could die. The left side of my brain could die but the right side could live....Mr. Gray wanted me to know the risks'" (193). The side effects of the two substances that actually manifest themselves in the novel are symmetrical inversions of each other: déjà vu, an unexpected onslaught of memory, is the most lasting observable aftereffect of Nyodene D. in Blacksmith, while Babette begins to suffer from memory lapses after taking Dylar. Jack Gladney, finally, articulates the complementarity of the two chemicals quite explicitly as he reflects on Dylar: "Would it ever work...? It was the benign counterpart of the Nyodene menace...releasing benevolent chemicals into my bloodstream, flooding the fear-of-death part of my brain....Technology with a human face" (211). The plot of *White Noise*, then, not only juxtaposes the deadly and life-giving facets of technology, but quite specifically confronts the protagonist's fear of lethal risk in one case with his willingness to accept the same risk in another. Similarly, the novel points up the implicit contradiction in Babette's attempts to lose weight for health reasons with her reckless acceptance of as serious a health risk as losing half of her brain capacity. In scenes such as these, *White Noise* showcases the difference in assessments of voluntary and involuntary risks that, as I pointed out in chapter 4, risk analysts have persistently found in their studies. Beyond that, it portrays the complex psychological and cultural rationalities characters deploy in their day-to-day encounters with risk in a society that surrounds them with all manner of technological artifacts and institutions.

Because it is difficult to justify these decisions on the part of the protagonists as rational choices, DeLillo may well be drawing a satirical portrait of the paradoxes risk awareness can lead to. But as many critics have noted, the Gladneys' fear of death seems irrational in the first place, not justified by any acute danger. This is true if, once again, one takes the poison gas accident to be the only instance of a real hazard in the novel; admittedly, Jack Gladney's fear of dying precedes rather than originates in his exposure to the gas, which merely confirms and reinforces it. But if the narrative aims at the broader portrayal of a society in which individuals and communities are exposed to multiple risks, many of which are completely new and at least partially unknown in their effects, then the Gladneys' existential fear may not be as unfounded as it seems: it is precisely the fact that so many of these risks are not yet known that justifies it. In other words, the portrayal of the risk society in *White Noise* is based on two dimensions: on the one hand, the novel refers not just to one technological disaster but to a range of risks from the trivial to the lethal; on the other hand, this wide spectrum of risk scenarios hints that there might be many others hidden in the plain sight of ordinary life, dangers that simply have not yet been detected. If, as Beck has argued, risk awareness is based not only on experience and secondhand experience but also on "secondhand nonexperience," that is, on the expectation of risks that no one has consciously experienced yet (*Risikogesellschaft* 96), then the Gladneys' fear of dying no longer appears completely unmotivated.

One might object that this analysis amounts to reading *White Noise* as a realist novel, a documentary of the risk society. Clearly, such an interpretation cannot hold true in any simple sense. *White Noise* is above all a satire of the contemporary, juxtaposing painfully realistic details from the world of supermarkets, credit cards, and brand-name advertising with obviously absurd, hyperbolic, and humorous elements: a department of Hitler studies chaired by a professor who does not speak German, a tourist attraction called "The Most Photographed Barn in America," pills that cause one to take words for objects, nuns who admit they do not believe in God but make believe they do for the sake of nonbelievers. To the extent that my analysis of the importance of risk for the plot is accurate, one might argue that DeLillo mocks contemporary risk perceptions rather than engaging them seriously. Undeniably, to the extent that the Gladney family's daily life is an object of satire in the novel, so are their experiences of risk. Yet the text is quite a bit more complex than that. Even calling it a satire and identifying its realistic and hyperbolic elements relies on the assumption that we as readers know what the real world is like and how DeLillo's narrative universe differs from it. But in practice, the line between realism and hyperbole turns out to be often difficult to draw: we may agree that a department of Hitler studies sounds implausible, but how about scholars who study narratives on cereal boxes and offer courses on car crash scenes in American movies? Pills that make one take words for things do not sound realistic, yet the sometimes uncanny side effects of psychopharmaceuticals are a matter of common knowledge. The description of media coverage of the Nyodene D. accident with its gradually intensifying euphemisms is undoubtedly very funny, but it would be easy to come up with comparable examples of the "social attenuation" of risk at the hands of the media in the "real" world. *White Noise* certainly functions as a satire at one level, then, but it is an uneasy satire that at another level seriously puts in question the reader's ability to distinguish the real from the fake and the hyperbolic.[10]

The ontological uncertainty that results from this deployment of the satiric mode has been theorized in a broader context as one of the hallmarks of postmodernist fiction by Brian McHale (chap. 1). But while McHale associates such uncertainty for the most part with clearly antirealist forms of narration, it is possible to claim, in the context of a risk-theoretical approach to narrative, that the destabilization of distinctions between the real and the nonreal can itself serve specific realist objectives. Making such distinctions is precisely the task the characters in DeLillo's novel have to perform repeatedly in their assessments of risk or "unreliable menace," as the text calls it at one point (184). The novel's narrative mode, which exacts similar decision-making from the readers, therefore mirrors in its narrative form the fundamental uncertainties that beset risk assessments in the "real world." Obviously, it is not necessary to assume that this use of satire aims exclusively at the portrayal of risk scenarios. Risk assessments are clearly not the only context in which DeLillo's protagonists have to make judgments about verisimilitude; the problem similarly arises in their encounters with mass media, advertisements, or scholarly arguments about culture. But decisions about risk do ultimately underlie many of these encounters, most obviously when media or advertising statements allude to real or imaginary hazards and miraculous remedies, or when discussions about popular culture turn on the way it portrays death. Because these topics recur so insistently, it is possible to argue that not so much in spite of as because of its use of satire, *White Noise* engages the problematic of risk both in its themes and its narrative form. Many of the hyperboles and simulations that have typically been read as examples of postmodern inauthenticity become, from this perspective, manifestations of daily encounters with risks whose reality, scope, and consequences cannot be assessed with certainty.

2. Toxic Systems: Richard Powers's *Gain*

Published more than a decade later than *White Noise,* Powers's *Gain* relies on a similar social scenario of white, middle-class U.S. citizens exposed to risk. Yet Powers reflects in far greater detail than DeLillo on what produces such risks and how they are bound into socioeconomic systems that span the globe. The novel is organized into two strands of plot that are narrated in alternating sections. The first outlines approximately 150 years in the development of a company that starts out as J. Clare & Sons, a family soap-and candle-making business in 1830s Boston. In the course of its long history of technological invention, shrewd business maneuvers, near failures, mergers, cutbacks, and expansions, this company has evolved by the 1990s into Clare International, a multinational chemical and pharmaceutical corporation that manufactures everything from detergents, cosmetics, and drugs to pesticides, fertilizers, and synthetic construction materials. Clare's Agricultural Division is headquartered in the midwestern town of Lacewood, where it has for decades been the community's major employer and financial mainstay. The other plot strand revolves around Laura Bodey, a middle-aged, divorced real estate agent with two children who lives in Lacewood. During a routine medical examination, she is diagnosed with ovarian cancer, and the novel follows her through surgery and chemotherapy to her final decline and death. In her last months, Bodey discovers not only that some of the chemicals Clare produces have been associated with cancer but also that a class action lawsuit is in progress against the company, which her ex-husband, Don, urges her to join. She does, after some resistance, and although the settlement money comes too late to benefit her, it is passed on to her children. A third narrative element is set apart from these two plots: descriptions and quotations of legal documents and above all, advertising materials referring to the Clare corporation and its products, which often form an ironic counterpoint to the evolving story of Bodey's cancer.[11]

Gain has some obvious similarities with *White Noise* in its portrayal of technological risk. Both focus on chemical exposure; both describe it as befalling a dysfunctional but all-too-normal family in a midwestern small town.[12] In both cases, the choice of location and type of family signal risk scenarios affecting a social class that formerly believed itself exempt from such environmental dangers. Most importantly, both novels attempt to capture the dual nature of chemical substances as killers and cures: the antithesis between poison and drug structures the juxtaposition between Nyodene D. and Dylar just as it does that between the herbicide that may have triggered Laura Bodey's cancer and the drugs she is given during chemotherapy. In both cases, the antithesis is an uneasy one, as the therapies fail and their side effects turn out to be potentially as serious as the symptoms they were designed to cure. But the play on toxins and drugs, on involuntary risk from chemical exposure and voluntary risk from substances that might bring benefit, is ultimately developed into a quite different conceptualization of risk in *Gain*.

White Noise puts considerable emphasis on the substances themselves, the way they enter human bodies and the time intervals and circumstances under which they take effect. This emphasis is obvious not only in the conversations Gladney has with doctors and technicians about his toxic gas exposure but also in the episode in which a neurochemist explains the sophisticated physical and chemical mechanisms of Dylar to him (187–89). Powers displays similar attention to detail in the description of Laura Bodey's chemotherapy, in which the names, quantities, ingestion times, and effects of all the medications are presented in excruciating detail. But the same is not true of the substance that might have caused Bodey's cancer, the herbicide she used in her gardening. The most obvious reason for this elision seems to be that there is no way of being sure. As Bodey discovers, once her awareness of environmental chemicals has been kindled, she is surrounded by chemicals, to the point where it is impossible to get rid of them:

> No longer her home, this place they have given her to inhabit. She cannot hike from the living room to the kitchen without passing an exhibit. Floor by Germ-Guard. Windows by Cleer-Thru. Table by Colonial-Cote. The Bodey mansion, that B-ticket, one-star museum of trade. But where else can she live?
>
> She vows a consumer boycott, a full spring cleaning. But the house is full of them. . . . They paper her cabinets. They perch on her microwave, camp out on her stove, hang from her shower head. Clare hiding under the sink, swarming in her medicine chest, lining the shelves in the basement, parked out in the garage, piled up in the shed.
>
> Her vow is hopeless. Too many to purge them all. Every hour of her life depends on more corporations than she can count. (303–4)

This profusion of potentially dangerous products eerily echoes Heinrich's remark in *White Noise* that " 'it's the things around you in your own house that'll get you sooner or later' " (175). The reason one is tempted to pick out the herbicide from this lineup is that it is the one that Bodey most obviously recognizes: when Don, in a whole list of Clare products that are suspected of being carcinogenic, mentions only the first two syllables of its name, "Atra-," Bodey immediately thinks of the garden she loves and agrees without further ado to join the lawsuit.[13] In part, what is at work here is unquestionably the rhetoric of "disrupted pastoral" that Lawrence Buell has diagnosed as one of the elements of discourse about toxicity (*Writing* 36–38): the garden, Bodey's own plot of unspoiled nature, turns out to be what may be slowly killing her. *May* be killing her: the novel never confirms that this is so, never even completes the name of the guilty product. This uncertainty is quite deliberate and points to a structure of causality quite different from the one that informs *White Noise*. In contrast to Jack Gladney, who declares, somewhat melodramatically, after his toxic exposure, "Death has entered. It is inside you" (141–42), no concrete moment of poisoning can be identified in *Gain*. For Powers, the real problem of toxicity derives not from any concrete substance but from the complex technoeconomic system that has evolved over more than a century to deliver chemical products to individuals.

It is above all the novel's narrative structure, with its stark juxtaposition of the rise of a company and the decline of an individual, that makes this point. From the outset, the inverted plotlines of these stories suggest that Clare is causally related to Bodey's illness, though the concrete circumstances only emerge later on.[14] The causal link is reinforced through the play on words related to the body. The female protagonist's name, of course, is merely a misspelling of the word "body," and her antagonist turns out to be an "incorporated" company:[15] "The law now declared the Clare Soap and Chemical Company one composite body: a single, whole, and statutorily enabled person...an artificial being, invisible, intangible, and existing only in contemplation of law" (158). In the historical narrative, Powers spends considerable time describing the rise of the incorporated enterprise as a legal concept in the late nineteenth century, which he characterizes as the transfer of individual rights to the business company. Part of the point in juxtaposing the two narrative strands, then, is to show how the corporate body and the individual body depend on each other, and how the corporate organism can become a lethal threat to the individual one. More than any single substance and more even than the whole array of products it delivers, it is the corporation as a social form that kills Laura Bodey.

But the play on incorporated and embodied beings already reveals that the relationship between the two narrative strands is not one of pure antagonism. If the metaphor of the body connects them, so does the metaphor of cancerous growth. Just as Bodey's cancer returns and spreads after surgery and chemotherapy, so the Clare Company keeps growing in spite of economic recessions, adverse legislation, and internal crises that sometimes take it to the brink of failure (see Caldwell C4; Williams, "Issue" para. 10). Through this continued expansion, the family business of the early nineteenth century evolves into a multinational by the end of the twentieth. And even money that Clare disburses to its opponents seems inevitably destined to further corporate growth, as is made clear by the settlement money Bodey's children receive from the class action lawsuit after her death. Years later, as Bodey's son Tim starts working in the computer industry, he helps develop software that predicts and even manipulates the behavior of certain protein sequences, producing a "chemical assembly plant at the level of the human cell" that will be able, it is hoped, to cure cancer (355). In order to put this software to use, he and his friends decide that with the help of his savings, they will incorporate. Indirectly and with considerable time delay, corporate money generates yet another corporate body. This new corporation may be able to cure the cancer the old one caused, but in that very process it can only worsen the other cancer that is incorporated business itself. The novel's ending, then, is curiously optimistic and pessimistic at the same time.

Because he portrays the multinational corporation as a lethal risk both in its products and by virtue of its structure, Powers has been accused by some reviewers of mounting an "assault on corporate America" (Caldwell C4; see also Kakutani E6). Others have pointed out that there is a good deal of admiration and optimism in his portrayal of capitalist enterprise (Kirn 103; Williams, "Issue" paras. 13–14). These diverging assessments are due to the fact that Powers, especially in the first half of the novel, considers risk in both its negative and its positive dimensions: not only as danger or hazard but also as opportunity, as the voluntary acceptance of uncertainty or danger in the expectation of profit. One of the Clare founding fathers, for example, is described as "handl[ing] cotton and indigo and potash. But above all else, he dealt in risk. Profit equaled uncertainty times distance. The harder it was to haul a thing to where it humanly belonged, the more one made" (10). There is indeed a good deal of admiration in Powers's descriptions of how the first few generations of Clares deal with economic risk and the frequent setbacks it imposes, and how they manage it with perseverance, ingenuity, and skill. But the breaking point seems to come with the rise of the incorporated enterprise, precisely because at that moment the company is allowed to continue making a profit without incurring all the risks it formerly had to confront. Powers places great emphasis on the concept of "limited liability" in this context: "If the Fifth and Fourteenth Amendments combined to extend due process to all individuals, and if the incorporated business had become a single person under the law, then the Clare Soap and Chemical Company now enjoyed all the legal protections afforded any individual by the spirit of the Constitution. And for the actions of that protected person, for its debts and indiscretions, no single shareholder could be held liable," he points out, and quotes the definition of a corporation from Ambrose Bierce's *Devil's Dictionary:* "An ingenious device for obtaining individual profit without individual responsibility" (159; see Williams "Issue" para. 5). Business that faces risk and engages it creatively is described approvingly, while business that is shielded from risk becomes a hazard to those in its environment.

In *Gain*, then, the risk of chemical exposure is represented not so much in terms of the mysterious and dangerous substances that occupy center stage in DeLillo; beyond such specific materials, it is a complex system of the kind described by Thomas Hughes that comes to embody risk in Powers's novel. While DeLillo focuses on the hazardous substances whose origins and effects are difficult for average individuals to discover and understand, Powers shifts the emphasis to the complex technoeconomic systems that deliver such substances, whose workings are even more impenetrable to the ordinary citizen. In fact, they are nearly impossible to control even by those who do understand sowme of them: toward the end, the novel gives a brief glimpse of Franklin Kennibar, CEO of Clare International, reflecting on his own powerlessness in crucial decisions about the company. These systems beyond comprehension and control really are the overarching risk that *Gain* seeks to address, a risk of which household toxins are only the most minor, if still potentially lethal, manifestations.

Resistance to these complex systems is as futile in Powers as it is unimaginable in DeLillo. Bodey's daughter and her friends publicly burn their Clare cosmetics in a televised protest against the company, but such temporary outbursts and the more protracted lawsuits against Clare in the end produce merely a shifting of the problem with no solution.[16] With lower ratings on the Stock Exchange, Clare sells its Agricultural Division to Monsanto some time after Laura Bodey's death, and Monsanto two years later relocates the agricultural products plant to a *maquiladora*, precipitating Lacewood into economic ruin. Corporate deals and global expansion thereby cancel any possibility of resistance. Ironically enough, the character that comes closest to offering some hope for opposition is Bodey's former husband, Don, whom she divorced because, among other things, she could not stand his habit of seeing connections, conspiracies, and cover-ups everywhere. Don is the one who, as she herself notes, knows how to ask all the right questions about her cancer diagnosis and therapy, studies the medical background, finds out about the Clare connection, and pushes her to join the lawsuit. Indefatigable in his search for accurate and comprehensive information, Don is the only one who achieves some measure of knowledge and success in the struggle with Clare.[17] But nothing he does approaches any serious challenge to the underlying system, and Powers's novel as a whole does not hold out prospects of any change. Against the complex system of Clare's global body, the local bodies of individuals or small communities are powerless.

But while *Gain* portrays, with astonishing conceptual sophistication, individuals' inability to resist or even comprehend the worldwide networks that entangle them, its narrative structure does not in the end offer a persuasive formal correlative for this approach to the global. Indeed, Powers's narrative strategies suggest that whatever difficulties the *characters* may encounter in their attempts to grapple with the global corporate world, the *readers* can rely on the comprehensive map that the self-assured omniscient narrator unfolds before them. It is precisely the novel's split into two narrative strands that creates this schism: the historical narrative acquaints the reader with a wealth of detail about the development and functioning of multinational corporations and their relation to risk scenarios, while such insight is not available to Laura Bodey and other characters, even though they may occasionally glimpse a fragment of this background. Mostly, the characters perceive the corporation through the kinds of language that are exemplified in the novel's third narrative component—snippets of advertising, corporate self-promotion, and legal documents gleaned from Clare's discursive archive. As noted earlier, these rhetorical samples often stand in ironic contrast to the actual evolution of Clare International, and even more so to its effects on the environment and public health as they are spelled out in the two narrative strands.

Powers here deploys a narrative technique derived from the modernist urban novels of John Dos Passos, James Joyce, and Alfred Döblin that I already discussed in chapter 2 in the context of John Brunner's *Stand on Zanzibar* and David Brin's *Earth:* the insertion of fragments of "authentic" discourse from a variety of modern institutions and media into a fictional story.[18] This transfer of a technique that originally served to illustrate the bewildering diversity and fragmentation of languages in the modernist metropolis to the portrayal of a multinational corporation is in and of itself not unproblematic, since Powers ultimately aims to capture not heterogeneity at all but precisely the dangerous singularity of purpose that lurks behind the apparent diversity of consumer products. But whatever effect these high modernist fragments might have is, at any rate, neutralized by their insertion into an omniscient narration that provides the reader with just the kind of overarching and authoritative information that is usually not available in *Manhattan Transfer, Ulysses,* or *Berlin Alexanderplatz.* The shock, surprise, and disorientation such fragments cause in high modernist novels and postmodernist descendants such as *Stand on Zanzibar* or *Earth* are absorbed, in *Gain,* by a mode of narration that consistently restores context, control, and orientation to the reader; narrative collage is reabsorbed into orderly progression.

In the last third of the novel, Powers resorts to a somewhat different technique to portray the workings of Clare International. In some sections, he juxtaposes snapshots of individuals in some way involved with the company and its products across the globe; in one, he focuses on a specific consumer product, a disposable camera, and traces back the processes and materials that went into its making to their places of origin around the planet. This stylistically intriguing and innovative passage centers on the insight that "plastic happens; that is all we need to know on earth. History heads steadily for a place where things need not be grasped to be used" (347). It counteracts this reification of consumer objects by showing one of them gradually emerging out of a network of globally dispersed raw materials and production and distribution processes:

> The camera jacket says: "Made In China With Film From Italy Or Germany." The film itself accretes from more places on the map than emulsion can cover. Silver halide, metal salts, dye couplers, bleach fixatives, ingredients gathered from Russia, Arizona, Brazil, and underwater seabeds, before being decanted in the former DDR. Camera in a pouch, the true multinational: trees from the Pacific Northwest and the southeastern coastal plain. Straw and recovered wood scrap from Canada. Synthetic adhesive from Korea. Bauxite from Australia, Jamaica, Guinea. Oil from the Gulf of Mexico or North Sea Brent Blend, turned to plastic in the Republic of China before being shipped to its mortal enemies on the Mainland for molding. Cinnabar from Spain. Nickel and titanium from South Africa. Flash elements stamped in Malaysia, electronics in Singapore. Design and color transfers drawn up in New York. Assembled and shipped from that address in California by a merchant fleet beyond description, completing the most heavily choreographed conference in existence. (347–48)

From what follows, it is clear that this globally assembled object was once in the possession of Laura Bodey, who left it behind in a drawer next to one of her hospital beds. It is, in fact, a memento mori of sorts, as its appearance follows the last scene in which the reader sees Bodey alive. But even if she were not yet dead by the time the narrator draws up the camera's map of global origins, it is clear that Bodey had no access to this kind of detailed information while the camera was in her possession. What presents itself to the character as a finished product that provides little information about itself—except, significantly, the manufacturer's warnings and disclaimers of liability—is portrayed for the reader as a shape that gradually emerges from the planetary dispersion of its raw materials. Interestingly, however, the human design, work, and organization that go into this emergence are downplayed in the foregoing passage, whose lack of inflected verbs and passive constructions foreground its elision of agency: the object seems to be assembling itself before the reader's eyes. The critique implicit in this description clearly aims less at capitalism's exploitation of human beings than at its waste of global resources: "The entire engineering magnificence was designed to be pitched. Labor, materials, assembly, shipping, sales markups and overheads, insurance, international tariffs—the whole prodigious creation costs less than ten dollars. The world sells to us at a loss, until we learn to afford it" (348).

Tracing a trajectory from photosynthesis to photography—from the trees that are felled for the camera's cardboard packaging ("[a] thing that once lived for light" [345]) to the pictures on its forgotten film—this section stands out in its conceptual sweep and industrial lyricism. But considered as part of the overall narrative structure, it presents a problem similar to the alternation of the two narrative strands with their punctuation by fragments of corporate discourse or, for that matter, the occasional allegorization of Clare International as the protagonist of an unfolding *Bildungsroman*.[19] All these strategies present to the reader a fictional world in which the individual is shaped by, dependent on, and intermittently threatened by networks of global capitalism that she has few resources to recognize and comprehend, let alone resist. Yet the fundamental challenges to ordinary conceptions of individuality, privacy, and freedom that this vision articulates are not translated into any disturbance in the reading process. While the novel shows in detail how individuals and local communities cannot know or control the corporate forces that shape their existence, this panorama is drawn up by a narrator who knows the corporation in both its historical and its geographical extension down to the most minute details, and who delivers them in an idiom that never questions the reader's ability to grasp and connect these details. This narrative strategy is, in the end, far removed from DeLillo's, whose subtle deployment of satire defies readers' sense of realism and reality as they encounter a fictional world whose risk scenarios challenge the characters in a similar way. It is even more fundamentally opposed to the narrative techniques of Burroughs or Pynchon, as whose literary successor Powers has often been designated. Burroughs, Pynchon, or Kathy Acker, all of whom similarly place their protagonists in worlds that are shaped by forces and institutions they are ill equipped to understand or combat, persistently refuse to reassure their readers that they, after all, can grasp this world with the help of omniscient narrators and realist narration. On the contrary, these authors constantly challenge their readers to reflect on the kinds of cognitive strategies and language that might be able to map global connections at which their own novels can only hint. In *Gain*, by contrast, the self-assurance of the narrator's command of the global and his transparent (though complex) language remain in tension with the scenario of individual powerlessness vis-à-vis the global that the novel portrays. In this respect, the novel's formal accomplishment lags behind its conceptual sophistication.

These differences notwithstanding, both Powers and DeLillo place their protagonists in environments fraught with multiple risks of the most varied kinds, and one of the characters' central challenges is to gain awareness of these riskscapes and find ways of living and dying within them. In both novels, chemical toxins become the most crucial of these risks—as agents that effectively blur the boundaries between body and environment, domestic and public spheres, and between beneficial and harmful technologies. It is in the territory between these realms that the uncertainties of risk perception and risk assessment play themselves out. Aesthetically, *White Noise* remains the more interesting novel, as it translates these uncertainties into the uneasy satire, the "unreliable menace" I analyzed earlier. But it is able to do so because it limits the conceptual horizon of risk perception to the individual and the local, while Powers attempts precisely to move beyond these limitations. As he delivers a detailed account of complex and global technoeconomic systems as a source of risk through an omniscient narrator, Powers takes an important step toward highlighting the ways local inhabitation is deterritorialized by global networks. Yet his narrative technique, for the most part, reverts to the "outside" view of the globe that was symbolized in the 1960s by the image of the Blue Planet, rather than suggesting how this perspective might formally be integrated with the multiple different viewpoints and approaches that, as theories of cosmopolitanism would insist, go into the making of images of the global. Like authors such as Brunner, Brin, and Cage, some of whose works I discussed in chapter 2, Powers seems to be aware of the possibilities that the techniques of the high modernist urban novel hold out for such an integration. But unlike these more experimental authors, he uses these narrative strategies in a way that remains decorative rather than structural. Nevertheless, in juxtaposing an apparently purely local story with a global institution, Powers moves toward a portrayal of transnational risk scenarios that are sure to gain steadily in importance as a central issue of concern for the literature and arts of the twenty-first century.

6

AFTERGLOW

Chernobyl and the Everyday

---

1. Global Chernobyl

"Then the third angel sounded and a great star fell from heaven, burning like a torch, and it fell on a third of the rivers and on the springs of water. The name of the star is Wormwood. A third of the waters became wormwood, and many men died from the water because it was bitter." This prediction from the Apocalypse of John (8: 10–11) took on a surprising new meaning in the early morning hours of April 26, 1986, when reactor 4 of the nuclear power plant at Chernobyl near the town of Pripyat, Ukraine, exploded and sent a plume of radioactive dust into the air. Called "Chornobyl" in Ukrainian, the place name is identical to the word for "wormwood," a particular kind of plant, in this language; in the aftermath of the accident, this coincidence was frequently referred to as a means of highlighting what many in the Soviet Union and around the world perceived as nothing less than an apocalyptic day of reckoning for modern technology. Scientists and writers alike seized on allusions to the "star Chernobyl" so as to impress upon their audiences the magnitude of a disaster many of whose most serious consequences remained eerily invisible to the senses. The millennial reference also helped to counteract the initial delays, obfuscations and distortions in information provided by the Gorbachev government, whose newly declared policy of *glasnost* here egregiously failed one of its first serious tests.

The causes of this event, whose probability had been rated as one in ten thousand years by Soviet scientists, nevertheless soon emerged under national and international pressure.[1] During the twenty-four hours leading up to the explosion, plant operators had conducted what was, ironically enough, intended to be a safety experiment—investigating how long the reactor would continue to provide turbine energy in case of a power failure. Over the course of this test, unsafe features of the RBMK-1000 reactor design combined with insufficient safety procedures and outright violation of some safety protocols on the part of the operators to produce the largest accident in the history of nuclear energy generation. Over two hundred people were diagnosed with radiation sickness, and thirty-one, most of them firefighters brought on the scene to extinguish the reactor core fire, died as a direct consequence of the accident. Approximately 116,000 people from surrounding areas were evacuated.[2] The radioactive cloud that arose from the explosion was initially driven northwest to Latvia, Lithuania, and Scandinavia by prevailing winds. On subsequent days, wind currents carried the radioactivity first west to Poland, Austria, parts of Germany, Switzerland, Italy, and France, then northwest to the rest of Germany, the Netherlands, and Great Britain, and later northeast into Russia. Local weather conditions crucially affected the amount of contamination in different places, since rain helped to bring down the radioactive dust to ground level. Altogether, more than twenty countries and four hundred million people were subject to fallout from Chernobyl, and some of the radiation was measurable as far away as the United States.

Chernobyl therefore turned into a truly transnational risk scenario. Not only the radioactive fallout crisscrossed national borders, however, but also information flows about the event. News about the accident emerged not in the Soviet Union but in Sweden, where authorities measured elevated radiation levels on April 28 and initiated inquiries about its origin. In response, the Gorbachev administration informed foreign governments before its own population, parts of which therefore learned about the accident from foreign sources. During the crisis, east and west Europeans relied on media newscasts as their main source of information about the accident, as well as for instructions on how to avoid exposure to radiation. These instructions varied from country to country, with some governments recommending consumption of iodine to prevent absorption of radioactive iodine into the thyroid glands, some warning against outdoor activities, others advising against the consumption of fresh foods such as milk and vegetables, and yet others ordering the destruction of certain harvests such as lettuce and cabbage. In the weeks that followed, information about the relaxation or termination of such safety measures also varied considerably. Inevitably, this variation generated a great deal of uncertainty among the affected populations as to the magnitude of the danger and the appropriate responses, producing a wide range of cultural reactions, from fears, rumors, and proposed home remedies against radiation sickness all the way to jokes. Chernobyl, therefore, turned into a paradigmatic example of how risk scenarios are socioculturally mediated, magnified, minimized, and understood in a variety of cultural contexts.

The complex intersections of technology, politics, media, and international relations in a catastrophe with regional and even global ramifications also made it an eerily perfect instantiation of the kinds of hazards that, according to Beck, characterize the emergent risk society of the late twentieth and early twenty-first centuries. As it traveled across borders, the fallout from the explosion did indeed affect individuals and communities of the most varied backgrounds without regard for national or social distinctions, but merely on the basis of the contingencies of wind and weather. Beck had already finished writing *Risikogesellschaft* when the Chernobyl accident occurred. According to his preface, dated May 1986, the disaster seemed to him to turn what he intended as predictions for the future into harsh reflections on an all-too-present state of things:

> The discourse about the (industrial) *risk society* ... has been given a bitter taste of truth. Much of the argument I still had to struggle for in the writing—the imperceptibility of hazards, their dependence on knowledge, their transnational character, "ecological expropriation," the switch from normalcy to absurdity etc.—reads like a flat description of the present after Chernobyl. Oh, that it had remained the evocation of a future to be prevented! (*Risikogesellschaft* 10–11)

Years later, he again reaffirmed the accident's paradigmatic status as an icon of the risk society:

> The entry into risk society occurs at the moment when the hazards which are now decided and consequently produced by society *undermine and/or cancel the established safety systems of the welfare state's existing risk calculations.*...[T]o express it by reference to a single example: the injured of Chernobyl are today, years after the catastrophe, not even all *born* yet.
>
> (*World Risk Society* 76–77)

If the Chernobyl disaster, in its scope as well as the number of populations affected by it, seemed like the realization of some critics' worst predictions of technological apocalypse, it also, as time went by, raised the question of how such a millennial event could or should become part of everyday life and awareness. Many of the literary texts that were written in response to the crisis take up this question. Most of them focus primarily on the fate of local residents and rescue workers who were directly exposed to radiation or evacuated from their homes in the intermediate aftermath of the explosion. In these texts, from folk ballads and poems to plays such as *Sarcophagus: A Tragedy* (1987), by Vladimir Gubaryev, and novels such as *The Star Chernobyl* (1987), by Russian émigré Julia Voznesenskaya, *Chernobyl* (1987), by American science fiction writer Frederik Pohl, and *The Sky Unwashed* (2000), by Ukrainian American novelist Irene Zabytko, the emphasis lies on the way catastrophe upsets and undermines everyday life and the assumptions and expectations that shape it.[3] But the literary texts that raise the most interesting cultural and linguistic issues in the representation of crisis and routine are those that focus on individuals who experience the crisis from far away in a highly mediated way, struggle to understand its consequences and translate their understanding into language and narrative form. *Störfall: Nachrichten eines Tages* (Accident: A day's news), by East German novelist Christa Wolf, and *Der Flötenton* (Sound of the Flute), by West German author Gabriele Wohmann, both published in 1987, raise the question of how individuals can and should live in a globalized environment where risks transcend national borders and are not readily accessible to our physical senses, linguistic conventions, or social institutions. Because such regional and global risk scenarios challenge conventional language as well as common-sense reasoning, addressing this question involves narrative style and strategy as much as content.

In Wolf's and Wohmann's novels, the protagonists are forced to reflect on the ways they inhabit their local places and daily routines at a moment when both are under threat from forces that originated far away, outside the reach of any immediate action or political engagement they could undertake to counter its effects. While Wolf describes one day, during which her main character undergoes the shock of first learning about the Chernobyl disaster, Wohmann focuses on its long-term impact over the months that follow in the lives of various characters, as consciousness of the accident increasingly becomes part of their experiential background. In spite of their considerable differences in perspective, scope, and style, three crucial concerns inform both novels. First and most centrally, both investigate how the rhythms and routines of daily life are affected by a transnational environmental crisis, and how daily life can and should be lived in the aftermath. Second, both novels foreground the way a regional risk scenario such as Chernobyl transforms the individual's relationship to the local and deterritorializes the experience of place, in the sense that it detaches cultural practices from the local as their most important shaping framework, in ways I have explored theoretically in chapters 1 and 4. Third, both texts portray the characters' increasingly deterritorialized relationship to the local in a context of social and emotional relationships that are already geographically removed and technologically mediated in much the same way the crisis itself is; in fact, these relationships ultimately function as a metaphor for the experience of risk in both novels. The relationship between environmental crisis and daily routine in an increasingly globalized world, therefore, requires a reformulation of basic environmentalist and ecocritical assumptions about the urgency of establishing a "sense of place": in Wolf's and Wohmann's novels, such a sense of place cannot be conceived outside of a sense of transnational connectedness.

2. Crisis: Christa Wolf's *Störfall*

Wolf's novel focuses on the day when news about the Chernobyl disaster was first disseminated by the media (most likely April 28, 1986), and on the perspective of a single character. The first person narrator, an aging writer living in a village in what was then the East German province of Mecklenburg, spends the day in ordinary activities: preparing meals, gardening, talking to neighbors, riding her bike, making phone calls, reading a book, listening to the radio, and watching TV. But these unremarkable pursuits contrast sharply with the invisible yet life-threatening events that occupy her thoughts from morning until night. On this day, her brother is undergoing brain surgery for a dangerous tumor, and for many hours she anxiously imagines the various steps of the operation and their possible consequences, until a phone call from her sister-in-law informs her of its successful outcome. During her wait, she follows the unfolding news about Chernobyl with increasing unease and outrage, reacting to the warnings and instructions on how to avoid radiation exposure with a mix of worry about its impact on her village and indignation about her neighbors' complacency. Throughout the day, she questions in her mind what the cultural and perhaps even evolutionary origins might be of the fascination with technology and the disdain for nature and human life that lead up to disasters such as Chernobyl. Only at the end of the day does she find solace in reading Joseph Conrad's novel about colonialism, *Heart of Darkness*, and in its emphasis that England, too, used to be one of the "dark places."

Wolf's portrayal of nuclear technology and its cultural roots attracted an enormous amount of attention on the part of scientists and technologists. Between 1988 and 1990, dozens of scientists and intellectuals fought over *Störfall* in the pages of the scientific magazine *spectrum* and in public debates at the East German Academy of Arts, in a rather unique instance of direct dialogue between literature and science.[4] Most of this ferocious debate revolved around the scientific accuracy and political thrust of Wolf's description of nuclear energy: many scientists and engineers interpreted Wolf's novel as an unqualified rejection of nuclear technology and either agreed with some of her critique or defended nuclear energy—among other things, by asking how she would address the risks accompanying alternative energy sources such as coal-burning plants. By contrast, scientists paid very little attention to the novel's engagement with advanced techniques of neurosurgery. Literary critics, however, have frequently commented on this bifurcation of the plot as a juxtaposition of destructive and creative, pathogenic and therapeutic technologies (Brandes 107; Eysel 293; Hebel 43; Kaufmann 256; Magenau 346; Rey 375; Weiss 102). At first sight, this seems like a plausible enough reading, given that the plot contrasts an industrial accident that might increase the incidence of cancer with a medical procedure designed to remove life-threatening tumors. Yet I would argue that such a straightforward dichotomy does as little justice to the actual unfolding of the plot in *Störfall* as the assumption that it is a simple indictment of nuclear technology. For much of the day, the narrator worries about both the spread of radiation and the ongoing surgery and weighs the dangers of both. She seeks to protect herself from fallout but is also concerned that her brother's tumor might not be removed entirely, that the operation might deprive him of vision or smell, that damage to some parts of his brain might induce severe personality changes or, worse, that injury to the pituitary gland might make him lose his mental and motor faculties on a permanent basis. In other words, for a good part of the day, the narrator perceives serious dangers in both scenarios.

Much of the novel's plot, therefore, revolves not so much around the contrast between good and bad technologies as the comparison between different kinds of risk. The risks that come with brain surgery are well known to the narrator, her brother, and her sister-in-law; they have discussed them with the surgeons and accept them knowingly in the expectation that the probability of success is higher than that of failure. As a highly individualized risk, surgery will not affect the health of anyone but the brother. By contrast, news about the nuclear meltdown at Chernobyl comes to the narrator as a completely unanticipated shock: the realization that her small village is contaminated by an event that happened without her knowledge hundreds of miles away upsets her daily routines and turns her perceptions of nature and of her own body upside down. For all its high-technological trappings, brain surgery appears to her as a much more conventional and more comprehensible kind of risk than large-scale radioactive pollution: it is local, visible, specific, anticipated, voluntary, and focused on an individual whom one can contact and feel sympathy for. Whom to empathize with in the case of the Chernobyl? Perhaps the thirty-one dead, or the thousands of evacuees whose plight is broadcast via the media; but in a broader sense, the narrator and her neighbors might also be counted among the victims. Much of the novel, then, contrasts a local and voluntarily incurred risk whose consequences can be predicted with a regional, collective, imperceptible, and involuntarily imposed one whose impact cannot be fully estimated in advance. It is, in a sense, a fictionalized study of risk perception that reflects on many of the dimensions that, as I showed in chapter 4, risk researchers have investigated.

The reason brain surgery appears as a more benign technology than nuclear energy in *Störfall*, therefore, is not only that it is designed to cure disease or that it ends successfully—it might not have. Rather, it seems acceptable mainly because the narrator's cultural context provides her with concepts, categories, and emotions that allow her to cope with its risks, while similar cultural templates are not available for the public, large-scale, and long-distance risks associated with nuclear disaster. Even though she has no specialized medical training, the narrator reflects at length on the structure of the human brain, on material details of the operation (such as what saws might be used to open up a skull, or how a brain lobe is pushed aside to as to reach the layer underneath), on possible mishaps and their consequences, and on her brother's sensations and perceptions after the surgery. By contrast, a risk such as Chernobyl forces average citizens to acquire an entirely new vocabulary. At one point, she reflects, "So setzen sich die Mütter vors Radio und bemühen sich, die neuen Wörter zu lernen. Becquerel....Halbwertszeit, lernen die Mütter heute. Jod 131. Caesium" (35; "So the mothers sit down by the radio and attempt to learn the new words. Becquerel....Half-life is what the mothers learn today. Iodine 131. Cesium"; 27).[5] Somewhat later she comments: "Die Physiker fahren fort, in ihrer uns unverständlichen Sprache zu uns zu sprechen. Was sind '15 Millirem fall-out pro Stunde'" (49; "The physicists continue talking to us in their incomprehensible language. What are 'fifteen millirems per hour'?" 41). While the narrator has no difficulty envisioning details of her brother's surgery and recovery, she lacks even the most basic parameters for understanding nuclear risk.

The complexity of the nuclear risk scenario arises not only from unfamiliar scientific concepts, however, but also from the unexpected double meanings and ironies it creates for nonscientific discourse, whether it be ordinary, lyrical, or religious language. A word such as "radiation," for example, acquires an odd ambiguity as it refers both to the radioactivity that might cause cancer and the procedure used to fight it. The narrator notes this uncomfortable polysemy repeatedly, commenting at one point: "Der strahlende Himmel. Das kann man nun auch nicht mehr denken. Auf Bestrahlung können wir aufgrund des histologischen Befunds verzichten, wird der Professor zu dir sagen" (30; "The radiant sky. Now one can't think that anymore, either. We can do without radiation treatment in view of the histological findings, your doctor will tell you"; 21–22). At another moment, she similarly combines a poetic reference to nature with nuclear technology when she alludes to a Brecht poem: "*O Himmel, strahlender Azur.* Nach welchen Gesetzen, wie schnell breitet sich Radioaktivität aus, günstigenfalls und ungünstigenfalls" (18; "*O heavens' radiant azure.* According to what laws and how quickly does radioactivity spread, at best and at worst?" 9). In both cases, what was originally said in praise of nature assumes a sinister connotation in the context of nuclear disaster, and leads the narrator to doubt that nature poetry has any more relevance to the present: "*Wie herrlich leuchtet mir die Natur.* Vielleicht ist es nicht die dringlichste Frage, was wir mit den Bibliotheken voller Naturgedichte machen. Aber eine Frage ist es schon, habe ich gedacht" (44–45; "*Marvellous Nature Shining on Me!* Perhaps the problem of what to do with the libraries full of nature poems is not the most urgent. But it is a problem all the same, I thought"; 37).

A similar series of puns, associations, and reflections accompanies the frequent appearances of the word "cloud" (*Wolke*), which in the context of the novel refers above all to the plume of radioactivity moving westward from Chernobyl. "Daß wir es 'Wolke' nennen, ist ja nur ein Zeichen unseres

Unvermögens, mit den Fortschritten der Wissenschaft sprachlich Schritt zu halten," the narrator comments at one point (36; "Calling it 'cloud' is merely an indication of our inability to keep pace linguistically with the progress of science"; 27). She wistfully thinks back to the time of her grandmother, when a cloud referred to something made up of evaporated water, and responds with sarcasm when a voice on the radio reads out a biblical passage about Christ's ascension to the heavens on a cloud. The use of clouds as a metaphor for whiteness and purity in poetry leads her to remark:

> Nun aber, habe ich gedacht... durfte man gespannt sein, welcher Dichter es als erster wieder wagen würde, eine weiße Wolke zu besingen. Eine unsichtbare Wolke von ganz anderer Substanz hatte es übernommen, unsere Gefühle—ganz andere Gefühle—auf sich zu ziehen. Und sie hat, habe ich wieder mit dieser finsteren Schadenfreude gedacht, die weiße Wolke der Poesie ins Archiv gestoßen. (61)

> But now... it should be interesting to see which poet would be the first to dare sing the praises of a white cloud. An invisible cloud of a completely different substance had seized the attention of our feelings—completely different feelings. And, I thought once again with that dark, malicious glee, it has knocked the white cloud of poetry into the archives. (55)[6]

The narrator's insistence on the obsolescence of nature poetry illustrates the more general collision between the conventions of lyrical language and the new meanings that surge up in the age of Chernobyl.

But beyond the failure of conventional poetic language, *Störfall* highlights the shortfall of ordinary discourse and ultimately of ordinary modes of experience. Critics of the novel have frequently pointed out that the narrator (and, by extension, Wolf herself) pits the realm of the domestic, the pastoral, and the everyday against the domain of science, technology and specialized knowledge (Brandes 111; Magenau 374; Nalewski 284–85; West 260). Chernobyl is referred to as DIE NACHRICHT (the news) in capital letters on one of the first pages, signaling even typographically its disruption of the ordinary.[7] As an alternative and a possible mode of resistance to the forces that created this threat, according to this reading, the novel dwells extensively on details of the narrator's cooking, cleaning, and gardening—so much so that some of its first reviewers declared the novel boring or trivial, wondering why nothing more momentous would have occurred to Wolf on the occasion.[8] But what neither the critics who indict Wolf's "triviality" nor those who defend it mention is that the narrator herself consistently puts in question any attempt to counter extraordinary risk by means of ordinary routines; more than once, she herself concedes that the realm of local everyday life cannot be separated from that of global science and technology, even in the rural setting of a Mecklenburg village.

Radioactive contamination is the most obvious indicator that the natural and the domestic can no longer be decoupled from the technological and transnational. Fresh, home-grown food, for example, is now a threat to both children and adults: even as the narrator prepares the soil in her garden for the planting of lettuce, spinach, and watercress, and even as she delights in the sprouting of her zucchini seedlings, she is also aware that such home-grown vegetables are no longer considered safe for consumption, due to the fallout (28–29/20).[9] Indeed, even contact with the soil itself is a source of risk, as the narrator discovers when a radio broadcast warns that garden chores, if unavoidable, should only be carried out with rubber gloves. She resists at first and continues to pull up weeds with her bare hands, uttering a "manic clarion call of triumph" (33/25). But on the very next page, we learn that she has donned rubber gloves after all—though perhaps in a last movement of defiance, she leaves it open whether this change of mind is because she is now working on nettles or because she does in the end accept the wisdom of the radio warning. In either case, this warning makes it clear that simple country life, an active engagement with nature, and loving care of the domestic realm offer no refuge from danger, but have themselves become a source of risk.

As she begins to understand this new riskscape, it occurs to her that what still separates her from those who design life-threatening technologies is the concern and care for nature:

> Plötzlich habe ich mich fragen müssen, ob die Betreiber jener Arten von Technik, deren höllische Gefährlichkeit in ihrem Wesen liegt, jemals in ihrem Leben winzigste Samenkörner, die einem an den Fingerspitzen kleben bleiben, in die Erde gesenkt haben, um sie später aufgehen zu sehen und über Wochen, Monate hin das Wachstum der Pflanzen zu verfolgen. (29)

> All of a sudden I found myself wondering whether the perpetrators of those kinds of technology whose hellish danger is part and parcel of their very essence have ever in their lives put into the soil kernels so minute that they stick to the fingertips, later to see them sprout and to watch plants' growth for weeks, for months. (20–21)

But she herself realizes at once that such a simple distinction does not hold up to scrutiny:

> Mein Denkfehler ist mir gleich bewußt geworden, jedermann hat schon gehört oder gelesen, daß gerade angestrengt arbeitende Wissenschaftler oder Techniker häufig Entspannung bei der Gartenarbeit suchen. Oder gilt diese These nur für die Älteren, und ist sie in bezug auf die Jüngeren, diejenigen, die jetzt das Sagen haben, überholt? Ich habe mir vorgenommen, eine Liste derjenigen Tätigkeiten und Freuden anzufertigen, die jene Männer der Wissenschaft und Technik wahrscheinlich nicht kennen. Was soll daraus folgen? Um die Wahrheit zu sagen: Ich weiß es nicht. (29)

I immediately recognized my fallacy, since everybody has heard or read that hardworking scientists and technicians are just the ones who frequently seek relaxation through gardening. Or does this thesis apply only to the older ones; is it outdated with regard to the younger generation, those who now have the final say? I resolved to make a list of those activities and pleasures which, more than likely, are foreign to those men of science and technology. To what end? In all honesty: I don't know. (21)

It is hard to imagine a more explicit concession that the attempt to separate out a realm of the ordinary uncontaminated by science and technology is a dead end from the start. Nevertheless, in her search for alternatives, the narrator returns to this idea a few pages later and draws up a

Liste der Tätigkeiten, die jene Männer von Wissenschaft und Technik vermutlich nicht ausüben oder die sie, dazu gezwungen, als Zeitvergeudung ansehen würden: Einen Säugling trockenlegen. Kochen, einkaufen gehn, mit einem Kind auf dem Arm oder im Kinderwagen. Wäsche waschen, aufhängen, abnehmen, zusammenlegen, bügeln, ausbessern. Fußböden fegen, wischen, bohnern, staubsaugen. Staubwischen. Nähen. Stricken. Häkeln. Sticken. Geschirr abwaschen. Geschirr abwaschen. Geschirr abwaschen. Ein krankes Kind pflegen. Ihm Geschichten erfinden. Lieder singen.—Und wieviele dieser Tätigkeiten sehe ich selbst als Zeitvergeudung an? (39)

List of the activities which these men of science and technology presumably do not pursue or which, if forced upon them, they would consider a waste of time: Changing a baby's diapers. Cooking, shopping with a child on one's arm or in the baby carriage. Doing the laundry, hanging it up to dry, taking it down, folding it, ironing it, darning it. Sweeping the floor, mopping it, polishing it, vacuuming it. Dusting. Sewing. Knitting. Crocheting. Embroidering. Doing the dishes. Doing the dishes. Doing the dishes. Taking care of a sick child. Thinking up stories to tell. Singing songs. And how many of these activities do I myself consider a waste of time? (31)

This time, the thrust of the final concession is not so much that men of science might indeed engage in the stereotypically feminine activities associated with home, garden, and children but that the woman writer herself, in her own sphere of art, may be as removed from this domestic foundation as those she criticizes are in their domain of science. Effectively, this implies that distance from the ordinary is not always destructive, just as immersion in it is not always necessarily benign.[10]

Even more forcefully, the narrator's idea that not only scientists but ordinary citizens carry a burden of "coresponsibility" (*Mitverantwortung*) for the Chernobyl disaster short-circuits any attempt to portray everyday pursuits as an alternative to deadly technologies. Her frequent references to the Nazi period and World War II serve above all to highlight this co-responsibility of common people in collective disasters: she remembers, for example, that a family had stopped near her house a week earlier and discussed with outrage how the woman's father had been arrested during World War II even though he was "only" a driver with the Gestapo. The relevance of this incident for Chernobyl emerges when the narrator observes with amazement

> wie schlafwandlerisch sicher alles ineinandergreift: der meisten Menschen Lust auf eine bequemes Leben, der meisten Neigung, den Rednern hinter den erhöhten Pulten und den Männern im weißen Kittel zu glauben, jedermanns Übereinstimmungssucht und Widerspruchsangst scheinen dem Machthunger und der Arroganz, der Gewinnsucht, der skrupellosen Neugier und der Selbstverliebtheit der wenigen zu entsprechen. (26)

> the way in which everything fits together with a sleepwalker's precision: the desire of most people for a comfortable life, their tendency to believe the speakers on raised platforms and the men in white coats; the addiction to harmony and the fear of contradiction of the many seem to correspond to the arrogance and hunger for power, the dedication to profit, unscrupulous inquisitiveness, and self-infatuation of the few. (17)

If the desire for a comfortable and undisturbed life is one of the factors that contributes to the emergence of large-scale technological risk scenarios (see Rechtien 236–39), it is hard to see how the comforts of the domestic and the everyday could at the same time function as an alternative to them. Admittedly, this may simply be one of the conceptual weaknesses of a novel that often seems to want to have it both ways. But if so, the weakness is systematic: *every time* the narrator evokes the local and the domestic as an alternative to transnational technologies and risk scenarios, she ends up conceding that they can in fact no longer be thought apart from such patterns of global technological and ecological connectedness. If some passages from *Störfall* might remind one of Michel de Certeau's analysis of everyday life as a reservoir of strategies for resisting hegemony, Wolf ultimately does not seem to share de Certeau's confidence that such strategies matter much in a world of transnational industry and technology.

The principal means by which the materialities of local, everyday life are embedded in larger networks of politics, economy, technology, and ecology in *Störfall* is the mass media. Without such information and communications technologies, the villagers would not even know that anything unusual had occurred. The narrator herself listens to a small Sanyo transistor radio for much of the day and switches to TV coverage of the disaster toward evening, which triggers some of her most direct political criticism.[11] Not only radio and TV but also the national government and scientific establishment that control the broadcasts are attacked for their hypocrisy, false reassurances, and censorship of important information. As she flips through various TV channels, the narrator describes how formulaic and predictable the (mostly male) establishment's justifications of the accident soon become, and she herself quickly learns to predict the answers to journalists' questions. On one occasion, however, she turns out to be wrong: when one of the TV reporters asks an expert whether error-free safety predictions can be made for a very advanced area of technology,

> nun haben der Moderator und ich zu unserer schmerzlichen Überraschung erleben müssen, daß der sich bei aller Bereitschaft zum Entgegenkommen auf diese Aussage nicht hat festnageln lassen wollen. Nun, haben wir ihn sagen hören. Absolut fehlerfreie Prognosen—die gebe es für einen so jungen Zweig der Technik allerdings nicht. Da müsse man, wie immer bei neuen technischen Entwicklungen, mit einem gewissen Risiko rechnen, bis man auch diese Technik vollkommen beherrsche. (106)

> the moderator and I were forced to learn, to our painful surprise, that this guy—despite his general willingness to be accommodating—was not about to be pinned down to this statement. Well, we heard him say, there was no such thing as an absolutely faultless prognosis in such a young branch of technology. As always with new technological developments, one would have to take certain risks into account until one fully mastered this technology as well. (102–3)

This statement brings the narrator's resistance to its climax:

> Ich habe ja gewußt, daß sie es wissen. Nur, daß sie es auch aussprechen würden, und sei es dieses eine Mal—das hätte ich nicht erwartet. Mir ist ein Brieftext durch den Kopf gegangen, in dem ich—beschwörend, wie denn sonst—irgend jemandem mitteilen sollte, daß das Risiko der Atomtechnik mit fast keinem anderen Risiko vergleichbar sei und daß man bei einem auch nur minimalen Unsicherheitsfaktor auf diese Technik unbedingt verzichten müsse. Mir ist für meinen Brief im Kopf keine reale Adresse eingefallen, also habe ich einige Schimpfwörter ausgestoßen und den Kanal abgeschaltet. (106–7)

> I knew very well that they knew it. Only, I had not expected that they would also say it—be it only this one time. The text for a letter went through my mind in which I—imploringly, how else—was to communicate to someone that the risk of nuclear technology was not comparable to [almost] any other risk and that one absolutely had to renounce this technology if there was even the slightest element of uncertainty. I could not think of a real address for the letter in my mind, so I swore out loud and switched channels. (103)[12]

The fundamental disagreement between expert and nonexpert over what constitutes socially acceptable risk is as remarkable in this scene as the collision of newer and older communication media. While the expert broadcasts his opinion from an unnamed location via a television screen, the narrator can only imagine her resistance in the form of the older medium of the written letter. But her need for a precise location to which she can address it quite literally finds no place in a society of mass media and risks that have moved beyond such geographical specificity. The conflict between expert and lay assessments of risk is here associated with communications technologies that structure place in very different ways, emphasizing that one of the most important problems the Chernobyl accident raises is how it might be possible to inhabit the local in a context of transnational connectedness.

But the claim that Chernobyl can be compared "to almost no other risk" also raises intriguing questions about Wolf's own text, which approaches the crisis precisely by way of repeated comparisons with brain surgery, with the World War II era, and with colonialism as portrayed in Joseph Conrad's *Heart of Darkness*. The most important comparison, as discussed earlier, is the one between a distant and imperceptible risk and a local and visible one—but phrasing it in this way understates the complexities of the "local" in *Störfall*. In fact, neither the narrator's brother nor the rest of her family—her daughters and grandchildren—live geographically close to her. While the use of second person pronouns in the narrative simulates a direct address to the brother, who is doubly absent by virtue of his geographical distance and his unconsciousness during most of the day, the narrator speaks to her sister-in-law, her daughters, and a friend in London over the phone no fewer than eight times. Her expectation that she will receive news about the nuclear accident every time she turns on the radio or TV finds an exact parallel in her expectation that she will hear about the outcome of the surgery every time the phone rings. Both of the novel's main events, therefore, are in different ways detached from place: radioactivity is everywhere; the surgery could be anywhere (its location is never specified).

This detachment is crucial for understanding how the novel configures the relationship between the routines of the everyday and the moment of crisis, as well as between the local and the transnational realms. While *Störfall*, like Richard Powers's *Gain* (see chapter 5 here), draws on some of the standard motifs of backyard pastoral in portraying the narrator's attachment to her house and garden, it stops short of associating this scenario with family life and emotional intimacy. But the authenticity and depth of her long-distance family relationships are never put in question in *Störfall*. On the contrary, it would seem that it is precisely such relationships that offer the best chance for understanding the experience of place and risk in an increasingly global context. However invisible or mediated these relationships may be, they shape the ordinary routines of life for the individual, and these routines cannot be properly understood without the nonlocal relationships embedded in them. The moment of crisis—industrial accident, fatal illness—starkly foregrounds what ordinary rhythms might conceal: namely, that attachments to both places and people in an age of global connectedness are, for better or for worse, increasingly shaped by forces far outside the bounds of the local and familial. It is this representation of risk as a staging of deterritorialized relationships that Wolf's *Störfall* shares with Wohmann's *Flötenton*.

3. Routine: Gabriele Wohmann's *Der Flötenton*

Like *Störfall, Der Flötenton* takes the Chernobyl accident as the ground on which to explore the routines of everyday life in their relationship to experiences of risk, place, and social networks. As in *Störfall*, the central relationship is one between a brother and a sister, Anton and Emily Asper, who are deeply attached to each other. But the narrative framework in which this relationship unfolds is quite different; in a typically modernist structure somewhat reminiscent of the novels of Virginia Woolf or William Faulkner, the novel delves into the perceptions, memories, and anticipations of about a dozen different characters. On the surface connected by no more than geographical proximity—all of them live in or around the town of Gerresheim—these characters turn out to be involved in each others' lives in various ways: as members of the same family, neighbors, current or former friends, or employees. The plot starts in May 1986, when Chernobyl is still constantly in the news but has moved beyond the initial crisis that Wolf's novel concentrates on, and the novel ends sometime in late October of the same year. By this time, most of the official warnings and safety measures have been suspended, suggesting a return to normalcy that some of the characters welcome with relief and others reject with skepticism or anger.

The variety of characters and the more extended time frame are crucial for Wohmann's narrative project, which is not to convey the first brutal encounter with a new environmental risk but to investigate the different ways people come to terms with a life from which such risk can no longer be eliminated. On one end of the spectrum, we find Sandra Hinholz, an optimistic and sensuous woman who is completely absorbed by the concreteness of everyday life: her family, her lover, her music lessons, and her academic career plans are the issues around which most of her thinking revolves. She considers Chernobyl only in terms of what food it might be best to avoid for her children, but cannot really understand why someone like her lover, Anton Asper, views it as a serious crisis. On the other end of the spectrum, Anton's sister, Emily, becomes gradually more obsessed with the nuclear threat and what it implies about the world, to the point where she suffers a nervous breakdown. She stays away from her work as a high school teacher without notifying the principal, and instead—in a manner reminiscent of Jack and Babette Gladney in DeLillo's *White Noise*, as discussed in chapter 5—attempts all kinds of minor deceptions to get hold of a prescription drug she thinks might alleviate her anxiety. In between these two extremes, the other characters evolve into and out of different positions of awareness and forgetfulness, rebellion and resignation, fear and hope.

In exploring the characters' evolution, Wohmann interweaves the transformations that a new environmental hazard imposes on everyday life with existential concerns that preceded Chernobyl—as Jack Gladney's fear of death precedes his exposure to Nyodene D.—but are condensed and precipitated by the crisis: career anxieties, fears about sexuality or old age, successes and shortfalls of social relationships all enter into uneasy conjunctions with nuclear risk in the texture of the characters' everyday experiences. This subtle imbrication of old and new fears has prompted one critic to argue that in fact Chernobyl itself is only of marginal importance to a novel whose real concern is the angst caused by the progressive dehumanization of the characters' lifeworld (Fritsch 426), an argument that parallels the analyses that dismiss the significance of DeLillo's "airborne toxic event" as merely one among many possible triggers of existential anxiety. But even if one accepts this approach—which leads to a possible but by no means the most compelling reading of the novel—it remains significant that such existential fears would crystallize around the Chernobyl accident rather than any of the countless other scenarios of danger and death that the media communicated to average German citizens in the 1980s. In other words, while it is true that the characters' concerns about Chernobyl are intertwined with other existential issues, nuclear risk is by no means only a screen onto which other fears are projected. In fact, the extent to which it functions as an important motivating force for different characters becomes a measure of their awareness that their lives are shaped by realities that transcend their local surroundings.

Anton Asper, the character whose reflections take up more space than those of anyone else in the novel, voices his concerns over the nuclear disaster so frequently that he comes to be called "unser Kollege mit dem Tschernobyl-Syndrom" ("our colleague with the Chernobyl syndrome") by his coworkers (472).[13] Painfully aware not only of the dangers of radiation but also other risks such as airplane accidents or the ozone hole, he overtly criticizes the excessive technological manipulation of nature, rejects nuclear power, and insists that others should become acquainted with the best scientific prognoses. But while his social criticism is at times very specific, it is also clear that his pessimism is rooted as much in personal guilt and self-doubt as in public shortfalls and disasters. Uncertain relationships to his past and present partners, doubts about his own masculinity, and especially latent guilt over his teenaged son Simon, who has Down syndrome and lives in a faraway residence for disabled youth, surface again and again in his thoughts and constellate around the more public but equally intangible threat of nuclear radiation. Similarly, his sister Emily's deterioration and breakdown are triggered by the daily experience of nuclear risk, but have their deeper roots in the long-term frustration of her career ambitions as an economist and latent tensions in her twenty-year relationship with the psychologist Samuel Speicher. For two of the aged characters, Mrs. Asper, Anton and Emily's mother, and the theologian Professor Hinholz, the aftermath of Chernobyl becomes the occasion for reflecting on the loss of their spouses, and on their own attachment to life and anxieties about approaching death. In each of these cases, Chernobyl is experienced in a context of other existential issues with which it comes to be amalgamated in complex ways.[14]

But the novel does make a clear distinction between those characters for whom Chernobyl is merely added on as just another element in a swirl of daily details and preoccupations that they cannot transcend and those for whom concern about Chernobyl becomes a motive for rethinking their own positions in the world. The novelist Richard Kast, whose memory loss allows him only a limited understanding of recent events, the widow Mrs. Asper, who begins a journey of self-discovery when she starts writing accounts of her daily life, and the flutist Sandra Hinholz, relentlessly absorbed in the details of her family life and career, are examples of characters for whom Chernobyl is only a vague outline on the conceptual horizon. None of them perceive it as an event that has any serious impact on their own lives, which are mostly consumed by ordinary routines. On the other hand, Mrs. Asper's son and daughter and Professor Hinholz are deeply shaken by the crisis and struggle throughout the novel to find some way of returning to a "normal" perspective on the banalities of everyday life.

Anton and Emily Asper are perhaps the clearest examples in the novel of characters whose experiential logic is turned upside down in ways reminiscent of Beck's analysis of the risk society. Anton's life is successful on the surface: he is the chief executive of his corporation's construction branch, travels widely throughout Germany, Europe, and occasionally other parts of the world, and lives with a lively and interesting partner who is somewhat of a television celebrity. Well informed though he may be about the consequences of Chernobyl, as well as many other risks of disease or accident in the contemporary world, he nonetheless ignores repeated warnings from friends and family that his own smoking puts him at greater health risk than any of the other scenarios that worry him. This detail may confirm that Chernobyl is a means of externalizing and displacing anxieties that really concern more intimate aspects of his life. Yet whatever the roots of his awareness may be, the novel makes it difficult not to agree with many of his factual assessments, as well as his stark indictments of media distortions and politicians' lack of foresight and honesty. While some of these comments are proffered in contexts where they needlessly thwart others' cheerfulness, enjoyment, or affection, they also serve as a measuring stick for all that many of the other characters choose to ignore or gloss over. This is particularly obvious in a direct conversation with a deputy minister (447–50), where Anton's acerbic insistence on the facts cuts through the politician's persistent attempts at minimizing and embellishing the disaster. Whatever the psychological roots of his concern, therefore, they do drive Anton to look facts in the face in a way that few other characters in the novel do, and they lead to a more accurate perception of what living in a "risk society" means.

Anton's sister Emily resists the social pressure to return to a "normal" life and viewpoint in more extreme ways than her brother, and her behavior clearly becomes pathological over the course of time. As in Anton's case, her concern about radioactive fallout is hard to divorce from her personal problems: outrage at her friend Jutta's pregnancy is as much due to her feelings of envy and inferiority as to health concerns, anger at her students' indifference as much to her career frustration as to political despair.[15] But reducing her development to a pathological case study would not do justice to the subtlety of Wohmann's text, as the characters, in spite of their mixed motivations, often do ultimately point to real social problems. In Emily's case, it is particularly the altered relationship to the local that comes to the fore. Unable to cope with bleak prospects, both personal and collective, she drives around aimlessly in her car and seeks relief in a drug, the painkiller Vendrix, which she and Anton experimented with in their college days. But since this drug is not available without a prescription, Emily begins to drive from pharmacy to pharmacy pretending to be a traveler in need of medication. When these performances fail, she rings the doorbells of private homes instead, in more and more desperate attempts to mobilize others' compassion. During one of these excursions, she ends up on Professor Hinholz's doorstep and casually confesses to him: "Wissen Sie, es ist so merkwürdig, ich habe seit ein paar Tagen das Gefühl, irgendwie nirgends zu sein" ("You know, it's so strange, I've had this feeling for a few days of somehow being nowhere"; 358). This helpless admission, beyond signaling her personal disorientation, also indicates quite accurately how tenuous the individual's rooting in a particular place becomes when the modes of local inhabitation can be fundamentally reshaped by catastrophic events elsewhere on the planet. Living through Chernobyl in Gerresheim, Emily Asper ends up nowhere.

After she leaves, Hinholz returns to his desk and makes a note: "The Chernobyl shock: anthropological in nature. Shock of the impotence of all individual experiences of the senses" (358). This note refers primarily to his own anxiety, since he took a walk in the rain on April 30, only a few days after the explosion, when each rainfall washed down radioactive particles.

Der Aprilregen hat mir wohlgetan, weil ich nichts über ihn wußte. Objektiv hat er mich verseucht. Sandras Kinder haben in Sand und Gras gespielt, weil beides aussah wie immer, die Blumen rochen wie immer,

Sandras Schnittlauch hat wie immer geschmeckt: Die Sinne des Menschen versagen.

The April rain felt good to me because I didn't know anything about it. Objectively, it has contaminated me. Sandra's kids played in the sand and grass because both of them looked as usual, the flowers smelled as usual, Sandra's chives tasted as usual: Human senses fail. (358–59)

But, coming as it does right after Emily's appearance at his house, Hinholz's note is hard not to read as the author's indirect comment on her predicament as well. It is hard to imagine a better fictionalization of Beck's "expropriation of the senses" and his comment that life in the risk society forces individuals to rely on the nonexperience of others rather than on their own senses. In this context, Emily's condition seems merely a more aggravated version of the general alienation from the physicality of the local landscape that Hinholz here describes with reference to himself and his grandchildren. As sense perception can no longer be trusted to convey important information about the environment, it detaches individuals from their spontaneous physical relationship to the local. But in both Emily's and Hinholz's case, it is also this detachment that allows them to view their own ordinary lives critically and to perceive their embeddedness in the regional and the global.

By contrast, Hinholz's daughter-in-law, the flute player Sandra, remains completely immersed in the immediacies of the local throughout the novel. Her cheerfulness, optimism, sensuality, and genuine care for the people around her make it hard not to sympathize with her, especially since she is surrounded by characters who are consumed by their own doubts and uncertainties. Yet her naïveté and utter inability to grasp abstract connections beyond concrete details also make her at times appear almost grotesque in a world of international commerce and high technology. Anton is struck, for example, by her account of a tour of the United States she took with her orchestra, "north to south and east to west," where what she says she liked most were freshly pressed fruit juices (123). This relentless fixation on the mundane both fascinates and repels Anton, who observes in a subsequent conversation, "Earrings. Freshly pressed fruit juices that impressed you most in the US. Alien world. You make the world seem very small" (145). And later on, he reflects:

Jede Minute in Sandras Tageslauf ist bis obenhin mit Inhalt vollgestopft, und den Inhalt erlebt sie als Sinn. Gemästete, mit Lebendigkeit überfütterte Tage. Ihr winziges Quantum an Teilnahme an dem übrigen Geschehen auf diesem Globus beschränkt sich auf die vermischten Nachrichten ihrer Lokalzeitung, letzte Seite.

Every minute of Sandra's daily life is stuffed with content all the way, and she experiences this content as meaning. Days spoon-fed, overfed with vitality. Her minuscule quantum of participation in other events on this planet limits itself to the miscellaneous news of her local newspaper, last page. (176)

Sandra's world is indeed an extremely reduced one; she delights in the discovery that her father-in-law is a neighbor of Anton's aunt: "Die Welt ist klein...und in diesem Sachverhalt fand sie neuen Grund zum Jubeln....Daß die Welt wirklich so klein war, wie sich eben herausgestellt hatte, schien Anton hingegen zu verstimmen" ("It's a small world...and she found new grounds for rejoicing in this fact....By contrast, the idea that the world really was as small as they had just discovered seemed to put Anton in a bad mood"; 99). The limits of her grasp of the contemporary world become obvious even to Sandra herself when she mentally compares herself to Anton's partner, the worldly, well-informed talk show host Lydia Tulpen:

> Und die Politik war gewiß nicht das einzige Gebiet, auf dem Sandra Antons Freundin Lydia unterliegen würde, bei einem Test. Vermutlich wäre es die Gegenwart im Allgemeinen, in der sich Sandra weniger gut als Lydia auskannte. Sie gab ja offen zu, sich über ihren eigenen Lebensumkreis hinaus nicht besonders aufzuregen. Hauptgrund: Zeitmangel. Gut, es war grauenhaft, was man so vom Raubbau an der Natur, von benzol- und asbestverseuchter Luft, vom geldverschlingenden Wettrüsten mitbekam, und jetzt, ganz furchtbar, da hatte Anton ja recht, dieser FALL OUT, wirklich ganz furchtbar—und doch, kurz vorm Abflug hierher, hatte ihr eine Kirmes in Gerresheim richtigen Spaß gemacht.

> And politics was certainly not the only area in which Sandra would lose out to Anton's girlfriend Lydia in a test. Probably it was the present in general that Sandra knew less well than Lydia. She readily admitted that she wasn't particularly concerned about anything beyond her own life circumstances. Main reason: lack of time. Yes, it was horrendous what one heard about the exploitation of nature, about air polluted by benzol and asbestos, about the money devoured by the arms race, and now, really awful, Anton was right, this FALL OUT, really absolutely awful—and yet, right before her flight here she'd had real fun at a carnival in Gerresheim. (139)

The final reaffirmation of the trivial reveals that even Sandra's bouts of awareness of her own ignorance do not lead to any change in her attitude—not even any profound desire for change.

Consequently, Sandra's naïveté, as well as her commitment to concrete detail and spatial proximity, persist throughout the novel. After starting an affair with Anton during a trip to Portugal, she assumes at first that she can easily integrate her new lover into her family life by having him move in with them. She only realizes gradually that such closeness would not only be far from Anton's own wishes but also quite atypical of the way he conducts his own family relations. As Sandra discovers, Anton, his sister Emily, and their mother only rarely see each other, even though they are deeply attached to one another emotionally and live in close proximity—in fact, Emily rents a small apartment in a house next door to her mother's and can sometimes observe her from her window. Instead of visits and face-to-face contact, the Aspers talk over the phone, just as Wolf's narrator does with her family and friends; even more remarkably, they write long reports for each other on their daily lives. Emily composes a seven-page letter for her mother every week describing the details of her everyday routines, perceptions, and emotions, and Mrs. Asper passes these letters on to Anton along with a written report of her own that Anton has requested. In turn, Anton sends her frequent postcards from his travels—in the novel, he mails the first one from the airport before even leaving Germany. Even though they often think of each other, the three Aspers never lay eyes on each other until the last two chapters of Wohmann's almost 500-page novel. Needless to say, this kind of family relationship is completely alien to Sandra.

But in the novel, it is Sandra who is the exception rather than the Asper family. Even though the twelve characters who play significant roles in the plot all turn out to live close to each other and to be related by virtue of family, friendship, neighborhood, or employment, they appear strangely distanced from each other in their modes of communication. Not only does Emily turn down invitations from her mother next door and write her letters instead, but her landlord, the one-time novelist Richard Kast, does the same: he is a little in love with Mrs. Asper and secretly drops off anonymous letters at her doorstep rather than engaging her directly. Kast also speaks regularly over the phone to Professor Hinholz, Sandra's father-in-law, who is a friend and companion from their college days. Hinholz, in turn, likes to spy in secret on Mrs. Asper's sister, Etta Gersteck, whose garden lies next to his. Through phone calls and occasional visits from Sandra, he also finds out about her affair with Anton. The telephone, moreover, turns out to be one of Sandra's obsessions, in spite of her much greater commitment to face-to-face contact; at the same time, it is also Anton's main means of communication not only with his sister but with two other women for whom he professes to have profound affection. Just as in Wolf's novel, then, the social networks in Wohmann's *Flötenton* are for the most part quite indirect and mediated by various technologies of communication; but somewhat more surprisingly, relationships function as if they took place at long distance even when the individuals involved are geographically close.

Once this basic pattern emerges in the novel, it makes sense that the only physical love relationship that is described in any detail in the novel, the one between Anton and Sandra, does not take place in their hometown, where they have never even met, but during a trip abroad. Indeed, the only reason they meet in Lisbon in the first place is because his national identification card has expired and her passport has been stolen, forcing them both to visit the German embassy. In other words, the coincidence of emotional and physical closeness between them, a rare occurrence in the novel, is enabled by their being both geographically and administratively deterritorialized from their home country. Once they return to Germany, by contrast, they hardly see each other anymore, and their relationship spins itself out mostly in prolonged phone conversations. In the narrative logic the novel develops, then, social relationships become more mediated and indirect the more they involve geographical proximity. Direct encounters and physical intimacy, for most of the characters, are incompatible with being in one's own place.

It is tempting to describe this inability to interact directly with those in one's immediate vicinity as a symptom of profound alienation, and at least some of the characters in Wohmann's novel intermittently perceive it as such. Yet one cannot introduce this concept without noting simultaneously that the text presents it for the most part as mere normalcy, and without explicit judgment. In addition, it is worth remembering that Sandra, the one character who seems to suffer from no such alienation, appears by no means as an unambiguously positive figure, but is rather presented as childish and ignorant as often as she is portrayed as warm, selfless, and generous. I would argue that it is not Wohmann's objective, at any rate, to present some attitudes and relationships as genuine and others as inauthentic, but rather to investigate how daily life is lived in this context of deterritorialization, and how such ordinariness might be translated into language.

This is the question that surfaces again and again in the various written versions that different characters give of their experiences. Emily changes formulations in her letters repeatedly when she considers how particular sentences might be read by her various audiences—her mother, her brother, and perhaps even her partner Samuel. Mrs. Asper oscillates between delight and fierce struggle as she sits down at her husband's long-unused typewriter and slowly, for the first time in her life, attempts to give a coherent account of her daily life and self, her confrontation with aging and loss. Anton appears to be writing down three different versions of his encounter with Sandra on postcards from Lisbon, until we find out that these different stories all just unfold in his head after he's already dispatched the actual postcards with the usual travel clichés. Richard Kast's anonymous missives to Mrs. Asper stand out in their unusually stark attention to the details of life as an aging person that also characterize his own daily struggles. To help him with the difficulty of such everyday errands and chores, he hires Sandra's friend Kirsten Zwingenberg without realizing that she has completed a master's degree in literature on his own works. She reads these books to him, which Alzheimer's disease prevents him from even recognizing as his own; throughout the long literary sessions, his mind incessantly wanders off to his daily tasks, and he wishes Kirsten would help him do his shopping and tie his shoelaces instead. Partly funny and partly melancholy, these sessions persistently raise the question of the relationship between the trivial details of everyday life and literary emplotment.

Wohmann's sustained exploration of such situations shows that for her, as much as for Wolf, the crucial question that arises from a disaster such as Chernobyl is how extraordinary risk scenarios relate to the ordinariness of daily life. Wolf, focusing on the moment of shock in which the two collide, attempts to mobilize the small, usually unnoticed routines that tie individuals to place and family as a possible means of resistance to the encroachments of increasingly uncontrollable and dangerous technologies, but also records how such attempts fall short, and ultimately has her protagonist seek refuge in literature. Wohmann, by contrast, is interested above all in the processes by means of which risk and disaster become integrated into everyday life and ultimately almost indistinguishable from it. She describes these processes as extremely varied, ranging from Sandra's easy oblivion to Anton's hard-won acceptance, from Professor Hinholz' broadening political horizon to Richard Kast's amnesia. With a reticence that may annoy the environmentalist and delight the literary critic, the narrative refuses to deliver any definitive judgment on these varying perspectives. Rather, what Wohmann emphasizes is the inexorable force of the process whereby even the most frightening risk scenarios and the most earth-shattering disasters become a part of ordinary routines—the path from apocalypse to way of life, in the words of Frederick Buell, whose work I discussed in chapter 4. Whether this process implies apathy and amnesia or a new understanding of the relevance of politics for daily life, it is a necessary and inevitable one in the novel: the alternative to this normalization is the paranoia and nervous breakdown the Asper siblings suffer from during most of the plot.

But this does not imply that the moment when Anton and Emily recuperate their normal sense of life is described as a return to an authentic and unproblematic mode of experience. Anton reaches his final moment of reconciliation in a scene that brings together most of the novel's major characters, during the filming of a TV documentary on the life and work of his long-deceased father, the poet Louis Asper, which has been instigated by Lydia Tulpen. As he watches his friends and family mill about his aunt's garden, he is overcome by a feeling of deep love and happiness in relation to those around him. He immediately and typically catches himself, however, and reflects with a sharp sense of irony that this harmonious family scene has been generated by that most inauthentic of media, television. But right afterward, he puts this ironic distance itself in question and reaffirms that regardless of authenticity or inauthenticity, he really is happy and enjoying the beautiful day. "He decided in favor of them all, in favor of the reunion and in favor of fear of flying," the section concludes (478), combining both mediated social relationships and technological risk scenarios in its final affirmation of everyday life, however inauthentic and deterritorialized.

4. Everyday Risk in the Age of Globalization

Both Wolf and Wohmann, then, describe Chernobyl as a large-scale, regional, and even global risk scenario in its impact on more or less average characters' daily lives. Both focus on the contrast that arises from the collision of a catastrophic industrial accident and the habits and routines that make up ordinary life, and both highlight the conceptual, linguistic, social, and affective difficulties this clash entails. The logic of "secondhand nonexperience" described by Beck shapes the protagonists' lives in both narratives. But as it turns out, the local setting in which this collision occurs is in both novels already a highly deterritorialized one. All of the characters are surrounded by mass media that crucially shape the way they inhabit their physical and social worlds, and almost all of them experience important social relationships, even quite intimate ones, mostly through the intermediary of various technologies of communication rather than in face-to-face encounters. This deterritorialization of local relationships functions to some extent as a symptom of modernist alienation, but it also metonymically conveys the dissociation from the local that is brought about by transnational ecological and technological connections, even when individuals continue to inhabit the same place. In this deterritorialized context, Wolf tries to maintain the tension between everyday life and technological risk by exploring them as potential opposites; her novel, in the end, is balanced uneasily between her attempt to keep these two areas separate—culminating in the narrator's claim that nuclear risk is difficult to compare to anything else—and the realization that risk scenarios will and must somehow be integrated into life practice. As I have pointed out, *Störfall* does not quite solve this conceptual problem. *Der Flötenton*, by contrast, takes such integration as a given and investigates by what means, under what circumstances, and at what cost different characters achieve it. Since it does not definitively condone or condemn the different accommodations characters arrive at, Wohmann's novel is in some ways a less "engaged" or "environmentalist" one than Wolf's; but at the same time, it avoids some of Wolf's conceptual tensions and presents a much broader and more nuanced portrait of life in the risk society.

Wolf's and Wohmann's novels, like many of the other texts and artworks I have discussed, challenge localisms through their reflection on how everyday life in its material practices, as well as in its social networks, has in fact detached itself from its local roots, even when it continues to be lived in specific places. While both authors show some of the negative consequences of this detachment—all the way from anxiety about one's gardening to existential feelings of solitude and emptiness—they also subtly but insistently highlight how precisely this detachment enables an understanding of the way local sites function in a network of global connectedness. Far from any simple appeals to Gaian-style holism, the central characters in both novels wrestle with the implications of risk scenarios that originate far away from their place of inhabitation and yet have the power to change their everyday experience of the local fundamentally. In their more or less successful attempts to integrate their awareness of such risks into their daily routines, these characters—none of them primarily nature lovers or environmental activists, but quite average people—seek a way of relating to the global that strikes a balance between an eco-paranoia that would paralyze everyday life and an absorption into the ordinary that would blot out this broader framework of thinking. To the environmentalist reader, this quest holds out the challenge of imagining deterritorialization not only as a threat to nature- and place-bound forms of inhabitation, but as a step toward an eco-cosmopolitan mode of inhabiting the ordinariness of the global in the risk society.

Two decades after the Chernobyl meltdown, the site's apocalyptic history is quietly being reappropriated for other purposes in the popular cultural imagination. When the town of Pripyat was opened for tourism in 2002, it initially attracted few visitors. But in 2004 and 2005, hundreds of tourists began to include it among their travel destinations, enrolling in guided walking tours of the area that include regular Geiger counter measurements of the remaining—by now relatively low—radioactivity. While some visit the site to commemorate and inform themselves about the accident and Soviet life of the period, others are drawn by an attraction to abandoned industrial sites, and yet others—in an ironical reversal—come to see what has by now become a remarkable nature sanctuary with resurgent bird, wolf, boar, and other wildlife populations (Chivers). Mary Mycio, in her *Wormwood Forest: A Natural History of Chernobyl*, refers to it as a "radioactive wilderness" of indisputable beauty. The juxtaposition of natural beauty with abandoned radioactive vehicles and machinery that *New York Times* correspondent C. J. Chivers describes in his brief account of the tour cannot but remind one of the junkyard ecology in Karen Tei Yamashita's *Through the Arc of the Rainforest* I discussed in chapter 3, while the conversion of the site of the worst nuclear accident into a tourist destination shares with Bacon and Welch's HazMaPo figures, analyzed in chapter 4, the uncanny ability of popular culture to transform risk scenarios into commodities and even art. Through the deterritorializations of international travel, Chernobyl is turned back from an abstract icon of technological disaster to its concrete materiality as a place; reterritorialized as a site to be visited rather than inhabited (by humans, at any rate), it has returned to the ordinariness of global tourism. One may reject this reappropriation as what Frederick Buell calls a domestication of crisis—but in doing so, it may be wise to remember that a good deal of environmentally oriented literature and film similarly relies, in one way or another, on the aestheticization of risk.

In the political arena, in the meantime, the Chernobyl disaster continues to generate controversy that arises mainly from the difficulty of determining its exact health consequences. Health experts had originally predicted long-term epidemics of various kinds of cancer among the affected populations, especially thyroid cancer and leukemia, as two of the most common consequences of exposure to radiation. Since the inhabitants of the area surrounding Chernobyl were evacuated and now live in a wide variety of locations across the former Soviet Union, it is not easy to pin down which of their illnesses should be traced back to Chernobyl and which ones would have arisen anyway or were due to other impacts, a difficulty that is compounded by the fact that some cancers remain latent for decades before manifesting themselves. Beyond the original residents of the area, it is difficult to determine who should even count as "affected population," given the very large number of individuals who were exposed to low levels of radiation in eastern, western, and northern Europe. As a consequence, estimates of the health effects of the disaster vary dramatically. In the fall of 2005, the United Nations' Chernobyl Forum issued a report that attributed approximately 4,000–9,000 additional deaths to the impact of the fall-out (Chernobyl Forum 14–21). In April 2006, as the United Nations commemorated the twentieth anniversary of the accident, Greenpeace issued a report that vigorously questioned these results; it attributed approximately 270,000 cancers, 93,000 fatal cases among them, to Chernobyl, and estimated that radiation had caused an additional 60,000 deaths in Russia from the early 1990s onward, with an expectation of a total additional death toll of 140,000 in the Ukraine and Belarus (*The Chernobyl Catastrophe*). Part of the discrepancy resulted from the fact that the World Health Organization, on whose studies part of the UN report was based, limited itself to the most affected countries—Ukraine, Belarus, and Russia—while Greenpeace's study referred to all of Europe. Other organizations, such as the International Agency for Research on Cancer, have pointed out that with the exception of thyroid cancer in the most contaminated areas, overall cancer rates in Europe did not increase after Chernobyl (Cardis 1233). Causal relations are, at any rate, extremely difficult to establish with regard to faraway regions that received low levels of radiation.

This debate over observed and expected health outcomes of Chernobyl was exacerbated by the fact that steadily growing concerns over global warming have recently led to a reconsideration of nuclear energy generation in countries that have foregone construction of nuclear plants for decades or even, as in the case of Germany, contemplated shutting down all existing ones. In a classical case of risk trade-off, even staunch opponents of nuclear energy such as Charles Perrow, whose work I discussed in chapter 4, have come to argue that the risks of climate change may well outweigh those of civilian nuclear technology, which does not emit greenhouse gases. Greenpeace remains firmly opposed to the technology and argues that low estimates of death rates from the aftermath of Chernobyl may be prompted by a desire to make nuclear energy palatable again to a public that has grown increasingly hostile to it from the 1970s onward. Even the study of a risk scenario that lies twenty years in the past rather than in the future, in other words, takes place within a political and cultural matrix that crucially shapes some of the basic assumptions being brought to bear on its investigation. The dangers of nuclear disasters that reach across geographical, national, and social borders continue to reconfigure themselves in the cultural imagination, as the more recent image of an entire planet undergoing climate change superimposes itself on the older risk scenarios. It is in the context of such shifting risk scenarios that cultural as well as material practices of inhabiting the local and the global redefine themselves at the turn of the third millennium.

CONCLUSION

Some Like It Hot: Climate Change
and Eco-Cosmopolitanism

W hile issues such as population growth, chemical pollution, nuclear contamination, and looming resource shortages dominated the environmental imagination of the global in the 1960s and 1970s, a new concern began to reshape it in the late 1980s. Initially called the "greenhouse effect," the gradual warming of the Earth's atmosphere due to emissions of heat-trapping gases later came to be referred to as "global warming" or "climate change." Scientists and environmentalists have sometimes worried that "global warming," perhaps the most straight-forward of the three phrases, does not sound risky enough to populations who associate heat with pleasant summers on the beach, and obscures the fact that some regions might actually experience more rainfall or lower temperatures. "Climate change," on the other hand, a far more neutral term, might not only convey no sense of risk at all but also concede terri-tory to political parties interested in minimizing its importance. And that is only the beginning of the difficulties. While the overwhelming majority of scientists agree that the atmosphere is warming up, and that the causes of the increasing temperature are anthropogenic, many of the ecological and social consequences that will follow from this change are extremely difficult to predict, especially for particular regions and locales.

In the course of the 1990s, climate change also began to make its way into the cultural imagination. Like other processes of global systemic transformation, ecological or not, climate change poses a challenge for narrative and lyrical forms that have conventionally focused above all on individuals, families, or nations, since it requires the articulation of con-nections between events at vastly different scales. Climatologist Stephen Schneider has pointedly foregrounded this problem even for scientific thinking:

Remember the famous photographs the astronauts took in space in the late 1960s that transformed global consciousness about the Earth? White clouds swirled around a blue globe with white ice caps and reddish deserts. The spiral patterns of storms stood out as bold features occupying regions the size of the New England states—1,000 kilometers or so in scale. That's one way of looking at the atmosphere. An airplane passenger on a turbulent flight might think the atmospheric action is at the scale of hundreds of meters as the plane is tossed about in the sky. A balloonist who can see individual rain droplets or snowflakes leisurely drift by might conclude that the atmosphere must be understood at the microscale of millimeters. . . . As the mathematical ecologist Simon Levin . . . once put it, the world looks very different, depending on the size of the window you are looking through. (1–2)

The texts, films, and other artworks I have discussed in this book all directly or indirectly reflect on such connections and disjunctures across ecological scales in their considerations of local, regional, and global forms of inhabitation. But this general challenge is compounded, in the case of climate change, by the newness of a concern that only appeared on the scientific and cultural horizon approximately twenty years ago; imagining how such a planetary transformation might affect particular places and individuals, therefore, amounts to a paradigmatic exercise in "secondhand nonexperience," envisioning a kind of change that has not occurred before.[1] Understanding climate change ecologically and conveying a sense of the quite divergent impacts it might have on communities around the globe is a task of such magnitude that relatively few writers and filmmakers have attempted it so far, and those who have—with a few exceptions—have done so with limited success.

In their portrayal of climate change as a global risk scenario, some films and novels—Robert Silverberg's novel *Hot Sky at Midnight* (1994), David Twohy's film *The Arrival* (1996), and Roland Emmerich's movie *The Day after Tomorrow* (2004), for example—fall back on apocalyptic narrative in some of its most dated and formulaic clichés of urban disaster and alien invasion. Michael Crichton's *State of Fear* (2004), a novel whose express purpose, as mentioned in chapter 1, is to expose global warming as a fiction cooked up by environmentalists and journalists, remains similarly simplistic in its one-dimensional characters and far-fetched conspiracy plot, which end up turning different risk perceptions into a black-and-white confrontation between heroes and villains. Cyberpunk novelist Bruce Sterling's *Heavy Weather* (1994) portrays climate-devastated American landscapes and cities as the context for an exploration of how personal relationships unfold in a context of social and ecological crisis, yet never rises above a rather shallow and haphazard analysis. Norman Spinrad's partly satirical and partly serious *Greenhouse Summer* (1999), set in a newly subtropical Paris, deviates from the typical apocalyptic plot by including both winners and losers from climate change, but ends with the frightening vision of a planet whose climate has spun so far out of control that not even its changes can be predicted anymore.[2] Novels that develop more complex story patterns—George Turner's *Drowning Towers* (1987), David Brin's *Earth* (1990), and Kim Stanley Robinson's climate change trilogy *Forty Signs of Rain* (2004), *Fifty Degrees Below* (2005), and *Sixty Days and Counting* (2007)—all evoke apocalyptic scenarios as templates for envisioning the effects of global warming but then proceed to displace, constrain, or frame millennial narrative in such a way that the texts as a whole take on quite different generic shapes.

Robinson's three novels, though the most recent, are the most conventional in their narrative strategy. The trilogy focuses on the effects of climate change in Washington, D.C., with the first novel describing a catastrophic flood and the second an extremely severe winter. These portrayals of disaster are framed by the professional and personal stories of scientists who investigate and develop policy proposals for global warming, through which Robinson explores in meticulous detail the complex institutional and political processes that frame the pursuit of scientific knowledge. While such analyses of scientific and political institutions tend to make for rather dry reading, the scientists' personal lives provide a symbolic frame for understanding global warming that emphasizes tropes of rootedness, home, and domesticity juxtaposed with those of homelessness, exile, and ferality. In this vein, one of the scientists combines her job at the National Science Administration (NSA) with her family obligations, while her husband takes care of their children at the same time that he serves as a policy advisor to a U.S. senator who by the third volume is elected president— dual tasks that lead to extended portrayals of domesticity and its difficulties. One of the other NSA scientists loses his apartment during the flood and begins to live in a tree house in a Washington park, encountering groups of homeless people as well as zoo animals that gradually turn feral after the inundation of the zoo. Both scientists become acquainted with a group of ambassadors from a fictional Asian island nation, Khembalung, who respond to the flooding of their homeland due to rising sea levels by redefining their identity in terms of a deterritorialized spiritual community. What is at stake in Robinson's portrayal of climate change, then, is clearly the attempt to envision less territorially defined forms of inhabitation; yet the narrative itself never develops any cultural perspective of the global. It remains for the most part stuck in Washington and American government perspectives (with the Asian climate refugees functioning as rather grotesque stereotypes of Buddhist wisdom and serenity), and the omniscient narrator never relinquishes his grip of this local scene to let other perspectives and discourses percolate.

Australian novelist George Turner's lyrically titled *The Sea and Summer*—a reference to rising sea levels and temperatures that was rather more sensationalistically retitled *Drowning Towers* at its American publication—looks back on the "greenhouse culture" of the late twentieth century through the eyes of a historian a thousand years in the future. In addition to her academic investigations, this historian decides to write a novel about the period entitled *The Sea and Summer*, which as an embedded narrative makes up the bulk of Turner's book. But it fails to inspire the playwright who reads it in preparation for a play he plans to write about the same era. "I should have seen from the beginning that these people struggled in the nets of local culture and their own personalities; they did not represent the collapsing world. It might be impossible, I feel, to create a group that *could* represent it," he writes to the historian (383), who files his letter "along with the academic reviews which disapproved of attempts to reduce history to flashes of insight through narrow tower windows" (384). In this intriguing conclusion to the novel, Turner seems to question his own narrative procedure and its ability to bridge precisely the gap between stories of individuals and accounts of global transformations that I mentioned earlier as one of the central challenges for cultural representations of climate change.

David Brin's novel *Earth*, which I already discussed in chapter 2 in terms of its portrayal of population growth, makes the most sustained attempt to develop a narrative architecture that might be able to accommodate a view of global systems along with local stories. As I explained, Brin recognizes the power of apocalyptic narrative and uses it, along with the trope of the physical "singularity," to signal a phase change in the way humankind relates to its planetary habitat. But he displaces the apocalyptic template from the quite plausible ecological crises that his imagined world society of 2038 just barely manages to control—global warming among them—to the far more fantastic narrative of a black hole that is in the process of destroying the Earth's crust from within. At the same time, he combines some of the plot elements of myth, epic and allegory with the fragmented, heterogeneous multivocality of the high modernist urban novel in an attempt to fuse a global perspective on the fate of the planet with the often divergent cultural realities and presuppositions of a wide variety of individuals and communities. As I argued in chapter 2, this innovative attempt to develop a narrative form commensurate with the complexities and heterogeneities of cultures joined in global crisis is one of the most daring (if not entirely successful) novelistic attempts to address both global ecological risk and global environmental connectedness. Through its juxtaposed plot strands of technological destruction and ecological crisis, this work reflects on different modes of narrativizing risk; through its combination of epic and modernist urban novel, it reaches for a formal materialization of the kind of eco-cosmopolitanism whose articulation I have pursued throughout this book.

Besides its reflections in literature and feature films, the issue of climate change has also given rise to numerous nonfiction books and some documentary films. Many of the books, as Greg Garrard has pointed out, take the form of travelogues in which the authors trace the manifestations of climatological crisis in various locations around the globe (personal communication). This basic structure is also reflected in Al Gore's Oscar-winning documentary *An Inconvenient Truth* (2006), which seeks to convey climate science principally through a lecture that Gore is seen delivering to a range of audiences around the globe over the course of the film. While the trailers for *An Inconvenient Truth* included phrases such as "the scariest movie you'll ever see" and thereby suggested a millennial panorama along the lines of *The Day after Tomorrow,* the rhetoric of the film itself studiously avoids any sustained allusion to apocalypse—in contrast to a competing climate change documentary such as *The 11th Hour* (2007), which uses disaster rhetoric extensively. The focus on the presentation of scientific knowledge and the choice of a didactic scenario as the structuring dramatic frame might be expected to produce the same nonnarrative dryness as that in Robinson's trilogy, but Gore, well aware of this danger, seeks to make his presentation more compelling through the interspersal of autobiographical elements as well as the foregrounding of digital technology.[3] While the references to Gore's autobiography are designed to anchor the presentation of scientific facts in the kind of *Bildungsroman* structure I discussed in chapter 4 as characteristic of certain kinds of risk narrative, the persistent focus on Gore's use of an Apple laptop to do research, present his findings, and be in touch with people around the world highlight computer technology as a means of both exploring nature and establishing sociopolitical networks.

This emphasis on digital technology links *An Inconvenient Truth* to Brin's *Earth*, which, as I mentioned earlier, describes with surprising prescience—in 1990, before the emergence of the first widely available internet browser—a world of digital connectedness including online news, virtual chat groups, and digital books. The digital network, indeed, is the counterpart and in some sense the master trope for the ecological connectivity with which it fuses at the end. At the same time, the computer appears again and again as a tool for modeling the planet, though the novel does not quite succeed in anticipating the ways the actually existing digital web of the early third millennium allows its users to map the planet through software applications such as Google Earth and other digital imaging tools that have recently attained great popularity. Brin's *Earth* and Google Earth offer the most far-reaching and comprehensive aesthetic models for considering ecological crisis and environmental as well as cultural connectedness across different spatial scales. John Klima's installation *Earth,* whose anticipation of some of the structures of Google Earth I discussed in chapter 1, presents a close analogue in a different cultural medium. John Brunner's novel *Stand on Zanzibar* and John Cage's poem "Overpopulation and Art," as I showed in chapter 2, also imagine a planet linked as much by digital and other structures of information and communication as by the crowds of people that, in these works' vision, embody serious ecological risks as much as utopian social possibilities. The other texts, films, and artworks I have examined in this book approach the ecological imagination of the global not so much by way of a digital aesthetic as through the detailed exploration of a local site that on close inspection turns out to be linked to the global in unanticipated, sometimes unsettling, and sometimes exhilarating ways. Lothar Baumgarten's *Der Ursprung der Nacht* and Karen Tei Yamashita's *Through the Arc of the Rainforest* focus on Amazon rainforest ecology only to reveal its literal and metaphorical imbrications into global economic and symbolic exchanges. Don DeLillo's *White Noise* and Richard Powers's *Gain* present characters whose inhabitation of small midwestern towns is unsettled through their exposure to risk scenarios that transcend conventional class distinctions and link individuals to corporations operating around the globe. Even more obviously, the protagonists of Wolf's and Wohmann's novels gradually awaken to risk scenarios that tie them to institutions and places beyond national borders, prompting them to resituate their own everyday practices in relation to this expanded scale of inhabitation.

All of these works, implicitly or explicitly, highlight the imbrication of local places, ecologies, and cultural practices in global networks that reconfigure them according to a logic that recent theories of globalization label "deterritorialization." But unlike many more explicitly "environmentalist" texts written in the United States, these works take an ambivalent stance toward this process, suggesting that it might sometimes need to be resisted by some form of "reterritorialization," but that it might in other cases become the basis for cosmopolitan forms of awareness and community, both ecologically and culturally. At the same time, all of them strive to find effective aesthetic templates by means of which to convey such a dual vision of the Earth as a whole and of the different earths that are shaped by varying cultural contexts. They thereby participate in the search for the stories and images of a new kind of eco-cosmopolitan environmentalism that might be able effectively to engage with steadily increasing patterns of global connectivity, including those created by broadening risk scenarios. This book understands itself as a part of the same search.

NOTES

Introduction

1. Romance languages have the advantage of two terms to describe what is covered by "globalization" in English. In French, for example, the term "mondialisation" originally covered the same semantic territory as "globalization" in English, but has in some contexts taken on more specific political, social, and cultural connotations since "globalisation" has emerged as a competing concept mostly focused on economic processes. In English, "globalization" has also taken on a more and more centrally economic meaning, but unfortunately no comparable term has emerged to foreground other processes of global connection. In my analysis, "globalization" therefore refers to such processes in their entirety, rather than just to the economic component, however fundamental one assumes its role to be.

2. Among those who see global ecological policies in particular as part of the North's hegemonic strategies are Vandana Shiva ("Greening the Global Reach") and Larry Lohmann ("Resisting Green Globalism"). For a different assessment of the role of the West in globalization processes that is not specifically focused on ecology, see Tomlinson (89–97). On the question of globalism and cultural homogenization, see Appadurai, Hannerz (*Transnational Connections* 102–11 and "Scenarios for Peripheral Cultures"), and Lull (147–64).

Chapter 1

1. The ellipsis is Le Guin's.

2. In the 1987 introduction to the story, Le Guin does not mention Lovelock's Gaia hypothesis explicitly but does refer to "*Deo, Demeter, the grain-mother, and her daughter/self Kore the Maiden called Persephone*" as ancient mythological paradigms for envisioning humans' relationship to the plant world (83).

3. See McLuhan (71) and Lovelock's preface to *Gaia* (x, xiv).

4. For a detailed analysis of how the satellite view of Earth constituted the planet as a new kind of scientific object through the hegemony of vision, see Sachs's *Satellitenblick* (esp. 15–34). A particularly strident critique of the Blue Planet image is that of Yaakov Jerome Garb, who points out that it privileges

vision over the direct experience of the other senses and associates it with patriarchal consciousness, monotheism, and pornography. This sweeping critique seems to me misguided, insofar as it dissociates the image from its specific sociohistorical context and casts it instead as the incarnation of social and philosophical tendencies that have prevailed for centuries. But Garb asks pointedly toward the end of his essay, "Isn't the fantasy that we can somehow contain the Earth within our imagination, bind it with a single metaphor, the most mistaken presumption of all? What would it be to live with multiple images of the Earth—fragmented, partial, and local representations that must always be less than the Earth we try to capture through them?" (278). As I will show at the end of this chapter and later, the most interesting contemporary artworks and technological tools attempt to combine images of the whole planet with such more partial representations.

5. Some of the popular scientific publications involving Gaia are listed in Serafin (135); Merchant provides a detailed list of events, conferences and products associated with Gaia in the 1980s and 1990s (5). It is worth noting that the Gaia hypothesis did not lead Lovelock himself to a stance that would qualify as "environmentalist" today, since he believed that the overall functioning of the planet could only be marginally affected by human activity—a view he subsequently found himself forced to qualify.

6. For detailed analyses of this rhetoric, see Garrard (*Ecocriticism* 85–107); L. Buell (*Environmental Imagination* 280–308); Killingsworth and Palmer; and F. Buell (177–208). I discuss apocalyptic narrative as a particular articulation of risk perceptions in chapter 4.

7. Shell and IG Farben also figured prominently in Pynchon's vision of corporate conspiracy in *Gravity's Rainbow*, published only two years before *The Monkey Wrench Gang*.

8. For a more detailed summary of the debates about the notion of human and/or economic development that surround these terms, see Hayden (121–51).

9. This tradition is far from obsolete today: for an analysis and critique, see Evans.

10. For more detailed readings, see Berthold-Bond's analysis of Leopold's sketch (23–24) and L. Buell's reading of Snyder's poem (*Environmental Imagination* 166–67).

11. See Williams, "Yellowstone," and Westling.

12. For Marx's reversal of his original analysis of the decline of pastoral, see his 1986 essay "Pastoralism in America." Raymond Williams's *The Country and the City* provides a similarly magisterial analysis for British literature. For recent ecocritical work on pastoral, see Bate; L. Buell (*Environmental Imagination* 31–52); Garrard ("Radical Pastoral?" and *Ecocriticism* 33–58); Gifford (*Pastoral* and "Gary Snyder and Post-Pastoral"); Love (65–88); and Scheese.

13. In spite of the postulation of such transcendental ties to place in quite a few environmental justice writings, however, their international dimension provides an important point of departure for developing more transnational forms of environmental and ecocritical thought, a point to which I will return in chapter 4. For a more detailed discussion of materialism and spirituality in environmentalist thought, see Plumwood, chap. 10.

14. For a detailed analysis of the image of the environmentally responsible Native American, see Krech. The celebration of premodern cultures also appears in other regional varieties of environmentalist thinking. Indian envi-

ronmentalist Vandana Shiva claims that traditional cultures of her country had an intuitive grasp of the ecological situatedness of their own place and its "connection to the universe....In most sustainable traditional cultures, the great and the small have been linked so that limits, restraints, responsibilities are always transparent and cannot be externalized. The great exists in the small and hence every act has not only global but cosmic implications. To tread gently on the earth becomes the natural way to be" (154).

15. On the relationship of Native American and other indigenous peoples to local places, see also Feld and Basso; Basso.

16. This opposition to modernity as a general sociopolitical structure is also clearly articulated by some environmentalist thinkers who draw on more leftist traditions of thought. British philosopher Mick Smith argues that "radical environmentalism is engaged in a fundamental critique of modernism; its alternative culture challenges modern life to its very core" (164–65). Yet in Smith's thought, "place" is quite deliberately used as an ambiguous concept that sometimes refers to actual localities (as in his discussion of the British antiroads movement) and sometimes to a more general reliance on the concrete rather than on abstract categories.

17. For a detailed analysis of the role of the body in twentieth-century philosophies of place, see Casey (202–42).

18. For the connections between European phenomenology and American environmentalism, see also Zimmerman, chap. 3; Brown and Toadvine; Abram; and Westling.

19. In fairness to Hardin, it should be added that he does acknowledge the existence of some truly global problems: the greenhouse effect, in his view, qualifies as such (*Filters against Folly* 145–69).

20. Haines's approach to what a sense of place might imply, at any rate, is interestingly varied. In some of his essays and poems he does celebrate a fairly straightforward, solitary, sensory, and self-sufficient immersion into a specific natural locale as an ideal: "To really know the place, I had to live there, build there, become intimate with it and know it for a long time" (11). But in other instances, he expresses unease with just this kind of intensely local inhabitation, and with an overly geographical conception of "place": "As a writer I have sometimes been uncomfortable with a purely local idea of place, as if I were attempting to wear a suit of clothes a size too small....I have wondered if we were not attempting to live in a world of continents and vaster entities with minds and senses conditioned by life in the village....I mean...that perhaps one reason for the difficulty we encounter when we speak about *community* and *place* is that our concepts of them are outmoded, and have been for a long time" (38–39). Both essays in which these statements appear date from the 1970s (1979 and 1975, respectively).

21. Thomashow articulated some of the essential points of his argument in *Bringing the Biosphere Back Home* in his earlier essay "Toward a Cosmopolitan Bioregionalism." In the latter, the concept of cosmopolitanism is used loosely, without reference to the body of theories I build on later in this chapter.

22. I would argue that a similar problem besets Patrick Murphy's much more thoughtful and nuanced attempt to formulate an approach to transnational community in his essay "Grounding Anotherness and Answerability in Allonational Ecoliterature Formations." Murphy sees the nation-state as problematic for environmentalist thought and argues for scales of identification and activism both below and above the nation. But ultimately, he sees

transnational formations still as founded on and identified through their ties to the local and the ethic of proximity: "These larger than nation and transnational formations, like the smaller than nation ones, maintain territorial identifications that generate loyalty to specific, concrete locations that are defined by a sense of shared threats and shared interests" (424). Fair enough: these are transnational formations that remain in their essence local; but surely, a "sense of shared threats and shared interests" is not necessarily defined by shared territorial location (especially not in the case of international nongovernmental organizations, to which Murphy refers as an example).

23. A renewed interest in the local and the experience of place characterized a variety of disciplines in the 1980s and 1990s, from literary and cultural studies (particularly in American studies) to anthropology, geography, and philosophy. Giving an adequate summary introduction to the vast amount of literature in these fields is beyond the scope of this chapter. Essays, monographs, and anthologies that convey a sense of this focus include Seamon and Mugerauer; Soja (*Postmodern Geographies* and *Thirdspace*); Franklin and Steiner; Bird et al.; Keith and Pile; Duncan and Ley; Hirsch and O'Hanlon; Ching and Creed; Harvey (*Justice*); Lovell; and Blair. For critiques of the way notions of the local have been deployed in literary and cultural studies, see Simpson (*Academic Postmodern*, chap. 5; *Situatedness*), as well as Robbins's arguments on behalf of cosmopolitanism and internationalism in "Comparative Cosmopolitanisms" and *Feeling Global*, to which I will return.

24. I am indebted to Rebecca Solnit for arguing this point in a panel discussion at the North American Interdisciplinary Conference on Environment and Community at the University of Nevada, Reno, February 19–21, 1998.

25. Leach himself participates in this tradition by deploring contemporary American placelessness throughout his book, from a cultural rather than an environmentalist viewpoint.

26. While Deleuze and Guattari's use of the concept does start out from a geographical basis in *Anti-Oedipus* (see 145–46), it becomes highly metaphorical in *Thousand Plateaus* (see 167–92 on the deterritorialization of the face). Due to the diffuseness and metaphoricity of the term in their work, it is less useful for the analysis I am proposing here than sociological and anthropological perspectives.

27. Lash and Urry emphasize the enormous importance of long-distance travel by car, train, or plane for modern societies, which they see as a much more centrally modern phenomenon than the oft-quoted movements of the Baudelairean flâneur through the metropolis (252). What they claim is quintessentially modern about such travel is not only its dependence on new technologies but also, and more decisively, the organizational innovations and cultural reconceptualizations that make these technologies accessible to large numbers of people and make them accept increased mobility as safe and desirable (253–54). Lash and Urry's analysis of these contexts leads them to claim that "the paradigmatic modern experience is that of rapid mobility often across long doistances" (253).

28. Cosmopolitanism is, obviously, not the only concept around which theories of identity and subjecthood in a global context have crystallized. Especially in American studies, competing terms such as "critical internationalism," "transnationalism," and "diaspora" have proliferated. Quite a few theoretical explorations of these terms overlap at least partially with the achievements, ambiguities, and shortfalls of theories of cosmopolitanism I

outline here and, given more time and space, would deserve to be discussed in parallel. I have focused on cosmopolitanism in particular because much of the work on this term is less tied to the specific disciplinary issues and configurations of American studies. I explore the relation between ecocriticism and some of the competing concepts, including transnationalism and diaspora, in "Ecocriticism and the Transnational Turn in American Studies."

In a comparatist context, Gayatri Spivak has proposed the notion of "planetarity" as an alternative to "globalization" and as a mode of identification that does not define itself in opposition to an Other. In *Death of a Discipline*, Spivak proposes that "if we imagine ourselves as planetary subjects rather than global agents, planetary creatures rather than global entities, alterity remains underived from us; it is not our dialectical negation, it contains us as much as it flings us away.... We must persistently educate ourselves into this peculiar mindset" (73). In a later essay, she elaborates (quoting her own earlier work): "I recommended planetarity because 'planet-thought opens up to embrace an inexhaustible taxonomy of such names including but not identical with animism as well as the spectral white mythology of post-rational science.' By 'planet-thought' I meant a mind-set that thought that we lived on, specifically, a planet. I continue to think that to be human is to be intended toward exteriority. And, if we can get to planet-feeling, the outside or other is indefinite.... If we planet-think, planet-feel, our 'other'—everything in the unbounded universe—cannot be the self-consolidating other, an other that is a neat and commensurate opposite of the self.... You see how very different it is from a sense of being the custodians of our very own planet, for god or for nature, although I have no objection to such a sense of accountability, where our own home is our other, as in self and world. But that is not the planetarity I was talking about. Planetarity, then, is not quite a dimension, because it cannot authorize itself over against a self-consolidating other. In that mind-set, there is no choosing between cultures" ("World Systems" 107–8). This kind of awareness sounds to a certain degree like that of the alien forest in Le Guin's "Vaster Than Empires and More Slow." To the extent that Spivak seems to include both other cultures and the nonhuman world in her conception of planetarity, it points in a theoretical direction of potential interest for ecocriticism. Yet theories surrounding the notion of cosmopolitanism have given far more detailed accounts of the processes involved in negotiating contemporary differences of nation, race, and culture than a planetarity that Spivak believes "is perhaps best imagined from the precapitalist cultures of the planet" ("World Systems" 101). Wai Chee Dimock, in elaborating the notion of planetarity, goes even further in seeking out a "deep time" dimension that she imagines on the scale of thousands of years as a way of overcoming the limitations inherent in current, nation-based forms of awareness (esp. chap. 6). One can readily agree with Dimock that if we think back to a time thousands of years ago, current differences of nationality lose their relevance; but what purchase such a vision might have on a present that *is* structured by differences of culture and nation unlikely to disappear anytime soon remains unclear in Dimock's account.

29. See also Posnock on the question of cosmopolitanism's historical associations with egalitarianism (803–4).

30. Some of the blandest conceptualizations of cosmopolitanism result from attempts to link these varied orientations without any explicit acknowledgment of the different theoretical and political agendas they entail. See, for example, Pollock et al.'s "Cosmopolitanisms," which claims that "Cosmopoli-

tanism may...be a project whose conceptual content and pragmatic character are not only as yet unspecified but also must always escape positive and definitive specification, precisely because specifying cosmopolitanism positively and definitely is an uncosmopolitan thing to do" (577), but also "that we already are and have always been cosmopolitan, though we may not always have known it....Cosmopolitanism is infinite ways of being" (588). See the critique of Pollock et al. in Skrbis et al. (118).

31. Nussbaum and Cohen's anthology *For Love of Country* contains both Nussbaum's essay and the varied responses to it. For an evaluation and critique of this debate, see Robbins (*Feeling Global*, chap. 8).

32. I am grateful to Catherine Diamond and Haruo Shirane for discussing perceptions of nature in Chinese and Japanese culture with me.

33. Environmentalists sometimes prefer the phrase "more-than-human world" to more conventional ones such as "nonhuman environment" because it deemphasizes the boundaries between human and nonhuman parts of the lifeworld. This term has become especially popular subsequent to the 1996 publication of David Abram's *Spell of the Sensuous*, which relies on a particular interpretation of Merleau-Ponty's brand of phenomenology.

34. I return to the question of what political structures this might entail in chapter 4.

35. Aihwa Ong makes a similar point when she compares different approaches to globalization: "Instead of embracing the totalizing view of globalization as economic rationality bereft of human agency, other social analysts have turned toward studying 'the local.'...This view is informed by a top-down model whereby the global is macro-political economic and the local is situated, culturally creative, and resistant. But a model that analytically defines the global as political economic and the local as cultural does not quite capture the *horizontal* and *relational* nature of the contemporary economic, social and cultural processes that stream across spaces" (*Flexible Citizenship* 4).

36. See the discussions in Worster (340–87); Phillips (42–82); and Garrard (*Ecocriticism* 56–58).

37. In December 2005, the *New York Times* reported on attempts by Russian officials to conceal the location of important oil fields by means of doctored maps, even though these installations can easily be identified on Google Earth (Kramer).

Chapter 2

1. UN (xix, 5, 11). The U.S. Census Bureau, which uses different forecasting procedures from the UN, similarly predicts a world population of nine billion for 2042 ("World Population Information").

2. On the divergent population developments in different regions, see Haub. Cultural concerns over the consequences of shrinking populations in some industrialized societies were expressed after the UN's *World Population Prospects: The 1996 Revision* in Crossette; Eberstadt, "Population Implosion" and "World Population Implosion"; Laing; and Wattenberg. For critiques of these views, see Gelbard and Haub, and the responses to Wattenberg's article, *New York Times Magazine*, 14 December 1997, 20–24.

3. I am grateful to Suki Hoagland for discussing this change with me.

4. See Laing (38) for a brief summary of U.S. concerns over population growth prior to the 1960s.

5. I am grateful to Deborah White for pointing me to this episode.

6. It would have been impossible for me to trace many of these texts without Brian Stableford's excellent survey article ("Overpopulation").

7. Carrying capacity is a more elusive term than appears at first sight: for an excellent discussion, see Cohen (pt. 4, 159–364). In recent years, the concept of a population's "ecological footprint" has replaced that of "carrying capacity" in many contexts.

8. Aldiss's *Earthworks* is an interesting exception from this rule, in that it focuses in part on the toxic agricultural hinterlands of big cities.

9. Killingsworth and Palmer, who quote this passage in their essay "Millennial Ecology," comment on its apocalyptic tone, its "bourgeois terror," and its fear of the crowds (33).

10. Quoted in isolation, this passage also appears tinged by racism in its juxtaposition of the affluent Western family and the poverty-stricken Eastern masses, as well as by Ehrlich's distinction between "our" problems and those of India, which excludes an Indian reader from the circle of those whom the author is addressing. Yet I would defend Ehrlich against such an accusation, given his persistent emphasis in many books that population growth, due to the West's disproportionate use of world resources, is as much a problem of the First as of the Third World: this is precisely the core of much of his argument, which he deliberately addresses to a mainly Western audience.

11. For a comparison of Disch's *334* with *1984*, see Swirski (170).

12. For two studies of the individual in mass society that were influential in the 1960s, see David Riesman's *The Lonely Crowd* (originally published in 1950; republished, slightly abridged, in 1961 and 1969, due to its extreme popularity) and Herbert Marcuse's *One-Dimensional Man* (1964). Riesman's claim that in advanced societies, "increasingly, *other people* are the problem, not the material environment" (18), is spelled out in overpopulation novels in a more literal sense than he intended.

13. "In this particular context, I thought of dos Passos [*sic*]. I went home, and I re-read *Midcentury*, not because it's a very good book, or even the best of his many novels, but because it's the one in which I think his technique of documentary association is most highly evolved" ("Genesis" 36).

14. See Goldman for an analysis of Brunner's protagonists from a moral rather than a narratological perspective.

15. This remark prefigures a very similar one uttered by one of the characters in Don DeLillo's *White Noise* (see chapter 5 here): "'For most people there are only two places in the world. Where they live and their TV set'" (66).

16. On the notion of the cyborg, see Donna Haraway's "Cyborg Manifesto" and Chris Hables Gray's anthology of essays; for an analysis of how computer users understand the relationship between their virtual-and-real-life stories, see Sherry Turkle's *Life on the Screen.*

17. The anthology *No Room for Man: Population and the Future through Science Fiction*, published in 1979 (Clem, Greenberg, and Olander) consists in large part of reprints of earlier short stories.

18. As early as 1947, Teilhard saw computers as part of this network of the future: see his essay "Une interprétation plausible de l'Histoire Humaine: La formation de la 'Noosphère.'"

19. See Amery's *Das Geheimnis der Krypta* for a much more sophisticated narrative confrontation with the question of overpopulation and genocide.

20 I have examined Brin's strategies and shortcomings in *Earth* in more detail in "Netzphantasien: Science Fiction zwischen Öko-Angst und Informationsutopie" (253–59).

21. The following interpretation of Cage's mesostics is based on Perloff's reading of this technique in her article on *Roaratorio*, "Music for Words Perhaps."

Chapter 3

1. I am quoting from the easily accessible translation of *Du miel aux cendres* by John and Doreen Weightman.

2. Some reviewers and critics read *Through the Arc of the Rainforest* as a straightforward antiglobalization story. Patrick Murphy, for example, interprets it as "a comic, cautionary tale about the destruction of many communities, and, by extension, virtually any community, by multinational capitalism's ubiquitous commodification of objects, peoples, practices, and beliefs" (*Farther Afield* 187). For a similar reading, see Sze. As I will show, such readings oversimplify the complexities of Yamashita's plot and narrative technique.

3. Rachel Lee's reading of the novel (106–38) remains unpersuasive because she strains to account for the novel purely within the framework of Asian American literature, never so much as mentioning the much more fundamental strategies that situate Yamashita's text in the tradition of twentieth-century Latin American narrative.

4. All translations from *Cien años de soledad* are mine.

5. Brian Conniff comments on the gypsies as representatives of global space and knowledge vis-à-vis Macondo (167–79). In almost all other respects, the reading of the novel's space I offer here diverges substantially from the one proposed by Conniff.

6. "All he knew was that Tania Aparecida was far away. It made very little difference how far. Batista's jealous imagination could follow Tania Aparecida to the next room or to the moon" (173).

7. The speaking parrot who is revealed, in the epilogue to *Macunaíma*, to be the one who conveyed the protagonist's story to the narrator has a humorous equivalent in the parrot accompanying the triple-breasted French ornithologist Michelle Mabelle (herself perhaps another parodic reincarnation of Andrade's one-breasted Amazon Ci); this bird, instead of telling stories, eats camembert and sings the Marseillaise.

8. Tweep, the three-armed American businessman, may well be Yamashita's version of the Peruvian businessman Venceslau Pietro Pietra, against whom Macunaíma struggles throughout most of Andrade's novel: Pietra is also described as a mythological figure, the giant Piaiman, Eater of Men, whose cannibalism provides an apt foil for Tweep's corporate imperialism.

9. "Um dos meus interesses foi desrespeitar lendariamente a geografia e a fauna e flora geográficas. Assim desregionalizava o mais possível a criação ao mesmo tempo que conseguia o mérito de conceber literariamente o Brasil como entidade homogênea—um concerto étnico e geográfico" ("One of my interests was to disregard geography and geographically specific fauna and flora completely. So I deregionalized nature as much as possible, at the same time that I succeeded in conceiving of Brazil literarily as a homogeneous entity— an ethnic and geographic concerto"); Mário de Andrade, quoted in Haroldo de Campos (78–79; my translation). See also Suárez and Tomlins (98).

10. But even in Andrade, this project is in some ways a paradoxical one: since in his portrait one of Brazil's most striking features is the endless transformability of the real, the character of Brazil ends up being no specific character at all—hence the novel's subtitle *The Hero without Any Character*. In an unpublished preface to his novel, Andrade himself comments on this lack of character: "'O que me interessou por Macunaíma foi inquestionavelmente a preocupação em que vivo de trabalhar e descobrir o mais que possa a entidade nacional dos brasileiros. Ora depois de pelejar muito verifiquei uma coisa me parece que certa: o brasileiro não tem caráter.... (O brasileiro não tem caráter porque não possui nem civilização própria nem consciência tradicional. Os franceses têm caráter e assim os jorubas e os mexicanos....) Brasileiro não'" ("What interested me about Macunaíma was unquestionably my concern to work out and discover as much as I could about the national essence of Brazilians. Now after struggling a lot, I found out something that seems certain to me: the Brazilian has no character.... [The Brazilian has no character because he possesses neither a civilization of his own nor a historical consciousness. The French have character, and so do the Yoruba and the Mexicans...]. Not the Brazilian"; quoted in Campos 75; my translation).

11. Just as Macunaíma's supernatural voyages lead him into Brazilian history as well as geography—he encounters indigenous artifacts and historical figures from the colonial period as well as the landscape of his present—Chicolándia is as much a simulation of history as it is of geographical and cultural difference.

12. Rody shares my sense of the narrator as a global presence when she argues that Yamashita aims "to engage us in a global community of concern. And how better to do this than with a narrator whose winning personality is unhampered by markers of national or ethnic identity? Yamashita and her hero Kazumasa Ishimaru may have evident ethnic origins, but the ball appears origin-free, and its bouncy conduct of the plot around the globe manages to transform an ethnic perspective into a credibly global historical witness. Yamashita's ball, then, is a performance of objectivity that retains the trace of its historical origins" (638).

13. I have explored the temporal structure of *Through the Arc of the Rainforest* in more detail in my essay "Die Zeitlichkeit des Risikos im amerikanischen Roman der Postmoderne" (The temporality of risk in the postmodern American novel).

Chapter 4

1. By tracing the academic analysis of ecological and technological risk back to Starr (especially his essay "Social Benefit versus Technological Risk"), I follow the accounts presented in Löfstedt and Frewer (3), and Lupton (chaps. 1–2); Löfstedt and Frewer also outline a different trajectory according to which the roots of this type of risk theory can be traced back to the Chicago School of geography and the attempt to explain human engagements with natural disasters such as periodic floods (3).

2. In economics, risk analysis has a far longer history than the one outlined here within the broader framework of decision theory. Most of the researchers who have shaped the field of technological and ecological risk analysis since the 1970s, however, do not tend to situate their work explicitly in relation to this theoretical framework, but in relation to the paradigms I focus on here.

3. Many of the basic factors that affect risk perception according to the psychometric model have been criticized, refined, or reformulated over time. For example, the distinction between voluntary and involuntary risks, as Charles Perrow has pointed out, is not always neat: driving one's car to work may seem more voluntary than inhaling secondhand smoke; yet if no alternative transportation is readily available, it may in fact be no more subject to one's own choice than, say, risks of injury at one's workplace (*Normal Accidents* 312–13).

4. Social trust is a crucial issue both for the analysis of risk perceptions and, much more generally, of modern societies. For a theory of social trust that not only analyzes its functioning in risk management as an exemplary case but defines it theoretically as a form of risk judgment, see Earle and Cvetkovich, *Social Trust: Toward a Cosmopolitan Society.* Earle and Cvetkovich are interested in how social trust can work to establish social relations across groups in a way that they refer to as "cosmopolitan," without specifically tying their reflections to theories of cosmopolitanism as a transnational mode of awareness.

5. Rayner ("Cultural Theory") provides a discussion of such objections and shows how cultural theory counters them.

6. For a critique and modification of some of the basic assumptions and concepts in Kasperson's framework, see Murdock et al.

7. On the question of pregnant women's regimentation, see also Lin Nelson's interesting suggestion that workplace rules intended to protect women, and especially pregnant women, from hazards can sometimes function in such a way as to shift the blame for the danger from the source of the risk itself to women's biological vulnerability (178). A fourth paradigm of research besides the psychometric model, cultural theory, and governmentality has developed from German sociologist Niklas Luhmann's brand of systems theory. As Luhmann's theory analyzes social phenomena on the basis of very different assumptions and by means of an entirely different vocabulary from most Anglo-Saxon sociology, it has not made a major impact on studies of risk outside Germany. For a sense of this type of risk theory, see Luhmann; and Japp (*Soziologische Risikotheorie* and *Risiko*).

8. Ingar Palmlund has suggested that risk controversies might be studied as a form of "social drama" with the vocabulary of theatrical characters, plots and conventions. While this approach is quite suggestive in some ways, Palmlund bases her analytic vocabulary mainly on Greek tragedy, without attention to other dramatic templates, especially the varying perspectives and divergent stories about an unfolding conflict that tend to take center stage in modern drama. Her account, therefore, remains ultimately very schematic and overly simple ("Social Drama and Risk Evaluation"). Other social scientists have deployed literary templates in a less systematic way. Sociologist Allan Mazur subtitled his detailed study of the Love Canal case *The Rashomon Effect at Love Canal* to indicate that the multiple different stories about the crisis told by different participants remain as contradictory and indeterminate as the competing stories in Akira Kurosawa's paradigmatically modernist film. Yet toward the end of his analysis, Mazur sums the crisis up as a "tragedy in the classic sense" (212), apparently with no awareness that a tragic narrative structure is hard to reconcile with the open-ended indeterminacy of *Rashomon.* For a more detailed narrative analysis of Mazur's and other accounts of Love Canal, see Heise, "Risk and Narrative at Love Canal."

9. On the whale as a synecdoche for the oceans, see L. Buell (*Writing* 196–223).

10. I will return to this question of the domestication of crisis in the context of the everyday lives of Wolf's and Wohmann's post-Chernobyl protagonists in chapter 6.

11. For a more recent discussion of nuclear technology, see also Perrow's *The Next Catastrophe* (chap. 5), and Feder for his admission that climate change may make nuclear power once again acceptable.

12. When Perrow claims that nuclear arms have done little harm to humans, he is of course referring to harm from accidents, not from their intentional usage as weapons.

13. See Beck, Giddens, and Lash for the somewhat different concepts of reflexive modernization each of these three theorists proposes.

14. All translations from Beck's *Risikogesellschaft* are mine.

15. For a well-articulated critique of this kind, see Goldblatt (chap. 5).

16. More detailed analyses of vulnerability can be found in Ezcurra et al.; Kasperson et al., "Vulnerability"; and Liverman.

17. It is tempting to relate Ulrich Beck's concept of "secondhand nonexperience" to Baudrillard's notion of the hyperreal, the copy without an original. But the context and import of the two concepts is ultimately different: Beck's argument is not so much about imitation as about anticipation, and his aim is to explore the ways new types of risk overturn the modes of common-sense reasoning, rather than to suggest the broader skepticism vis-à-vis the authenticity of contemporary culture that Baudrillard proposes.

18. The notion of "stigma" was proposed by Flynn, Slovic, and Kunreuther to characterize such adverse effects of risk perceptions. In the same volume, however, Vern Walker warns that stigma, far from being a neutral term, usually suggests an irrational or objectively unfounded social process by means of which people, places, or objects are singled out for opprobrium. Introducing this term into risk theory, he warns, might well surreptitiously reintroduce old biases against lay perceptions that the field overcame in the 1980s and 1990s (354–57). Most likely for this reason, the term has not found wide usage in the field.

19. Eckersley principally explores Habermas's *Die postnationale Konstellation* and Held's *Democracy and the Global Order*. As is obvious from this juxtaposition, Eckersley works with a somewhat different definition of cosmopolitanism than the cultural theories I have mostly relied on in my discussion.

20. In view of the argument I made in chapter 1, I would want to qualify Eckersley's insistence on the ontological priority of the local, which she here seems to equate with the specific—even as she also mentions solidarities with people or species that do not of necessity have to be local. But the more important point is Eckersley's own admission that an ethic of proximity will not suffice.

21. For empirical studies of cross-cultural risk perceptions, see Renn and Rohrmann.

Chapter 5

1. Like many other authors and critics, Buell also perpetuates the amalgamation of chemical with nuclear risk by including among his exemplary texts

Terry Tempest Williams's *Refuge*, which deals with cancer perhaps caused by nuclear testing in the American West.

2. See Mark Osteen's introduction to the Viking critical edition of *White Noise* (vii), which also contains materials documenting the novel's parallels with the Bhopal accident (353–62).

3. See, for example, Michael Valdez Moses's Heideggerian interpretation of the scene in "Lust Removed from Nature."

4. For discussions of spectacle, simulation, and the role of media in shaping reality in *White Noise*, see Duvall; Lentricchia; Reeve and Kerridge; Kerridge. A different interpretation is proposed by Paul Maltby, who argues that a Romantic sense of transcendence does emerge in some crucial scenes of the novel, so that the postmodern scene of the simulacrum does ultimately lead to some experience of authenticity ("Romantic Metaphysic").

5. Interestingly, this remark occurs in a book review of Richard Powers's *Gain*, which I will discuss later. In *Gain*, unlike *White Noise*, Scott contends, chemical risk is not symbolic (41). But simply rephrasing "ambient dread" as "environmental dread" in Scott's claim would restore full materiality to the toxic event.

6. In highlighting the importance of the risk concept for *White Noise*, it may also be worth remembering that DeLillo's earlier novel *The Names* (1982) features a political risk analyst as its protagonist.

7. The term *riskscape* is Susan Cutter's, as quoted in Deitering (200).

8. I have explored the temporal perspective that arises from this focus on the risk society in *White Noise* in "Die Zeitlichkeit des Risikos."

9. Bianca Theisen, for example, accounts for DeLillo's narrative strategy by arguing that it is aimed at "the paradoxical enterprise . . . of dissolving plot by means of plot" (132; my translation).

10. Reeve and Kerridge argue similarly that "for all the satirical pressure it applies to so many aspects of the contemporary world, *White Noise* recognises that the positions from which any such overview can proceed are themselves continually at risk of undermining" (305).

11. The juxtaposition of two storylines, which also features in Powers's other novels, has been widely commented on by his reviewers: see Kirn (103), Quinn (22), and Scott (40). For a perceptive discussion of how the relation between the two strands of plot in *Gain* differs from that in earlier texts due to the absence of a mediating figure, see Harris's essay on the role of the reader (esp. 98–99).

12. These two similarities are noted by A. O. Scott (who otherwise dismisses *White Noise's* engagement with chemically induced illness) as well as Michiko Kakutani.

13. Powers was no doubt thinking of Atrazine, an herbicide whose possible carcinogenic and endocrine-disrupting effects have long been the subject of controversy.

14. This inversion is discussed by Jeffrey Williams in his review of *Gain* (para. 9) as well as by Bruce Bawer (11).

15. This play on words is also discussed in Scott (38).

16. Williams notes the absence of a "utopian prospect" and describes Powers's political program as "modest," but praises him for avoiding "rote political judgment" ("Issue " paras. 13, 16, 14). Buell also points to the "never-had-a-chance quixoticism of the resistance effort" in the novel (*Writing* 290 n. 5) but argues that corporate hegemony can at least be questioned through

an examination of its impacts in the realm of the local and the individual body (56).

17. My interpretation of Don differs from Tom LeClair's, who claims that the novel rejects Don's "paranoid style" (35). That Don is cast as a much more positive figure than LeClair recognizes is also indicated by the fact that Powers puts into his mouth one of the most crucial insights in the novel: that human activities have subdued the Earth to the point where it can bear no more (353). See Powers's own comment on this scene in his interview with Jeffrey Williams: "This insight, on the part of a character who shouldn't have been able to reach it, is for me the emotional core of the book."

18. The echoes of Dos Passos's and Joyce's techniques are mentioned briefly in Williams ("Issue" para. 9), and those of Dos Passos also in Buell (*Writing* 55).

19. Scott notes that Powers's "chronicle of Clare, Inc.... [is] less the company's history than its life story" (38).

Chapter 6

1. My brief summary here is indebted to Medvedev, Gale and Hauser, and *Back to Chernobyl*, as well as the more technical accounts in Mould and Vargo.

2. The initial estimate, and the one still given in most accounts of the accident, is 135,000 evacuees. Mould indicates that this figure was later revised down (103).

3. Surveys and analyses of these texts can be found in Kononenko, Onyshkevych, and Weiss. Rudloff reviews some of the German literature on the subject but does not mention Gabriele Wohmann's work.

4. The contributions to *spectrum*, the scientists' correspondence with Wolf, and the debates were collected in a book entitled *Verblendung: Disput über einen Störfall* (Blinding: Dispute about an accident), which was later combined with the novel itself in one volume.

5. Page references following quotations from *Störfall* in English are keyed to Schwarzbauer and Takvorian's translation.

6. Brandes analyzes Wolf's puns on "Wolke" by arguing that "'Wolke' as an ideal concept is the almost dreamlike symbol of 'die weiße Wolke der Poesie,' derived from Brecht's 'Erinnerung an Marie A.' The cloud here represents the utopian, ethereal realm of pure poetry which floats in a sphere so far removed from this day's reality that it must now be relegated to the archives of sentimentality" (108). See also Saalmann (242–43).

7. As several critics have noted, it is also one of Wolf's many references to her own earlier work. In her novel *Der geteilte Himmel* (The divided sky, 1963), the capitalized "NEWS" was that of Yuri Gagarin as the first human in outer space, presented as a symbol of utopian hope for the association of socialism and technological progress. By using the same device in reference to Chernobyl, Wolf signals the end of this hope (Brandes 107; Fox 472; Magenau 344; Nalewski 274; Winnard 72).

8. See Brandes's discussion of these reviews (111).

9. Here as elsewhere in the discussion of *Störfall*, when two parenthetical page references are combined, the first one refers to the German edition and the second to Schwarzbauer and Takvorian's translation.

10. Karin Eysel, commenting on this list, argues that "Gender roles—namely the traditional assignment of daily concerns to women and scientific

ones to men—have resulted in a split between everyday practices and science; this split lies at the heart of Wolf's critique" (290). Andrew Winnard similarly considers this list as evidence of a clear split between women and men, the domestic and the scientific in the novel (79); see also West (260). None of them mentions that the immediately following reference to the narrator's own disregard for such everyday concerns calls precisely this split in question.

11. Andrew Winnard points out that the choice of a Japanese radio to convey the news of nuclear disaster may well be intended as a reminder of the nuclear attacks on Hiroshima and Nagasaki, a hypothesis that is supported by other allusions to Hiroshima and Japan in the text (Winnard 76–77).

12. Schwarzbauer and Takvorian omit the German adverb "fast" in their translation.

13. Page references are keyed to the second German edition; all translations of *Der Flötenton* are mine, as no English translation of the novel is currently available.

14. See the analysis of fear in Fritsch.

15. Wohmann develops the specifically feminist issues of Emily's career problems and environmental engagement further in her short story "Die weibliche Komponente" (The female element), whose protagonist resembles Emily Asper in many ways. This short story was published in a collection entitled *Ein russischer Sommer* (A Russian summer), which includes several other short stories that revolve around Chernobyl.

Conclusion

1. Previous climate reversals in the Earth's history were neither caused by human activity nor did they impact a human population that by the middle of this century is likely to number nine billion.

2. I am grateful to Patrick D. Murphy for pointing me to this novel.

3. I would like to thank Martin Puchner for discussing the theatrical aspects of Gore's film with me.

WORKS CITED

Abbey, Edward. *Desert Solitaire: A Season in the Wilderness.* New York: Ballantine, 1998.

Abbey, Edward. *The Monkey Wrench Gang.* New York: Perennial, 2000.

Abram, David. *The Spell of the Sensuous: Perception and Language in a More-Than-Human World.* New York: Vintage, 1996.

Adams, Douglas. *The More Than Complete Hitchhiker's Guide: Complete and Unabridged.* New York: Wings Books, 1986.

Adamson, Joni, Mei Mei Evans, and Rachel Stein, eds. *The Environmental Justice Reader: Politics, Poetics, and Pedagogy.* Tucson: University of Arizona Press, 2002.

Albrow, Martin. *The Global Age: State and Society beyond Modernity.* Cambridge: Polity Press, 1996.

Aldiss, Brian. *Earthworks.* Holborn, England: Four Square, 1967.

Aldiss, Brian. "Total Environment." In Clem, Greenberg, and Olander, 24–65.

Alexander, Donald. "Bioregionalism: Science or Sensibility?" *Environmental Ethics* 12 (1990): 161–73.

Amery, Carl. *Das Geheimnis der Krypta.* Munich: List, 1990.

Anderson, Benedict. *Imagined Communities: Reflections on the Origins and Spread of Nationalism.* Rev. ed. London: Verso, 2006.

Andrade, Mário de. *Macunaíma: O herói sem nenhum caráter.* Belo Horizonte, Brazil: Itatiaia, 1987.

Andrade, Mário de. *Macunaíma.* Translated by E. A. Goodland. New York: Random House, 1984.

Antonetta, Susanne. *Body Toxic: An Environmental Memoir.* Washington, D.C.: Counterpoint, 2002.

Appadurai, Arjun. *Modernity at Large: Cultural Dimensions of Globalization.* Minneapolis: University of Minnesota Press, 1996.

Appiah, Kwame Anthony. *Cosmopolitanism: Ethics in a World of Strangers.* New York: Norton, 2006.

The Arrival. Dir. David Twohy. Perf. Charlie Sheen. Artisan, Santa Monica, Calif., 1996.

Atkins, Robert. "Chernobyl and Beyond: Green Issues in the Recent Works of Gabriele Wohmann." *Carleton Germanic Papers* 24 (1996): 197–214.

Back to Chernobyl. Dir. Bill Kurtis. WGBH Educational Foundation, 1989.

Bahn, Paul G., and John Flenley. *Easter Island, Earth Island.* New York: Thames and Hudson, 1992.

Ballard, J. G. "Billennium." In *The Best Short Stories of J. G. Ballard.* New York: Holt, 1995, 125–40.

Ballard, J. "The Concentration City." In *The Best Short Stories of J. G. Ballard.* New York: Holt, 1995, 1–20.

Basso, Keith. *Wisdom Sits in Places: Landscape and Language among the Western Apache.* Albuquerque: University of New Mexico Press, 1996.

Bate, Jonathan. *Romantic Ecology: Wordsworth and the Environmental Tradition.* London: Routledge, 1991.

Bauman, Zygmunt. *Postmodern Ethics.* Oxford: Blackwell, 1993.

Baumgarten, Lothar. Personal communication, March 25, 2005.

Bawer, Bruce. "Bad Company." Review of *Gain*, by Richard Powers. *New York Times Book Review,* June 21, 1998, 11.

Beck, Ulrich. *Der kosmopolitische Blick oder: Krieg ist Frieden.* Frankfurt: Suhrkamp, 2004.

Beck, Ulrich. *Risikogesellschaft: Auf dem Weg in eine andere Moderne.* Frankfurt: Suhrkamp, 1986.

Beck, Ulrich. *World Risk Society.* Cambridge: Polity Press, 1999.

Beck, Ulrich, Anthony Giddens, and Scott Lash. *Reflexive Modernization: Politics, Tradition and Aesthetics in the Modern Social Order.* Cambridge: Polity Press, 1994.

Berry, Wendell. "Farming and the Global Economy." In *Another Turn of the Crank.* Washington, D.C.: Counterpoint, 1995, 1–7.

Berry, Wendell. "The Regional Motive." In *A Continuous Harmony: Essays Cultural and Agricultural.* New York: Harcourt Brace Jovanovich, 1972, 63–70.

Berry, Wendell. "Word and Flesh." In *What Are People For?* New York: North Point Press, 1990, 197–203.

Berthold-Bond, Daniel. "The Ethics of 'Place': Reflections on Bioregionalism." *Environmental Ethics* 22 (spring 2000): 5–24.

Bhabha, Homi K. "Unsatisfied: Notes on Vernacular Cosmopolitanism." In *Text and Nation: Cross-disciplinary Essays on Cultural and National Identities,* edited by Laura García-Moreno and Peter C. Pfeiffer. Columbia, S.C.: Camden House, 1996, 191–207.

Biehl, Janet. "'Ecology' and the Modernization of Fascism in the German Ultra-Right." *Society and Nature* 1 (1993): 130–70.

Biehl, Janet, and Peter Staudenmaier. *Ecofascism: Lessons from the German Experience.* Edinburgh: AK Press, 1995.

Bird, Jon, Barry Curtis, Tim Putnam, George Robertson, and Lisa Tickner, eds. *Mapping the Futures: Local Cultures, Global Change.* London: Routledge, 1993.

Blair, Sara. "Cultural Geography and the Place of the Literary." *American Literary History* 10 (1998): 544–67.

Blish, James. "Statistician's Day." In Clem, Greenberg, and Olander, 212–22.

Blish, James, and Norman L. Knight. *A Torrent of Faces.* Garden City, N.Y.: Doubleday, 1967.

Botkin, Daniel B. *Discordant Harmonies: A New Ecology for the Twenty-first Century.* New York: Oxford University Press, 1990.

Boulding, Kenneth E. "The Economics of the Coming Spaceship Earth." In *Environmental Quality in a Growing Economy: Essays from the Sixth RFF Forum,* edited by Henry Jarrett. Baltimore: Johns Hopkins University Press, 1966, 3–14.

Bramwell, Anna. *Blood and Soil: Richard Walther Darré and Hitler's "Green Party."* Bourne End, Buckinghamshire, England: Kensal Press, 1985.

Brandes, Ute. "Probing the Blind Spot: Utopia and Dystopia in Christa Wolf's *Störfall.*" In *Selected Papers from the Fourteenth New Hampshire Symposium on the German Democratic Republic,* edited by Margy Gerber et al. Lanham, Md.: University Press of America, 1989, 101–14.

Brennan, Timothy. *At Home in the World: Cosmopolitanism Now.* Cambridge, Mass.: Harvard University Press, 1997.

Brin, David. *Earth.* New York: Bantam, 1991.

Brown, Charles S., and Ted Toadvine, eds. *Eco-Phenomenology: Back to the Earth Itself.* Albany: State University of New York Press, 2003.

Brown, Lester R. *The Twenty-ninth Day: Accommodating Human Needs and Numbers to the Earth's Resources.* New York: Norton, 1978.

Brunner, John. "The Genesis of 'Stand on Zanzibar' and Digressions." *Extrapolation* 11.2 (1970): 34–43.

Brunner, John. *The Sheep Look Up.* New York: Harper and Row, 1972.

Brunner, John. *Stand on Zanzibar.* New York: Ballantine, 1969.

Buell, Frederick. *From Apocalypse to Way of Life: Environmental Crisis in the American Century.* New York: Routledge, 2003.

Buell, Lawrence. *The Environmental Imagination: Thoreau, Nature Writing, and the Formation of American Culture.* Cambridge, Mass.: Harvard University Press, 1995.

Buell, Lawrence. *The Future of Environmental Criticism: Environmental Crisis and Literary Imagination.* Oxford: Blackwell, 2005.

Buell, Lawrence. *Writing for an Endangered World: Literature, Culture, and Environment in the U.S. and Beyond.* Cambridge, Mass.: Harvard University Press, 2001.

Burgess, Anthony. *The Wanting Seed.* London: Heinemann, 1962.

Cage, John. "Overpopulation and Art." In *John Cage: Composed in America,* edited by Marjorie Perloff and Charles Junkerman. Chicago: University of Chicago Press, 1994, 14–38.

Caldwell, Gail. "On the Soapbox." Review of *Gain,* by Richard Powers. *Boston Globe,* June 7, 1998, C1+.

Calvino, Italo. *Invisible Cities.* Translated by William Weaver. San Diego: Harcourt Brace Jovanovich, 1974.

Campos, Haroldo de. *Morfologia do Macunaíma.* São Paulo: Perspectiva, 1973.

Cardis, Elisabeth, et al. "Estimates of the Cancer Burden in Europe from Radioactive Fallout from Chernobyl." *International Journal of Cancer* 119 (2006): 1224–35.

Carroll, Joseph. *Evolution and Literary Theory.* Columbia: University of Missouri Press, 1995.

Carroll, Joseph. *Literary Darwinism: Evolution, Human Nature, and Literature.* New York: Routledge, 2004.

Carson, Rachel. *Silent Spring.* Boston: Houghton Mifflin, 1962.

Casey, Edward S. *The Fate of Place: A Philosophical History.* Berkeley: University of California Press, 1998.

Castel, R. "From Dangerousness to Risk." In *The Foucault Effect: Studies in Governmentality,* edited by Graham Burchell, Colin Gordon, and Peter Miller. London: Harvester, 1991, 281–98.

Certeau, Michel de, Luce Giard, and Pierre Mayol. *L'invention du quotidien*. Paris: Union générale d'éditions, 1980.

Chang, Chris. "Sound and Lothar Baumgarten." *Film Comment* 40.1 (January–February 2004): 17.

Cheah, Pheng, and Bruce Robbins, eds. *Cosmopolitics: Thinking and Feeling beyond the Nation*. Minneapolis: University of Minnesota Press, 1998.

Chernobyl Forum 2003–2005. *The Legacy of Chernobyl: Health, Environmental, and Socio-economic Impacts and Recommendations to the Governments of Belarus, the Russian Federation and Ukraine*. 2nd rev. version. Vienna: International Atomic Energy Agency, 2006. www.iaea.org/Publications/Booklets/Chernobyl/chernobyl.pdf.

Ching, Barbara, and Gerald W. Creed, eds. *Knowing Your Place: Rural Identity and Cultural Hierarchy*. New York: Routledge, 1997.

Chivers, C. J. "New Sight in Chernobyl's Dead Zone: Tourists." *New York Times*, June 15, 2005.

A Civil Action. Dir. Steven Zaillian. Perf. John Travolta, Robert Duvall, Stephen Fry, James Gandolfini. Touchstone Pictures, Burbank, Calif., 1999.

Clem, Ralph S., Martin Harry Greenberg, and Joseph D. Olander, eds. *No Room for Man: Population and the Future through Science Fiction*. Totowa, N.J.: Rowman and Littlefield, 1979.

Clifford, James. *Routes: Travel and Translation in the Late Twentieth Century*. Cambridge, Mass.: Harvard University Press, 1997.

Cohen, Joel E. *How Many People Can the Earth Support?* New York: Norton, 1995.

Colborn, Theo, Dianne Dumanoski, and John Peterson Myers. *Our Stolen Future: Are We Threatening Our Fertility, Intelligence, and Survival? A Scientific Detective Story*. New York: Dutton, 1996.

Conniff, Brian. "The Dark Side of Magical Realism: Science, Oppression and Apocalypse in *One Hundred Years of Solitude*." *Modern Fiction Studies* 36.2 (1990): 167–79.

Crichton, Michael. *State of Fear*. New York: HarperCollins, 2004.

Cronon, William. "The Trouble with Wilderness; Or, Getting Back to the Wrong Nature." In *Uncommon Ground: Rethinking the Human Place in Nature*, edited by William Cronon. New York: Norton, 1995, 69–90.

Crossette, Barbara. "How to Fix a Crowded World: Add People." *New York Times*, November 2, 1997, sec. 4, 1+.

Cvetkovich, George, and Patricia L. Winter. "Trust and Social Representations of the Management of Threatened and Endangered Species." *Environment and Behavior* 35 (2003): 286–305.

The Day after Tomorrow. Dir. Roland Emmerich. Perf. Dennis Quaid, Jake Gyllenhaal, Emmy Rossum, Dash Mihok. Twentieth-Century Fox, Beverly Hills, Calif., 2004.

Deitering, Cynthia. "The Postnatural Novel: Toxic Consciousness in Fiction of the 1980s." In Glotfelty and Fromm, 196–203.

Deleuze, Gilles, and Félix Guattari. *Anti-Oedipus: Capitalism and Schizophrenia*. Translated by Robert Hurley, Helen R. Lane, and Mark Seem. New York: Viking, 1977.

Deleuze, Gilles, and Félix Guattari. *A Thousand Plateaus: Capitalism and Schizophrenia*. Translated by Brian Massumi. Minneapolis: University of Minnesota Press, 1987.

DeLillo, Don. *The Names*. New York: Knopf, 1982.

DeLillo, Don. *White Noise: Text and Criticism.* Edited by Mark Osteen. Viking critical edition. New York: Penguin, 1998.

Del Rey, Lester. *The Eleventh Commandment.* Evanston, Ill.: Regency, 1962.

Del Rey, Lester. *The Eleventh Commandment.* Rev. ed. New York: Ballantine, 1970.

Diamond, Irene, and Gloria Feman Orenstein, eds. *Reweaving the World: The Emergence of Ecofeminism.* San Francisco: Sierra Club, 1990.

Diamond, Jared M. *Collapse: How Societies Choose to Fail or Succeed.* New York: Viking, 2005.

Dimock, Wai Chee. *Through Other Continents: American Literature across Deep Time.* Princeton: Princeton University Press, 2006.

Dirlik, Arif. "Place-Based Imagination: Globalism and the Politics of Place." In Prazniak and Dirlik, 15–51.

Disch, Thomas M., ed. *The Ruins of Earth: An Anthology of Stories of the Immediate Future.* New York: Berkley, 1971.

Disch, Thomas M. *334.* New York: Avon, 1974.

Douglas, Mary. *Risk and Blame: Essays in Cultural Theory.* London: Routledge, 1992.

Douglas, Mary, and Aaron Wildavsky. *Risk and Culture: An Essay on the Selection of Technological and Environmental Dangers.* Berkeley: University of California Press, 1982.

Duncan, James, and David Ley, eds. *Place/Culture/Representation.* London: Routledge, 1993.

Duvall, John N. "The (Super)Marketplace of Images: Television as Unmediated Mediation in DeLillo's *White Noise.*" In Osteen, 432–55.

Earle, Timothy C., and George T. Cvetkovich. *Social Trust: Toward a Cosmopolitan Society.* Westport, Conn.: Praeger, 1995.

Eberstadt, Nicholas. "The Population Implosion." *Wall Street Journal,* October 16, 1997, sec. A, 22.

Eberstadt, Nicholas. "World Population Implosion?" *Public Interest* 129 (fall 1997): 3–22.

Eckersley, Robyn. *The Green State: Rethinking Democracy and Sovereignty.* Cambridge, Mass.: MIT Press, 2004.

Ehrlich, Paul R. *The Population Bomb.* Cutchogue, N.Y.: Buccaneer, 1971.

Ehrlich, Paul R. *The Population Explosion.* New York: Simon and Schuster, 1990.

Ehrlich, Paul R., and Anne H. Ehrlich. *One with Nineveh: Politics, Consumption, and the Human Future.* Washington, D.C.: Island Press, 2004.

Ehrlich, Paul R., Anne H. Ehrlich, and Gretchen C. Daily. *The Stork and the Plow: The Equity Answer to the Human Dilemma.* New Haven, Conn.: Yale University Press, 1995.

11th Hour, The. Dir. Nadia Conners and Leila Conners Petersen. Perf. Leonardo DiCaprio. Appian Way, 2007.

Erin Brockovich. Dir. Steven Soderbergh. Perf. Julia Roberts, Albert Finney, Aaron Eckhart. Universal Pictures, Universal City, Calif., 2000.

Evans, Mei Mei. "'Nature' and Environmental Justice." In Adamson, Evans, and Stein, 181–93.

Evernden, Neil. "Beyond Ecology: Self, Place and the Pathetic Fallacy." In Glotfelty and Fromm, 92–104.

Ewald, François. "Insurance and Risks." In *The Foucault Effect: Studies in Governmentality,* edited by Graham Burchell, Colin Gordon, and Peter Miller. London: Harvester, 1991, 197–210.

Ewald, François. "Two Infinities of Risk." In *The Politics of Everyday Fear,* edited by Brian Massumi. Minneapolis: University of Minnesota Press, 1993, 221–28.

Eysel, Karin. "History, Fiction, Gender: The Politics of Narrative Intervention in Christa Wolf's *Störfall*." *Monatshefte* 84 (1992): 284–98.

Ezcurra, Exequiel, Alfonso Valiente-Banuet, Oscar Flores-Villela, and Ella Vázquez-Domínguez. "Vulnerability to Global Environmental Change in Natural Ecosystems and Rural Areas: A Question of Latitude?" In Kasperson and Kasperson, 217–46.

Fahrenheit 9/11. Dir. Michael Moore. Columbia TriStar, Culver City, Calif., 2004.

Farmer, Philip José. *Dayworld*. New York: Putnam, 1985.

Feder, Barnaby. "Technology's Future: A Look at the Dark Side." *New York Times*, May 17, 2006.

Feld, Steven, and Keith Basso, eds. *Senses of Place*. Santa Fe: School of American Research Press, 1996.

Ferreira, Celio, Åsa Boholm, and Ragnar Löfstedt. "From Vision to Catastrophe: A Risk Event in Search of Images." In Flynn, Slovic, and Kunreuther, 283–99.

Finucane, Melissa L., Ali Alhakami, Paul Slovic, and Stephen M. Johnson. "The Affect Heuristic in Judgments of Risks and Benefits." *Journal of Behavioral Decision Making* 13 (2000): 1–17.

Fischhoff, Baruch, Sarah Lichtenstein, Paul Slovic, Stephen L. Derby, and Ralph L. Keeney. *Acceptable Risk*. Cambridge: Cambridge University Press, 1981.

Fischhoff, Baruch, Paul Slovic, and Sarah Lichtenstein. "Lay Foibles and Expert Fables in Judgments about Risks." In *Progress in Resource Management and Environmental Planning*, vol. 3, edited by Timothy O'Riordan and R. Kerry Turner. Chichester, England: Wiley, 1981, 161–202.

Flynn, James, Paul Slovic, and Howard Kunreuther, eds. *Risk, Media, and Stigma: Understanding Public Challenges to Modern Science and Technology*. London: Earthscan, 2001.

Flynn, James, Paul Slovic, and C. K. Mertz. "Gender, Race, and Perception of Environmental Health Risks." *Risk Analysis* 14 (1994): 1101–8.

Fox, Thomas C. "Feminist Revisions: Christa Wolf's *Störfall*." *German Quarterly* 63 (1990): 471–77.

Franklin, Wayne, and Michael Steiner, eds. *Mapping American Culture*. Iowa City: University of Iowa Press, 1992.

Fritsch, Hildegard. "Spielarten der Angst in Gabriele Wohmanns *Der Flötenton*." *Neophilologus* 74 (1990): 426–33.

Fuller, R. Buckminster. *Operating Manual for Spaceship Earth*. Carbondale: Southern Illinois University Press, 1969.

Gale, Robert Peter, and Thomas Hauser. *Final Warning: The Legacy of Chernobyl*. New York: Warner, 1988.

Gallagher, Tim. *The Grail Bird*. Boston: Houghton Mifflin, 2005.

Garb, Yaakov Jerome. "Perspective or Escape? Ecofeminist Musings on Contemporary Earth Imagery." In Diamond and Orenstein, 264–78.

García Canclini, Néstor. *Hybrid Cultures: Strategies for Entering and Leaving Modernity*. Translated by Christopher L. Chiappari and Silvia L. López. Minneapolis: University of Minnesota Press, 1995.

García Márquez, Gabriel. *Cien años de soledad*. Barcelona: Plaza y Janés, 1999.

Garrard, Greg. *Ecocriticism*. London: Routledge, 2004.

Garrard, Greg. "Radical Pastoral?" *Studies in Romanticism* 35 (1996): 451–56.

Gelbard, Alene, and Carl Haub. "Population 'Explosion' Not Over for Half the World." *Population Today* 26.3 (March 1998): 1–2.

Gibbs, Lois Marie. *Love Canal: My Story, as Told to Murray Levine.* Albany: State University of New York Press, 1982.

Giddens, Anthony. *The Consequences of Modernity.* Cambridge: Polity Press, 1990.

Giddens, Anthony. *Modernity and Self-Identity: Self and Society in the Late Modern Age.* Stanford, Calif.: Stanford University Press, 1991.

Gifford, Terry. "Gary Snyder and Post-Pastoral." In *Ecopoetry: A Critical Introduction,* edited by J. Scott Bryson. Salt Lake City: University of Utah Press, 2002, 77–87.

Gifford, Terry. *Pastoral.* London: Routledge, 1999.

Ginsberg, Allen. "In a Moonlit Hermit's Cabin." In *Collected Poems 1947–1980.* New York: Harper and Row, 1984, 527–28.

Glotfelty, Cheryll. "Introduction: Literary Studies in an Age of Environmental Crisis." In Glotfelty and Fromm, xv–xxxvii.

Glotfelty, Cheryll, and Harold Fromm, eds. *The Ecocriticism Reader: Landmarks in Literary Ecology.* Athens: University of Georgia Press, 1996.

Goldblatt, David. *Social Theory and the Environment.* Cambridge: Polity Press, 1996.

Golding, Dominic. "A Social and Programmatic History of Risk Research." In Krimsky and Golding, 23–52.

Goldman, Stephen H. "John Brunner's Dystopias: Heroic Man in Unheroic Society." *Science-Fiction Studies* 5 (1978): 260–70.

Gray, Chris Hables, ed. *The Cyborg Handbook.* New York: Routledge, 1995.

Greenpeace. *The Chernobyl Catastrophe: Consequences on Human Health.* 2006. www.greenpeace. org / international / press / reports / chernobylhealthre port.

Gubaryev, Vladimir. *Sarcophagus: A Tragedy.* Translated by Michael Glenny. New York: Vintage, 1987.

Guha, Ramachandra. "Radical American Environmentalism and Wilderness Preservation: A Third World Critique." *Environmental Ethics* 11.1 (1989): 71–84. Reprinted in Guha and Martínez-Alier, 92–108.

Guha, Ramachandra, and Juan Martínez-Alier. *Varieties of Environmentalism: Essays North and South.* London: Earthscan, 1997.

Habermas, Jürgen. *Die postnationale Konstellation: Politische Essays.* Frankfurt: Suhrkamp, 1998.

Haines, John. *Living off the Country: Essays on Poetry and Place.* Ann Arbor: University of Michigan Press, 1981.

Hamilton, Joan. "Nature 101." *Sierra* November–December 2000: 48–55. Republished at http://www.asle.umn.edu/archive/intro/sierra.html.

Hannerz, Ulf. "Scenarios for Peripheral Cultures." In *Culture, Globalization and the World-System: Contemporary Conditions for the Representation of Identity,* edited by Anthony D. King. Binghamton: State University of New York, Department of Art and Art History, 1991, 107–28.

Hannerz, Ulf. *Transnational Connections: Culture, People, Places.* London: Routledge, 1996.

Haraway, Donna J. "A Cyborg Manifesto: Science, Technology, and Socialist-Feminism in the Late Twentieth Century." In *Simians, Cyborgs, and Women: The Reinvention of Nature.* New York: Routledge, 1991, 149–81.

Hardin, Garrett. *Filters against Folly: How to Survive despite Economists, Ecologists, and the Merely Eloquent.* New York: Viking, 1985.

Hardin, Garrett. "The Tragedy of the Commons." *Science* 162 (1968): 1243–48.

Harris, Charles B. "'The Stereo View': Politics and the Role of the Reader in *Gain.*" *Review of Contemporary Fiction* 18.3 (1998): 97–109.

Harrison, Harry. *Make Room! Make Room!* New York: Berkley, 1967.

Harvey, David. *The Condition of Postmodernity: An Enquiry into the Origins of Cultural Change.* Oxford: Blackwell, 1990.

Harvey, David. *Justice, Nature and the Geography of Difference.* Oxford: Blackwell, 1996.

Haub, Carl. "New UN Projections Depict a Variety of Demographic Futures." *Population Today* 25.4 (April 1997): 1–3.

Hayden, Patrick. *Cosmopolitan Global Politics.* Hants, England: Ashgate, 2005.

Hebel, Franz. "Technikentwicklung und Technikfolgen in der Literatur." *Der Deutschunterricht* 41 (1989): 35–45.

Heidegger, Martin. "Bauen Wohnen Denken." In *Vorträge und Aufsätze,* edited by Friedrich-Wilhelm von Herrmann. Frankfurt: Vittorio Klostermann, 2000, 145–64.

Heise, Ursula K. "Ecocriticism and the Transnational Turn in American Studies." *American Literary History* 20 (2008): 381–404.

Heise, Ursula K. "Netzphantasien: Science Fiction zwischen Öko-Angst und Informationsutopie." In *Klassiker und Strömungen des englischen Romans im 20. Jahrhundert: Festschrift zum 65. Geburtstag von Gerhard Haefner,* edited by Vera and Ansgar Nünning. Trier: Wissenschaftlicher Verlag Trier, 2000, 243–61.

Heise, Ursula K. "Risk and Narrative at Love Canal." In *Literature and Linguistics: Approaches, Models, and Applications. Essays in Honor of Jon Erickson,* edited by Marion Gymnich, Vera Nünning, and Ansgar Nünning. Trier: Wissenschaftlicher Verlag, 2002, 77–99.

Heise, Ursula K. "Die Zeitlichkeit des Risikos im amerikanischen Roman der Postmoderne." In *Zeit und Roman: Zeiterfahrung im historischen Wandel und ästhetischen Paradigmenwechsel vom achtzehnten Jahrhundert bis zur Postmoderne,* edited by Martin Middeke. Würzburg: Königshausen und Neumann, 2003, 373–94.

Held, David. "Cosmopolitanism: Ideas, Realities and Deficits." In *Governing Globalization: Power, Authority, and Global Governance,* edited by David Held and Anthony McGrew. Malden, Mass.: Polity, 2002, 305–24.

Held, David. *Democracy and the Global Order: From the Modern State to Cosmopolitan Governance.* Stanford, Calif.: Stanford University Press, 1995.

Herber, Lewis [Murray Bookchin]. *Our Synthetic Environment.* New York: Knopf, 1962.

Hersey, John. *My Petition for More Space.* New York: Knopf, 1974.

Hirsch, Eric, and Michael O'Hanlon, eds. *The Anthropology of Landscape: Perspectives on Space and Place.* Oxford: Clarendon, 1995.

Hughes, Thomas P. *American Genesis: A Century of Invention and Technological Enthusiasm, 1870–1970.* New York: Viking, 1989.

Image Science and Analysis Laboratory, NASA-Johnson Space Center. "The Gateway to Astronaut Photography of Earth." http://eol.jsc.nasa.gov/sseop/images/EO/highres/ AS17/AS17–148–22727.TIF.

An Inconvenient Truth. Dir. Davis Guggenheim. Perf. Albert Gore. Paramount, Hollywood, Calif., 2006.

Jameson, Fredric. "Notes on Globalization as a Philosophical Issue." In *The Cultures of Globalization,* edited by Fredric Jameson and Masao Miyoshi. Durham, N.C.: Duke University Press, 1998, 54–77.

Jameson, Fredric. *Postmodernism, or, The Cultural Logic of Late Capitalism.* Durham, N.C.: Duke University Press, 1991.

Japp, Klaus Peter. *Risiko.* Bielefeld, Germany: Transcript, 2000.

Japp, Klaus Peter. *Soziologische Risikotheorie.* Weinheim, Germany: Juventa, 1996.

Jasanoff, Sheila. "Heaven and Earth: The Politics of Environmental Images." In Jasanoff and Martello, 31–52.

Jasanoff, Sheila, and Marybeth Long Martello, eds. *Earthly Politics: Local and Global in Environmental Governance.* Cambridge, Mass.: MIT Press, 2004.

Kakutani, Michiko. "Company Town's Prosperity and Pain." Review of *Gain,* by Richard Powers. *New York Times,* August 11, 1998, E6.

Kaplan, Caren. *Questions of Travel: Postmodern Discourses of Displacement.* Durham, N.C.: Duke University Press, 1996.

Kasperson, Jeanne X., and Roger E. Kasperson, eds. *Global Environmental Risk.* London: Earthscan, 2001.

Kasperson, Roger E. "The Social Amplification of Risk: Progress in Developing an Integrative Framework." In Krimsky and Golding, 153–78.

Kasperson, Roger E., et al. "The Social Amplification of Risk: A Conceptual Framework." *Risk Analysis* 8.2 (1988): 177–87.

Kasperson, Roger E., Jeanne X. Kasperson, and Kirstin Dow. "Vulnerability, Equity, and Global Environmental Change." In Kasperson and Kasperson, 247–72.

Kasperson, Roger E., Jeanne X. Kasperson, and Kirstin Dow. "Introduction: Global Environmental Risk and Society." In Kasperson and Kasperson, 1–48.

Kaufmann, Eva. "'Unerschrocken ins Herz der Finsternis': Zu Christa Wolfs 'Störfall.'" In *Christa Wolf: Ein Arbeitsbuch,* edited by Angela Drescher. Berlin: Aufbau, 1989, 252–69.

Keith, Michael, and Steve Pile, eds. *Place and the Politics of Identity.* London: Routledge, 1993.

Kerouac, Jack. *On the Road.* Edited by Ann Charters. New York: Penguin, 1991.

Kern, Robert. "Ecocriticism: What Is It Good For?" *ISLE* 7.1 (winter 2000): 9–32. Reprinted in *The ISLE Reader: Ecocriticism, 1993–2003,* edited by Michael P. Branch and Scott Slovic. Athens: University of Georgia Press, 2003, 258–81.

Kerridge, Richard. "Small Rooms and the Ecosystem: Environmentalism and Don DeLillo's *White Noise.*" In *Writing the Environment: Ecocriticism and Literature,* edited by Richard Kerridge and Neil Sammells. London: Zed Books, 1998, 182–95.

Kiefer, Chris, and Medea Benjamin. "Solidarity with the Third World: Building an International Environmental-Justice Movement." In *Toxic Struggles: The Theory and Practice of Environmental Justice,* edited by Richard Hofrichter. Philadelphia: New Society, 1993, 226–36.

Killingsworth, M. Jimmie, and Jacqueline S. Palmer. "Millennial Ecology: The Apocalyptic Narrative from *Silent Spring* to *Global Warming.*" In *Green Culture: Environmental Rhetoric in Contemporary America,* edited by Carl G. Herndl and Stuart C. Brown. Madison: University of Wisconsin Press, 1996, 21–45.

Kirn, Walter. "Commercial Fiction." Review of *Gain,* by Richard Powers. *New York,* June 15, 1998, 51+.

Klima, John. *Earth.* http://www.cityarts.com/earth/, 2001.

Kononenko, Natalie. "'*Duma Pro Chornobyl*': Old Genres, New Topics." *Journal of Folklore Research* 29 (1992): 133–54.

Kornbluth, Cyril. "Shark Ship." In *Voyages: Scenarios for a Spaceship Called Earth*, edited by Rob Sauer. New York: Ballantine, 1971, 268–305.

Kramer, Andrew E. "Mapmakers and Mythmakers: Russian Disinformation Practices Obscure Even Today's Oil Fields." *New York Times*, December 1, 2005.

Krech, Shepard. *The Ecological Indian*. New York: Norton, 1999.

Krimsky, Sheldon, and Dominic Golding, eds. *Social Theories of Risk*. Westport, Conn.: Praeger, 1992.

Laing, Jonathan R. "Baby Bust Ahead." *Barron's*, December 8, 1997, 37–42.

Lash, Scott, and John Urry. *Economies of Signs and Space*. London: Sage, 1994.

Laumer, Keith. "The Lawgiver." In *The Year 2000*, edited by Harry Harrison. Garden City, N.Y.: Doubleday, 1970, 213–26.

Leach, William. *Country of Exiles: The Destruction of Place in American Life*. New York: Pantheon, 1999.

LeClair, Tom. "Powers of Invention." Review of *Gain*, by Richard Powers. *Nation*, July 27–August 3, 1998, 33–35.

Lee, Rachel C. *The Americas of Asian American Literature: Gendered Fictions of Nation and Transnation*. Princeton, N.J.: Princeton University Press, 1999.

Lefebvre, Henri. *The Production of Space*. Translated by Donald Nicholson-Smith. Oxford: Blackwell, 1991.

Le Guin, Ursula K. "Vaster Than Empires and More Slow." In *Buffalo Gals and Other Animal Presences*. New York: Plume, 1987, 83–128.

Lentricchia, Frank, ed. *New Essays on* White Noise. Cambridge: Cambridge University Press, 1991.

Lentricchia, Frank, ed. "Tales of the Electronic Tribe." In Lentricchia, 87–113.

Leopold, Aldo. *A Sand Country Almanac and Sketches Here and There*. London: Oxford University Press, 1949.

Lévi-Strauss, Claude. *From Honey to Ashes: Introduction to a Science of Mythology: 2*. Translated by John and Doreen Weightman. New York: Harper and Row, 1973.

Lévi-Strauss, Claude. *Mythologiques*. Vol. 2. *Du miel aux cendres*. Paris: Plon, 1966.

Liverman, Diana M. "Vulnerability to Global Environmental Change." In Kasperson and Kasperson, 201–16.

Löfstedt, Ragnar E., and Lynn Frewer. Introduction to *The Earthscan Reader in Risk and Modern Society*. London: Earthscan, 1998, 3–27.

Love, Glen A. *Practical Ecocriticism: Literature, Biology, and the Environment*. Charlottesville: University of Virginia Press, 2003.

Lovell, Nadia, ed. *Locality and Belonging*. London: Routledge, 1998.

Lovelock, James E. *Gaia: A New Look at Life on Earth*. Rev. ed. Oxford: Oxford University Press, 1995.

Lovelock, James E. "Gaia as Seen through the Atmosphere." *Atmospheric Environment* 6 (1972): 579–80.

Lovelock, James E., and Sidney Epton. "The Quest for Gaia." *New Scientist* 65 (1975): 304–6.

Lovelock, James E., and Lynn Margulis. "Atmospheric Homeostasis by and for the Biosphere." *Tellus* 26 (1974): 1–10.

Luhmann, Niklas. *Soziologie des Risikos*. Berlin: de Gruyter, 1991.

Lull, James. *Media, Communication, Culture: A Global Approach*. New York: Columbia University Press, 1995.

Lupton, Deborah. *Risk*. London: Routledge, 1999.

Magenau, Jörg. *Christa Wolf: Eine Biographie.* Berlin: Kindler, 2002.

Maltby, Paul. "The Romantic Metaphysics of Don DeLillo." In Osteen, 498–516.

Manovich, Lev. *The Language of New Media.* Cambridge, Mass.: MIT Press, 2001.

Marcuse, Herbert. *One-Dimensional Man: Studies in the Ideology of Advanced Industrial Society.* Boston: Beacon, 1964.

"The Mark of Gideon." Episode of *Star Trek.* Dir. Jud Taylor. Perf. William Shatner, Leonard Nimoy, Sharon Acker, David Hurst. Paramount, Hollywood, Calif., 1969.

Marx, Leo. *The Machine in the Garden: Technology and the Pastoral Ideal in America.* London: Oxford University Press, 1964.

Marx, Leo. "Pastoralism in America." In *Ideology and Classic American Literature,* edited by Sacvan Bercovitch and Myra Jehlen. New York: Cambridge University Press, 1986, 36–69.

Massey, Doreen B. *Space, Place, and Gender.* Minneapolis: University of Minnesota Press, 1994.

Mazur, Allan. *Hazardous Inquiry: The Rashomon Effect at Love Canal.* Cambridge, Mass.: Harvard University Press, 1998.

McGrew, Anthony. "Liberal Internationalism: Between Realism and Cosmopolitanism." In *Governing Globalization: Power, Authority, and Global Governance,* edited by David Held and Anthony McGrew. Malden, Mass.: Polity, 2002, 267–89.

McHale, Brian. *Postmodernist Fiction.* New York: Methuen, 1987.

McKibben, Bill. *Maybe One: A Personal and Environmental Argument for Single-Child Families.* New York: Simon and Schuster, 1998.

McLuhan, Marshall. "At the Moment of Sputnik the Planet Becomes a Global Theater in Which There Are No Spectators but Only Actors." In *Marshall McLuhan: The Man and His Message,* edited by George Sanderson and Frank Macdonald. Golden, Colo.: Fulcrum, 1989, 70–80.

Meadows, Donella, Dennis L. Meadows, and Jørgen Randers. *Beyond the Limits: Confronting Global Collapse, Envisioning a Sustainable Future.* Post Mills, Vt.: Chelsea Green, 1992.

Meadows, Donella, Dennis L. Meadows, Jørgen Randers, and William W. Behrens III. *The Limits to Growth: A Report for the Club of Rome's Project on the Predicament of Mankind.* New York: Universe, 1972.

Meadows, Donella, Jørgen Randers, and Dennis L. Meadows. *Limits to Growth: The 30-Year Update.* White River Junction, Vt.: Chelsea Green, 2004.

Medvedev, Grigori. *The Truth about Chernobyl.* Translated by Evelyn Rossiter. New York: Basic Books, 1991.

Merchant, Carolyn. *Earthcare: Women and the Environment.* New York: Routledge, 1995.

Meyrowitz, Joshua. *No Sense of Place: The Impact of Electronic Media on Social Behavior.* New York: Oxford University Press, 1985.

Mignolo, Walter. "The Many Faces of Cosmo-polis: Border Thinking and Critical Cosmopolitanism." *Public Culture* 12 (2000): 721–745.

Mirsepassi, Ali, Amrita Basu, and Frederick Weaver, eds. *Localizing Knowledge in a Globalizing World: Recasting the Area Studies Debate.* Syracuse, N.Y.: Syracuse University Press, 2003.

Moses, Michael Valdez. "Lust Removed from Nature." In Lentricchia, 63–86.

Mould, R. F. *Chernobyl Record: The Definitive History of the Chernobyl Catastrophe.* Bristol, England: Institute of Physics, 2000.

Muir, John. "My First Summer in the Sierra." In *Nature Writings*, edited by William Cronon. New York: Library of America, 1997, 147–309.

Murdock, Graham, Judith Petts, and Tom Horlick-Jones. "After Amplification: Rethinking the Role of the Media in Risk Communication." *In The Social Amplification of Risk*, edited by Nick F. Pidgeon, Roger E. Kasperson, and Paul Slovic. Cambridge: Cambridge University Press, 2003, 156–78.

Murphy, Patrick D. *Farther Afield in the Study of Nature-Oriented Literature.* Charlottesville: University of Virginia Press, 2000.

Murphy, Patrick D. "Grounding Anotherness and Answerability through Allonational Ecoliterature Formations." In *Nature in Literary and Cultural Studies: Transatlantic Conversations on Ecocriticism*, edited by Catrin Gersdorf and Sylvia Mayer. Amsterdam: Rodopi, 2006, 417–34.

Mycio, Mary. *Wormwood Forest: A Natural History of Chernobyl.* Washington, D.C.: Joseph Henry Press, 2005.

Nabhan, Gary. *Coming Home to Eat: The Pleasures and Politics of Local Foods.* New York: Norton, 2002.

Nadler, Maggie. "The Secret." In Clem, Greenberg, and Olander, 194–204.

Naess, Arne. *Ecology, Community and Lifestyle.* Translated by David Rothenberg. Cambridge: Cambridge University Press, 1989.

Naess, Arne. "Identification as a Source of Deep Ecological Attitudes." In *Deep Ecology*, edited by Michael Tobias. San Diego: Avant Books, 1985, 256–70.

Nalewski, Horst. "Ernstfall: Störfall." In *Christa Wolf: Ein Arbeitsbuch*, edited by Angela Drescher. Berlin: Aufbau, 1989, 270–91.

Nelkin, Dorothy. "Blunders in the Business of Risk." *Nature* 298 (1982): 775–76.

Nelson, Lin. "The Place of Women in Polluted Places." In Diamond and Orenstein, 173–88.

Niven, Larry, and Jerry E. Pournelle. *The Mote in God's Eye.* New York: Simon and Schuster, 1974.

Nussbaum, Martha C., and Joshua Cohen, eds. *For Love of Country: Debating the Limits of Patriotism.* Boston: Beacon Press, 1996.

O'Malley, P. "Risk, Power and Crime Prevention." *Economy and Society* 21 (1992): 252–75.

Ong, Aihwa. *Flexible Citizenship: The Cultural Logics of Transnationality.* Durham, N.C.: Duke University Press, 1999.

Onyshkevych, Larissa M. L. Zaleska. "Echoes of Chornobyl in Soviet Ukrainian Literature." *Agni* 29–30 (1990): 279–91.

Otway, Harry. "Public Wisdom, Expert Fallibility: Toward a Contextual Theory of Risk." In Krimsky and Golding, 215–28.

Palmlund, Ingar. "Social Drama and Risk Evaluation." In Krimsky and Golding, 197–212.

Peña, Devon G. "Endangered Landscapes and Disappearing Peoples? Identity, Place, and Community in Ecological Politics." In Adamson, Evans, and Stein, 58–81.

Perloff, Marjorie. "Music for Words Perhaps: Reading/Hearing/Seeing John Cage's *Roaratorio*." In *Postmodern Genres*, edited by Marjorie Perloff. Norman: University of Oklahoma Press, 1989, 193–228.

Perrow, Charles. *The Next Catastrophe: Reducing Our Vulnerabilities to Natural, Industrial, and Terrorist Disasters.* Princeton, N.J.: Princeton University Press, 2007.

Perrow, Charles. *Normal Accidents: Living with High-Risk Technologies.* 2nd ed. Princeton, N.J.: Princeton University Press, 1999.

Peters, Ellen M., and Paul Slovic. "The Role of Affect and Worldviews as Orienting Dispositions in the Perception and Acceptance of Nuclear Power." *Journal of Applied Social Psychology* 26 (1996): 1427–53.

Phillips, Dana. *The Truth of Ecology: Nature, Culture, and Literature in America.* Oxford: Oxford University Press, 2003.

Plumwood, Val. *Environmental Culture: The Ecological Crisis of Reason.* London: Routledge, 2002.

Pohl, Frederik. "The Census Takers." In Pohl, *Nightmare Age,* 39–46.

Pohl, Frederik. *Chernobyl.* Toronto: Bantam, 1987.

Pohl, Frederik., ed. *Nightmare Age.* New York: Ballantine, 1970.

Pohl, Frederik, and C. M. Kornbluth. *The Space Merchants.* New York: Ballantine, 1953.

Pollock, Sheldon, Homi K. Bhabha, Carol A. Breckenridge, and Dipesh Chakrabarty. "Cosmopolitanisms." *Public Culture* 12 (2000): 577–90.

Posnock, Ross. "The Dream of Deracination: The Uses of Cosmopolitanism." *American Literary History* 12 (2002): 802–18.

Powers, Richard. *Gain.* New York: Farrar, Straus and Giroux, 1998.

Prazniak, Roxann, and Arif Dirlik, eds. *Places and Politics in an Age of Globalization.* Lanham: Rowman and Littlefield, 2001.

Quinn, Paul. "On the Tracks of the Rhino." Review of *Gain,* by Richard Powers. *Times Literary Supplement,* March 17, 2000, 22.

Rayner, Steve. "Cultural Theory and Risk Analysis." In Krimsky and Golding, 83–115.

Rechtien, Renate. "'Prinzip Hoffnung' oder 'Herz der Finsternis'? Zu Christa Wolfs 'Störfall.'" *New German Studies* 17 (1992–93): 229–53.

Reed, T. V. "Toward an Environmental Justice Ecocriticism." In Adamson, Evans, and Stein, 145–62.

Reeve, N. H., and Richard Kerridge. "Toxic Events: Postmodernism and Don DeLillo's *White Noise.*" *Cambridge Quarterly* 23 (1994): 303–23.

Regna, Joseph. "Assessing Risk: Making Toxics Acceptable." *Science for the People* 18.3 (1986): 12–15, 27.

Renn, Ortwin, and Bernd Rohrmann, eds. *Cross-Cultural Risk Perception: A Survey of Empirical Studies.* Dordrecht, Netherlands: Kluwer, 2000.

Rey, William H. "Blitze im Herzen der Finsternis: Die neue Anthropologie in Christa Wolfs *Störfall.*" *German Quarterly* 62 (1989): 373–83.

Riesman, David, with Nathan Glazer and Reuel Dennehy. *The Lonely Crowd: A Study of the Changing American Character.* Abr. ed. with 1969 preface. New Haven, Conn.: Yale University Press, 1969.

Robbins, Bruce. "Comparative Cosmopolitanisms." In Cheah and Robbins, 246–64.

Robbins, Bruce. *Feeling Global: Internationalism in Distress.* New York: New York University Press, 1999.

Roberts, Keith. "Therapy 2000." In *World's Best Science Fiction: 1970,* edited by Donald A. Wollheim and Terry Carr, 171–88.

Robertson, Roland. "Glocalization: Time-Space and Homogeneity-Heterogeneity." In *Global Modernities,* edited by Mike Featherstone, Scott Lash, and Roland Robertson. London: Sage, 1995, 25–44.

Robinson, Kim Stanley. *Fifty Degrees Below.* New York: Random House, 2005.

Robinson, Kim Stanley. *Forty Signs of Rain.* New York: Random House, 2004.

Robinson, Kim Stanley. *Sixty Days and Counting.* New York: Random House, 2007.

Rody, Caroline. "Impossible Voices: Ethnic Postmodern Narration in Toni Morrison's *Jazz* and Karen Tei Yamashita's *Through the Arc of the Rain Forest*." *Contemporary Literature* 41 (2000): 618–41.

Ross, Andrew. *The Chicago Gangster Theory of Life: Nature's Debt to Society.* London: Verso, 1994.

Ross, Andrew. *Strange Weather: Culture, Science, and Technology in an Age of Limits.* London: Verso, 1991.

Rudd, Robert L. *Pesticides and the Living Landscape.* Madison: University of Wisconsin Press, 1964.

Rudloff, Holger. "Literatur nach Tschernobyl." *Mitteilungen des deutschen Germanistenverbandes* 37 (1990): 11–19.

Saalmann, Dieter. "Elective Affinities: Christa Wolf's *Störfall* and Joseph Conrad's *Heart of Darkness*." *Comparative Literature Studies* 29 (1992): 238–58.

Sachs, Wolfgang. *Planet Dialectics: Explorations in Environment and Development.* Halifax, Nova Scotia: Fernwood, 1999.

Sachs, Wolfgang. *Satellitenblick: Die Visualisierung der Erde im Zuge der Weltraumfahrt.* Berlin: Wissenschaftszentrum Berlin für Sozialforschung, 1992.

Safe. Dir. Todd Haynes. Perf. Julianne Moore, Peter Friedman, Xander Berkeley. Columbia Pictures, Culver City, Calif., 1995.

Sale, Kirkpatrick. *Dwellers in the Land.* 2nd ed. Athens: University of Georgia Press, 2000.

Sanders, Scott Russell. *Staying Put: Making a Home in a Restless World.* Boston: Beacon Press, 1993.

Sauer, Rob, ed. *Voyages: Scenarios for a Spaceship Called Earth.* New York: Zero Population Growth/Ballantine, 1971.

Scheese, Don. *Nature Writing: The Pastoral Impulse in America.* New York: Twayne, 1996.

Schneider, Stephen H. *Laboratory Earth: The Planetary Gamble We Can't Afford to Lose.* London: Weidenfeld and Nicolson, 1996.

Scott, A. O. "A Matter of Life and Death." Review of *Gain*, by Richard Powers. *New York Review of Books*, December 17, 1998, 38–42.

Seamon, David, and Robert Mugerauer, eds. *Dwelling, Place and Environment: Towards a Phenomenology of Person and World.* New York: Columbia University Press, 1985.

Serafin, Rafal. "Noosphere, Gaia, and the Science of the Biosphere." *Environmental Ethics* 10 (1988): 121–37.

Shepard, Paul. "Place in American Culture." *North American Review* 262.3 (fall 1977): 22–32.

Shiva, Vandana. "The Greening of the Global Reach." In *Global Ecology: A New Arena of Conflict*, edited by Wolfgang Sachs. London: Zed Books, 1993, 149–56.

Silko, Leslie Marmon. "Landscape, History, and the Pueblo Imagination." In Glotfelty and Fromm, 264–75.

Silverberg, Robert. *Hot Sky at Midnight.* New York: Bantam, 1995.

Silverberg, Robert. *The World Inside.* Toronto: Bantam, 1983.

Simpson, David. *The Academic Postmodern and the Rule of Literature: A Report on Half-Knowledge.* Chicago: University of Chicago Press, 1995.

Simpson, David. *Situatedness, or, Why We Keep Saying Where We're Coming From.* Durham, N.C.: Duke University Press, 2002.

Sjöberg, Lennart. "Are Received Risk Perception Models Alive and Well?" *Risk Analysis* 22 (2002): 665–69.

Sjöberg, Lennart. "Principles of Risk Perception Applied to Gene Technology." *European Molecular Biology Organization* 5 (2004): S47–S51.

Sklair, Leslie. *Sociology of the Global System.* Hemel Hempstead, England: Harvester Wheatsheaf, 1991.

Skrbis, Zlatko, Gavin Kendall, and Ian Woodward. "Locating Cosmopolitanism: Between Humanist Ideal and Grounded Social Category." *Theory, Culture and Society* 21 (2004): 115–36.

Slovic, Paul. "Perception of Risk." *Science,* April 17, 1987, 280–85. Reprinted in *The Perception of Risk.* London: Earthscan, 2000, 220–31.

Slovic, Paul. "Trust, Emotion, Sex, Politics, and Science: Surveying the Risk-Assessment Battlefield." *Risk Analysis* 19 (1999): 689–701. Reprinted in *The Perception of Risk.* London: Earthscan, 2000, 390–412.

Smith, Mick. *An Ethics of Place: Radical Ecology, Postmodernity, and Social Theory.* Albany: State University of New York Press, 2001.

Smith, Neil. *Uneven Development: Nature, Capital, and the Production of Space.* New York: Blackwell, 1984.

Smith, Roberta. "If the Actual Amazon Is Far Away, Invent One Nearby." Review of *Der Ursprung der Nacht (Amazonas-Kosmos),* by Lothar Baumgarten. *New York Times,* September 5, 2003.

Snyder, Gary. *Back on the Fire: Essays.* N.p. : Shoemaker and Hoard, 2007.

Snyder, Gary. *Myths and Texts.* New York: Totem Press, 1960.

Snyder, Gary. *No Nature: New and Selected Poems.* New York: Pantheon, 1992.

Snyder, Gary. "The Place, the Region, and the Commons." In *The Practice of the Wild.* San Francisco: North Point, 1990, 25–47.

Snyder, Gary. *"Reinhabitation."* In *A Place in Space: Ethics, Aesthetics, and Watersheds.* Washington, D.C.: Counterpoint, 1995, 183–91.

Snyder, Gary. *Turtle Island.* New York: New Directions, 1974.

Soja, Edward W. *Postmodern Geographies: The Reassertion of Space in Critical Social Theory.* London: Verso, 1989.

Soja, Edward W. *Thirdspace: Journeys to Los Angeles and Other Real-and-Imagined Places.* Oxford: Blackwell, 1996.

Soylent Green. Dir Richard Fleischer. Perf. Charlton Heston, Edward G. Robinson, Leigh Taylor-Young, Chuck Connors, Joseph Cotten, Paula Kelly. MGM, New York, 1973.

Spiegelman, Art. *In the Shadow of No Towers.* New York: Pantheon, 2004.

Spigner, Clarence, Wesley Hawkins, and Wendy Loren. "Gender Differences Associated with Alcohol and Drug Use among College Students." *Women and Health* 20 (1993): 87–97.

Spinrad, Norman. *Greenhouse Summer.* New York: Tor, 1999.

Spinrad, Norman. "Stand on Zanzibar: The Novel as Film." In *SF: The Other Side of Realism: Essays on Modern Fantasy and Science Fiction,* edited by Thomas D. Clareson. Bowling Green, Ohio: Bowling Green University Popular Press, 1971, 181–85.

Spivak, Gayatri Chakravorty. *Death of a Discipline.* New York: Columbia University Press, 2003.

Spivak, Gayatri Chakravorty. "World Systems and the Creole." *Narrative* 14.6 (2006): 102–12.

Stableford, Brian. "Overpopulation." In *Grolier Science Fiction: The Multimedia Encyclopedia of Science Fiction.* CD-ROM. Danbury, Conn.: Grolier Electronic, 1995.

Starr, Chauncey. "Social Benefit versus Technological Risk." *Science* 165 (1969): 1232–38.

Steger, Mary Ann E., and Stephanie L. Witte. "Gender Differences in Environmental Orientations: A Comparison of Publics and Activists in Canada and the US." *Western Political Quarterly* 42 (1989): 627–49.

Steingraber, Sandra. *Living Downstream: A Scientist's Personal Investigation of Cancer and the Environment*. New York: Vintage, 1998.

Sterling, Bruce. *Heavy Weather*. New York: Bantam, 1994.

Stern, Paul C., Thomas Dietz, and Linda Kalof. "Value Orientations, Gender, and Environmental Concern." *Environment and Behavior* 25 (1993): 322–48.

Stone, Christopher D. *Should Trees Have Standing? And Other Essays on Law, Morals, and the Environment*. 25th anniversary ed. Dobbs Ferry, N.Y.: Oceana Publications, 1996.

Suárez, José I., and Jack E. Tomlins. *Mário de Andrade: The Creative Works*. Lewisburg, Penn.: Bucknell University Press, 2000.

Sukenick, Ronald. *Mosaic Man*. Normal, Ill.: FC2, 1999.

Swirski, Peter. "Dystopia or Dischtopia? The Science-Fiction Paradigms of Thomas M. Disch." *Science-Fiction Studies* 18 (1991): 161–79.

Sze, Julie. "From Environmental Justice Literature to the Literature of Environmental Justice." In Adamson, Evans, and Stein, 163–80.

Teilhard de Chardin, Pierre. "Une interprétation plausible de l'Histoire Humaine: La formation de la 'Noosphère.'" *Revue des questions scientifiques* 118 (1947): 7–37.

Tepper, Sheri S. *The Family Tree*. New York: Avon, 1997.

Theisen, Bianca. "White Noise." In *Im Bann der Zeichen: Die Angst vor Verantwortung in Literatur und Literaturwissenschaft*, edited by Markus Heilmann und Thomas Wägenbaur. Würzburg: Königshausen und Neumann, 1998, 131–41.

Thomashow, Mitchell. *Bringing the Biosphere Home: Learning to Perceive Global Environmental Change*. Cambridge, Mass.: MIT Press, 2002.

Thomashow, Mitchell. "Toward a Cosmopolitan Bioregionalism." In *Bioregionalism*, edited by Michael Vincent McGinnis. London: Routledge, 1999, 121–32.

Tocqueville, Alexis de. *Democracy in America and Two Essays on America*. Translated by Gerald E. Bevan. Edited by Isaac Kramnick. London: Penguin, 2003.

Tomlinson, John. *Globalization and Culture*. Chicago: University of Chicago Press, 1999.

Tuan, Yi-Fu. *Topophilia: A Study of Environmental Perception, Attitudes, and Values*. Englewood Cliffs, N.J.: Prentice-Hall, 1974.

Tung, Lee. *The Wind Obeys Lama Toru*. Bombay: Kutub-Popular, 1967.

Turkle, Sherry. *Life on the Screen: Identity in the Age of the Internet*. New York: Simon and Schuster, 1995.

Turner, B. L. II, Roger E. Kasperson, William B. Meyer, Kirstin M. Dow, Dominic Golding, Jeanne X. Kasperson, Robert C. Mitchell, and Samuel J. Ratick. "Two Types of Global Environmental Change: Definitional and Spatial-Scale Issues in Their Human Dimensions." *Global Environmental Change* 1 (1990): 14–22.

Turner, George. *Drowning Towers*. New York: Avon, 1996.

Turney, Jon. *Frankenstein's Footsteps: Science, Genetics and Popular Culture*. New Haven, Conn.: Yale University Press, 1998.

UN Department of Economic and Social Affairs. Population Division. *World Population Prospects: The 2004 Revision*. Vol. 3. *Analytical Report*. New York: United Nations, 2006.

Der Ursprung der Nacht (Amazonas-Kosmos). Dir. Lothar Baumgarten. 1973–77.

U.S. Bureau of the Census. "World Population Information." www.census.gov/ ipc/www/world.html.

Vargo, George J., ed. *Chernobyl: A Comprehensive Risk Assessment*. Columbus, Ohio: Battelle Press, 2000.

Vonnegut, Kurt. "Tomorrow and Tomorrow and Tomorrow." In *Welcome to the Monkey House*. New York: Delacorte, 1968, 284–98.

Vonnegut, Kurt. "Welcome to the Monkey House." In *Welcome to the Monkey House*. New York: Delacorte, 1968, 27–45.

Voznesenskaya, Julia. *The Star Chernobyl*. Translated by Alan Myers. London: Quartet Books, 1987.

Walker, Vern R. "Defining and Identifying 'Stigma.'" In Flynn, Slovic, and Kunreuther, 353–59.

Wallerstein, Immanuel. *The Modern World System*. New York: Academic Press, 1974.

Wark, McKenzie. "Third Nature." *Cultural Studies* 8 (1994): 115–32.

Wattenberg, Ben J. "The Population Explosion Is Over." *New York Times Magazine*, November 23, 1997, 60–63.

Weinkauf, Mary. "Aesthetics and Overpopulation." *Extrapolation* 13 (1972): 152–64.

Weiss, Sydna Stern. "From Hiroshima to Chernobyl: Literary Warnings in the Nuclear Age." *Papers on Language and Literature* 26 (1990): 90–111.

West, Russell. "Christa Wolf Reads Joseph Conrad: *Störfall* and *Heart of Darkness*." *German Life and Letters* 50 (1997): 254–65.

Westling, Louise. "Virginia Woolf and the Flesh of the World." *New Literary History* 30 (1999): 855–75.

Wildavsky, Aaron, and Karl Dake. "Theories of Risk Perception: Who Fears What and Why?" *Daedalus* 119.4 (1990): 41–60.

Williams, Jeffrey. "The Issue of Corporations: Richard Powers' *Gain*." Review of *Gain*, by Richard Powers. *Cultural Logic* 2.2. (1999): http://eserver.org/ clogic/2–2/ Williamsrev.html.

Williams, Jeffrey. "The Last Generalist: An Interview with Richard Powers." *Cultural Logic* 2.2 (1999): http://eserver.org/clogic/2–2/williams.html.

Williams, Raymond. *The Country and the City*. New York: Oxford University Press, 1973.

Williams, Terry Tempest. *Refuge: An Unnatural History of Family and Place*. New York: Pantheon, 1991.

Williams, Terry Tempest. "Yellowstone: An Erotics of Place." In *An Unspoken Hunger: Stories from the Field*. New York: Pantheon, 1994, 81–87.

Winnard, Andrew. "Divisions and Transformations: Christa Wolf's *Störfall*." *German Life and Letters* 41 (1987): 72–81.

Winner, Langdon. *The Whale and the Reactor: A Search for Limits in an Age of High Technology*. Chicago: University of Chicago Press, 1986.

Wohmann, Gabriele. *Der Flötenton*. 2nd ed. Darmstadt, Germany: Luchterhand, 1987.

Wohmann, Gabriele. *Ein russischer Sommer*. 2nd ed. Darmstadt, Germany: Luchterhand, 1988.

Wolf, Christa. *Accident: A Day's News*. Translated by Heike Schwarzbauer and Rick Takvorian. New York: Farrar, Straus and Giroux, 1989.

Wolf, Christa. *Störfall: Nachrichten eines Tages. Verblendung: Disput über einen Störfall*. Munich: Luchterhand, 2001.

World Commission on Environment and Development. *Our Common Future.* Oxford: Oxford University Press, 1987.

Worster, Donald. *Nature's Economy: A History of Ecological Ideas.* 2nd ed. Cambridge: Cambridge University Press, 1994.

Wynne, Brian. "Institutional Mythologies and Dual Societies in the Management of Risk." In *The Risk Analysis Controversy: An Institutional Perspective,* edited by Howard C. Kunreuther and Eryl V. Ley. Berlin: Springer, 1982, 127–43.

Wynne, Brian. "May the Sheep Safely Graze? A Reflexive View of the Expert-Lay Knowledge Divide." In *Risk, Environment and Modernity: Towards a New Ecology,* edited by Scott Lash, Bronislaw Szerszynski, and Brian Wynne. London: Sage, 1996, 44–83.

Yamashita, Karen Tei. *Through the Arc of the Rainforest.* Minneapolis: Coffee House Press, 1990.

Zabytko, Irene. *The Sky Unwashed.* Chapel Hill, N.C.: Algonquin Press, 2000.

Zero Population Growth (Z.P.G.). Dir. Michael Campus. Perf. Geraldine Chaplin, Diane Cilento, Don Gordon, Oliver Reed, Sheila Reid. Sagittarius, 1971.

Zimmerman, Michael E. *Contesting Earth's Future: Radical Ecology and Postmodernity.* Berkeley: University of California Press, 1994.

INDEX

5, 45, 50; and modernization, 51–55, 145; and resistance to globalization, 6–7, 222n16; and situated knowledge, 5, 28, 37, 40–41, 43–44, 53–56, 213n20; the translocal, 121, 153. *See also* place

Löfstedt, Ragnar E., 138, 219n1
Lohmann, Larry, 211n2
Lopez, Barry, 42
Loren, Wendy, 126
Love Canal, 126, 133, 153, 160, 220n8
Love, Glen, 42, 212n12
Lovell, Nadia, 214n23
Lovelock, James, 19, 22–27, 63, 112, 140, 150, 211nn2–3, 212n5. *See also* Gaia hypothesis
Luhmann, Niklas, 220n7
Lull, James, 211n2
Lupton, Deborah, 129, 131, 133, 136, 219n1

Magenau, Jörg, 182, 185, 223n7
Maltby, Paul, 222n4
Malthus, Thomas, 71, 74, 79, 84
Manovich, Lev, 67
Marcuse, Herbert, 217n12
Marsh, George Perkins, 49, 140
Martello, Marybeth Long, 7
Martínez-Alier, Juan, 149
Marvell, Andrew, 18–19
Marx, Karl, 32, 45, 57, 156
Marx, Leo, 30, 212n12
Massey, Doreen, 46
Mazur, Allan, 126, 220n8
McGrew, Anthony, 6, 57
McHale, Brian, 169
McKibben, Bill, 80
McLuhan, Marshall, 22, 63, 87, 211n3
Meadows, Dennis, 25, 80, 132
Meadows, Donella, 22, 25, 80, 132
media, 22, 40, 52, 54–55, 65–67, 70, 77, 81, 84, 87–88, 91, 92, 100, 101, 111, 126, 128–29, 130, 138, 162, 163, 168, 169, 174, 179, 182, 183, 188–90, 192, 193, 199, 200, 222n4
Medvedev, Grigori 223n1
Mendes, Chico, 91, 100

Merchant, Carolyn, 212n5
Merleau-Ponty, Maurice, 35, 216n33
Meyrowitz, Joshua, 54
Mignolo, Walter, 6, 57–58
migration, 5–6, 31, 40–41, 44, 51, 55–58, 70;
Mirsepassi, Ali, 7
mobility, 5–6, 19, 31, 33, 40–41, 44, 48–51, 55–58, 70, 111, 112, 152; and modernization/globalization, 52–53, 214n27; in the U.S., 9, 31, 48–49
modernization, 4, 12, 32, 36, 51–54, 94, 122–24, 137, 143–46, 151, 221n13; postmodernization, 51
Monet, Claude, 94, 96
Moore, Michael, 129
Moses, Michael Valdez, 222n3
Mould, R. F., 223nn1–2
Mugerauer, Robert, 214n23
Muir, John, 24, 42
Murphy, Patrick D., 61, 213–14n22, 218n2, 224n2
Musil, Robert, 77
Mycio, Mary, 201

Nabhan, Gary, 61
Nadler, Maggie, 72
Naess, Arne, 31, 34–35, 40
Nalewski, Horst, 185, 223n7
nation/nationalism, and environmentalism, 8–9, 37, 43–44, 47, 60, 156–57; and identity, 4–7, 42, 45, 57–58, 61–62; critiques of, 5, 30, 34, 37, 56–57, 213–14n22; as "imagined community," 5, 57; and resistance to globalization, 6–7; and postnationalism, 45, 155; and transnationalism, 6, 12, 43–44, 50–51, 57;
Nelkin, Dorothy, 135
Nelson, Lin, 220n7
networks, 18, 20, 35, 40, 50, 51, 54, 55, 56, 61, 65, 67, 70, 71, 81, 82, 90, 100, 101, 102, 123, 130, 140, 145, 146, 155, 174, 175, 176, 177, 188, 191, 197, 200, 201, 210, 217n18; technological networks as metaphor for ecological networks, 65, 77, 90, 209

Lightning Source UK Ltd.
Milton Keynes UK
UKHW02f2212130718
325693UK00004B/152/P